Perfecting Man From Lockup

Perfecting Man From Lockup

Minister Jeff Mathews

THE REGENCY PUBLISHERS

Copyright © 2022 by Jeffery Mathews.

All rights reserved. No part of this book may be reproduced in any form or by any electronic or mechanical means, including information storage and retrieval systems, without permission in writing from the author and publisher, except by reviewers, who may quote brief passages in a review.

ISBN: 978-1-958517-04-8 (Paperback Edition)
ISBN: 978-1-958517-05-5 (Hardcover Edition)
ISBN: 978-1-958517-03-1 (E-book Edition)

Book Ordering Information

The Regency Publishers, US
521 5th Ave 17th floor NY, NY10175
Phone Number: (315)537-3088 ext 1007
Email: info@theregencypublishers.com
www.theregencypublishers.com

Printed in the United States of America

INTRODUCTION

From March of 2004-March 2005, I was deployed to Baghdad Iraq in the war on terrorism. Now, what is significant about Iraq is it is the former Garden of Eden where God created the man Adam. While I was deployed there, God deposited much in me in understanding the purpose of the man. What the spirit later revealed to me was I was on an assignment of hope for men. In this assignment in Iraq, I received insight from God on how man wins every battle with hope. This hope is the God of hope. While in Iraq God allowed me and demonstrated to me that man has been given much authority. Without hope this authority falls in the hand of the enemy. Much was given to the man Adam from God when He made him out of His own image. My assignment from God is to evaluate this man and to determine what has robbed this man of his authority. Once discovered, I am to expose the enemy and his exact weapon of defeat and give it a name. This is what I have done in this book spending six years working with men in lockup. In November of 2012, I was hired at Kilby prison for men as a supply clerk. This would be an assignment that only God could have done with my calling and the anointing on my life. What I discovered in this assignment is man is in real trouble without God.

Contents

Chapter 1 What Is Man 1

    A Man Of Power 5
    The Power Of Man's Word 16
    Understanding The Old And New Man 24
    The Man As God's Masterpiece 30

Chapter 2 The Mind Of Man 37

    How Satan Blinded The Mind 41
    As A Man Thinks 48
    The Mind Of Overcoming 55
    The Purpose Minded Man 61

Chapter 3 The Common Denominator Of Troubled
    Men 69

    Tips For Troubleshooting 78
    Know Your Friends 80
    Know Family History Tip 85
    The Danger Of Losing Hope 90
    The Seed Of The Troubled Man 97

Chapter 4 The Needs Of The Troubled Man 105

    What Love Has To Do With It 108
    A Listening Ear For The Troubled Man 114
    A Heart That Cares For The Troubled Man 121
    A Vision For The Troubled Man 128

Chapter 5 A Message For All Boys And Athletes..............135

    The Basketball Courts Vs The Probate Courts....141
    High School Dropout Trouble............................149
    What In The Jail Do You Want 158
    Identity And Lockup 167

Chapter 6 Satans Weapons Of Mass To Lockup 173

    How Great Men Get Locked Up 176
    An Achilles Heel To Great Men-Sex Crimes........183
    The Man And A Gun 192
    The Gun Vs The Keeper 199
    Guns Down And Hands Up 204

Chapter 7 Fisherman Of Men 212

    God's Make A Difference Man 218
    The Restored Man 225
    The Wise Man 232

Chapter 8 Faith Over Lockup 238

    The Law Of Faith And Law Of The Land 244
    Faith And Yes I Can..251

Chapter 9 Satan's Demasking Of The Man..........................259

    Who Are You To You 266
    The Man And The Masterpiece..........................272

Chapter 10 Man Up Or Lockup 280

    The Call On The Man 287
    New Man New Life..293

Chapter 1

WHAT IS MAN

As a man created by God, I have many possibilities for greatness. What shall be significant for me as a man is understanding my image and design. The moment I embrace this with confidence there is no place I can fall and not recover. What the devil hopes is that I lose focus of my creator, and the creativity I embrace. What I have discovered is that it is important for every man to discover uniqueness. I say this because what I have learned is, if you do not know who you are, the world will tell you. Man is not here on this earth for the world to tell him who he is, but for man to show the world whose he is.

The bible says "And God said, Let us make man in our image, after our likeness; and let them have dominion over the fish of the sea, and over the fowl of the air, and over the cattle, and overall the earth, and over every creeping thing that creepeth upon the earth. (Gen: 1.26). What I see is a man, once he truly embraces his full potential on the earth, he is unstoppable. What I mean is, if he knows who he is, he can fulfill his purpose. What I see in God's creation of man is, he has placed all of himself in man to dominate his world.

Growing up in the projects of Trenholm Court in Montgomery, Alabama, I witnessed the world trying to label me. What they didn't know was great people came out of Trenholm Court. I was blessed to have great parents that would not go for living below the bar. As I began to grow in Christ, something began to take root in me that there is more. Now, the enemy wants the man again to stay bound with no hope, that he listens to his voice. When the man is out of touch with who he is, and what he is capable of doing, then he is suspected of evil. I believe as long as I stay in touch with God as a man, I now am in line with His image. The moment that I am out of step with God's image, I am again controlled by the god of this world, the devil. (2 Corr:4.4)

In November 2012, I started working at Kilby Prison for men in Mt. Meigs, Al., and I did not like what I saw. I began to see a tremendously overcrowded prison for men who are just out of touch with their purpose. I was not shocked because I had done prison ministry in the past. While working five days a week, I now get up close and personal with inmates and hear their stories. What is interesting to me is how the enemy went around the man to attack his purpose. Now, I know I may have someone puzzled here, but stay with me, and I will give clarity. What we as Christians must understand is the devil fights hard to keep you in the flesh.

What I have discovered in every situation was, if the devil could keep me in my flesh, my real image diminishes. When my real image of God diminishes, the man in me falls prey to the enemy and I fall. What I have witnessed is many men are falling because the flesh is overpowering them. I was on an assignment from God years after my deployment to Iraq. Iraq is located where the Garden of Eden was and man was created. Preaching the gospel in Iraq was amazing and I developed and learned more about the man. I believe my assignment at the men's prison was to see what the devil is doing to the man and do something about it. What I do know is the devil is allowing sons to kill sons. The Bible says

"And he said When ye do the office of a midwife to the Hebrew women and see them upon the stools; if it be a son, then ye shall kill him. (Exodus1.16). Now, here's the key, this should never happen to a man who has been given dominion in the earth. Living in the projects, and witnessing trouble, I had the opportunity to fall. Now, I am not saying I did the right thing all the time because I made mistakes. What I am saying is man is an amazing being when he knows who he is in Christ.

The enemy today is still after taking the lives of sons. What hurt me working at the prison was the great men used by the enemy. Yes, I had the pleasure of meeting great men at the prison to inspire and encourage. What they needed to know was God still loved them and He can turn them around. What I wanted to do was to let them also know that God can do a mighty work in their life if they allow Him.

I am one who that believes if the man can capture himself under pressure, he can overcome. This is who we are as men with capabilities given by God in His image when we believe. In my nearly thirty years of travel in the military, in some men, I have found this to be so. I have witnessed potentially great men who didn't know who they were and stumbled under temptation. Beloved, I come with an assignment from God to alert you that you are greater. You are much greater as a man who has the DNA of God to overtake and recover. (1Sam:30.8). It just tore my heart daily as I walked through the prison seeing so many men held hostage of their calling. Now, when the man is held hostage by the world around him, the devil attacks, and his troubles begin. When the man's troubles begin, and he fights in his strength, many roads lead to lockup.

Men are held hostage of their calling when they never discover their purpose. Yes sir, when you can discover quickly as possible why you are here, trouble is **returned to sender.** Here's what's important, it doesn't matter how big or small the trouble, it bows down to your discovery. The discovery is connected to the image in the man that is connected to God that brings hope. I believe at this point; the man gets the strength to fight off every fiery dart that comes his way. What I noticed every temptation the devil brought my way, he also was reaching at my image. See, the enemy is not reaching only at the man, he is reaching at the image that is just like God.

This is why I spend a lot of time teaching men about having the image of God. What I discovered in me as a man was I will never go any farther than my image in me. I believe if my image in me is distorted, I now give place to the enemy to call me again anyone. The enemy now knows he can call me robber, murderer, thief, rapist, deceiver, etc… and I may answer. Child of God, as a man, you are bigger than any of these, and you never have to answer to these. Once you recover to the image inside of you as a man, God has positioned Himself for you. It does not matter what the circumstances look like outside of you, it is what is inside of you.

As a man, you are more than a conquer, and with God, in you, there is much greater. I also believe there is too much greatness in you to be locked up, and give the devil pleasure. Yes, the devil takes pleasure in seeing great men like you giving in to the pressure on you. The enemy knows if you get locked up, another great mind is locked up. Now, the enemy knows that another image has been deceived. I say deceived because the devil knows a man who walks in the image of God is mighty. The bible says "And the Lord said, Behold, they are one people and they have all one language; and this is only the beginning of what they will do, and now nothing they have imagined they can do will be impossible. Gen:11.6amp). Please get this, man is bound by the limits of his imagination. When I understand as a man I have the image of God, nothing is out of my reach. This is why the devil desires to keep my image distorted, knowing imagination comes from the word image. When the man understands these principles, I believe he can take back what was stolen from, and out of him.

A Man Of Power

I believe every man created by God, and who knows who he is, has the power to defeat his enemy. The key here is the man knowing who he is will determine the power within him. What is so amazing about this man is his economic status has no bearing. This is what the world has used for years to deceive the man of the power that he embraces lack. Sir, regardless of what you may be facing, you were made a man of power. Your God who created you sees you as a man of power because He put Himself in you. By faith, you need to know that you may be the only one on your block, or in your family, with this revelation.

I want you to know yes, this is a divine revelation from God right now to me for you. What I mean here is, if you are on the edge, take a look at the real you and breathe. I promise you that if you know of the power that is in you, there will be no compromise. Sir, trust me when I say that it may look bad right now, but you have in you turn around power. This power is in you and the devil is trying to keep it from you that lockup robs your power. I say this because I talked to inmates daily that had incredible power and minds that have been robbed. Most of these are men with minor offenses but are locked up because they were unaware.

These are men that were unaware that they were men of power, with no knowledge. What I have noticed is the world will allow a man a title, as long as his trust is in the world. When the man has placed all his trust in the world, he never exercises his power, only the power with his position. What this mindset has done in the man is shut down his ability to know he is full of power. God thought so much of the man and his power of him that he filled him with glory and honor. The moment this is set and rests on the heart of the man, his days of feeling inferior are over. Sir, the glory alone that is upon you and me as men give us the power that we can succeed in every area.

The bible says "What is man, that thou art mindful of him? And the son of man, that thou visitest him? For thou hast made him a little lower than the angels, and hast crowned him with glory and honor. (Psalm 8.4) Sir, you are very powerful when you can see yourself as God sees you. I am here to tell you that the devil will always get you to look at your current situation in life. By faith, as a man, you need to know that you are always on the mind of God because He cares for you. Now, my prayer is to get the man to get his mind on God. I am also on assignment to help the man get his **CROWN** back. Notice what this verse says about you and I, that we are **crowned** and a little lower than the angels. You may be in a place where your circumstances may make you feel that you are a lot lower than your problem.

Let me encourage you that because you are crowned with glory from God, you are far above your problem. The enemy might be trying to keep your eyes on the problem and take your power to lock up. Beloved, trust me when I say that we need no more men of power in lockup now, or never. We need these men in the homes, the communities, churches, that other men see and witness your light. I believe as other men see your light, they will witness the power in you from God. I also believe they can build something, or plant a seed of power in them seeing you. Every morning when I would arrive at work in the prison, many men are sitting waiting to see the doctor. As many as I see each morning, I speak to them and shake their hand in the hope to plant a seed. I believe each of us who know of the power in us from God with His glory has that ability.

I am here again to let the man know that the devil is at your **crown** to take you **down**. Let me say it another way. The devil wants your **Crown Down.** What I have learned is the devil works overtime to keep you blind to your crown. The devil is afraid you may discover you are a king. (Rev.5.10). Now, what I have discovered from working at the prison is the devil has used 3 ways to take the man's crown. The first takedown is **Distraction.** Now, by causing a distraction on the man, the devil knows he can lose his sense of direction. The devil can lead the man to trouble by taking his eyes off his purpose. The enemy desires to distract man with the world's possessions and goods. When the man has his crown and is focused, he knows God provides all to him as promised. Now, all this man needs is faith, and he can become great and recover from wherever he has fallen and become a difference-maker.

The second take down the devil uses is **Disappointment.** What the devil will do here is bring enough disappointment on the man to push him to his limits. At this point, the man has a tendency of giving up the right way for the wrong way. Now, this man gets comfortable with the wrong way of doing things, and it becomes a habit. In most cases, his habit leads to risks, risks, leads to trouble, then to lock up. The third takedown I have witnessed in these men in lockup is **Depression.** The devil attempts to bring depression to affect the man's way of thinking. The devil knows when he does this long enough, he could get the man unstable in emotions. Unless this man is trusting in God, and strong in faith, the enemy takes him down. This man usually stays depressed, and his mind if not strong weakens. The next step could be detrimental to his overall functioning in the mind. Medication is required for his benefit. When this man has his crown, he realizes by faith he has the mind of Christ. (1Corr:2.16) Unfortunately, I witnessed this in the prison more than I desired. In our State and many others, the prisons mental health crisis has become a huge factor, and out of control.

Once again, my goal is to help the man get his crown back, that he can defeat the devil with confidence. One may say how did I see these 3 things among the men at the prison? Great question. Not only through daily communication with these men at work, but also when I performed monthly eye clinic. I worked with the optometrist, and I used what was called a refractor to look into the patient's eyes. This machine allows me to see in their eyes, and print a small sheet with numbers. I give this sheet to the patient, for them to give to the optometrist. Now, these number tells the doctor whether the patient is farsighted or near-sighted along with other concerns. I saw in the spirit some things the optometrist couldn't see.

The bible says "Blessed are the eyes which see the things that ye see. (Luke 10.23). What caught my attention was many of the inmates would say to me when they look in this machine "**It Looks Like a tree in there**" This reminded me of a blind man who was brought to Jesus. The bible says "And he looked up and said, I see men as trees walking. (Mark 8.24). Notice here, there is a tree mentality in this man that is out of focus. What I discovered working with the inmates is the tree can be planted in him and bind his perception. This tends to lead the man to corruption that can bring him to violence. When this man attempts to do good, evil rings his mental doorbell.

Now, the devil brings him corruption. The bible says "Even so every good tree bringeth forth good fruit, but a corrupt tree bringeth forth evil fruit. (Matt:7.17). The devil can try to distort man's vision until a touch from God. The devil will attempt all he can through the eyes of man to disable him. Now, he does this to keep the man blind to his God-given abilities. The enemy knows if man ever can see himself as God created him, he can have dominion in the earth as God intended. (Gen1.26). During the pandemic with Coronavirus, a virologist from a major television network contacted the virus. This virologist stated that he believed he caught the virus through his eyes. This was stated because the virologist said he was wearing a mask and gloves when in the public.

I said "WOW" the devil is truly after the eyes of man through every means possible.

Later it was discovered that the Coronavirus can be transmitted through the eyes. The doctors then recommended wearing shields for the eyes. This is why I was confident in my assignment with the eye clinic while performing this monthly with inmates. I believe there is yet more to be discovered in this. I discovered after this that this is not the time for man to keep his eyes off the word. The moment the man's eyes are off the word, the enemy will destroy him. The bible says "My son, attend to my words; incline thy ear unto my sayings. Let them not depart from thine eyes; keep them in the midst of thine heart. (Prov:4.20-21). I want to stop here and say to men, if you can keep your eyes on the word, you will keep your eyes on your purpose. I was also able to see in their eyes what I call **P.A.D.**

This stands for **Potential, Abilities, Desires.** I believe all of us by faith is gifted with some of these. I saw much of this in many of the great guys. Unfortunately for some, the desires went a little too far due to distorted vision as the blind man. These are the desires that lead most to sexual abuse. I believe the devil can contaminate desires. He can do this through sin, greed, etc... We must remember, the devil seeks to devour (1Peter 5.8). Now, nothing wrong with desires the bible says "Delight thyself also in the Lord, and he shall give thee the desires of thine heart. (Psalm 37.4.5). I believe the key here is staying in the word that you get a touch from God. When a man is not connected with God in his desires, the devil brings a takedown.

Now, for me by faith, I was able also to see the 3 takedowns I mentioned above. The bible says " The eyes of your heart flooded with light so that you can know and understand the hope to which He has called you. (Epes:1.18amp). Notice how the bible teaches us that your heart has eyes. By faith, I was able to see other factors in these men through my calling. In fact, it was in a short time they confirmed to me what I saw in their eyes. Precious one, by faith, God gives us this kind of power when we apply what is in us as His children. Now, everybody can't see what those who walk in the spirit see.

What the spirit of God allowed me to see was without the man having his crown, the devil can control his vision. Now, I want men to get this. The enemy can keep the man far-sighted in his **Hope,** and nearsighted in **No Hope.** The devil desires to keep **Hope** as far as possible, and **No Hope** as close and clear as possible. My goal for men is to plant a seed in them that they are men of power and hope. The question on the floor is, what will it take for the man to get his crown back? What I do know is we will have to uproot some things out of him to get started. What I want to do with the man is encourage him that all the things this world said about him is a liar.

The bible says "Every plant, which my heavenly Father hath not planted, shall be rooted up. (Matt:15.13). We must get rooted up all the lies this world has put in the heart of men. These are lies such as lack, nobody cares for me, racism, I will always be in debt, bad health because it's in my family, etc. We also must uproot generational curses that bind the man. These were not planted in man by God, but by the system. I say let's root them up. I believe in the hour that we are in as men, to get their crown back will take 3 things. The first thing I would say is that man must **reconnect with God**. Here's what's real. The enemy knows the moment there is a disconnect of man from God, he is all alone. Now, the enemy can come after him with the power that no one man can handle by himself.

This man reconnects with God through His word with prayer and fasting. Once the man reconnects with God, he gains new strength to endure the pressures of the world. With the man's connection with God and new strength, he's now a victor than a victim. This man now becomes a **prisoner of hope** (Zechariah:9.12). Here's the key, the enemy knows if the man loses his hope, he loses his crown. Now, for the man to get his crown back, he must get his hope back. What am I saying about this man? This man needs a 1 on 1 with God. This is what I call **Relationship 101**. This is an intimate relationship between God and man as man's purpose is revealed. This shall be a relationship like God established 1 on 1 with Adam and Moses. I believe the man now can be restored to be the man God intended him to be before the fall in the garden of Eden. All this shall come by way of a 1 on 1 visitation from God upon the man praying to God for His visit.

The second thing the man must do is to **identify with his purpose.** I believe when the man experiences a 101 visitation from God, a new spirit of hope with purpose comes upon him. He can now see himself as significant in the earth, and the lives of others. When the man's purpose is identified, his past has no bearing on who he can become. This is because with his purpose identified, he develops mountain-moving faith to accomplish his goals. The third thing the man must do is **embrace possibilities.** We know that with God all things are possible. When the man reconnects with God through faith, he can do all things. When man embraces possibilities, he can finish what God started in him.

God started greatness in him because he has the image of God. Those things that appear to be impossible for him now are within his reach if he can only believe. When the man makes these changes, there is no pitfall in his past that cannot be used as a platform for his comeback. The bible says "I am coming quickly; hold fast what you have, so that no one may rob you and deprive you of your crown. (Rev:3.11amp). I have watched more than enough great men get robbed of their crowns. This was done by the world's ability to strip a man who relies totally on himself and his earthly achievements.

What I am trying to get to men today is that power can keep you, but you must know of the power in you. God saw something amazing in the man that he made him a little lower than the angels. This means by faith for me that all I need to do when trouble comes is know that I am somebody. I am somebody that God thought so much of me as a man that angels and I were nearby.

Beloved, what this means for you and me as a man is we are mightier than the world will ever know. What needs to be clear with you and me is we do not have to go down the way men are going down. I am on a mission for God to get a man to walk in his power and watch his world change. All it is to it to me is to get the man to believe that he is who God said he is. When I can get this to all men, I believe I am going to see the violence diminish. I believe it will diminish out of our communities, our schools, and turn them into leaders. I also believe when the man recognizes who he is, we are going to fix the divorce rate, crime rate, and many others.

When man was made, he also was made to have dominion including a loving family. The problem is he has lost his ability to reap due to his inability to walk in his power. This is what is amazing about it all is once he believes in the power, God will do the rest. When I went to the Army Warrant Officer Course in Fort Rucker Al., I knew I was going against huge odds. The first obstacle was there were no fulltime African American men as a Warrant Officer in the Alabama Army National Guard technician program. When I heard the voice of God saying, go to the school, I didn't question God. When I attended, I was sent home three times a failure for physical fitness failure.

What I knew was when God called me to go to the school, he knew I had the power in me to finish. Now, God did not tell me about the test between Him saying go and finish the course. I had to believe that if God called me as a man to do something that have not been done, I needed power. I first needed to know that with the image of God and His power in me, there was nothing impossible. When I graduated from the course, I walked out the power of God in me as the first fulltime African American male in the program. Sir, you and I have the power of God in us to accomplish the worst. What God is searching for in this hour is for men who are ready to know of His power. I believe the power that is in a man once it is activated, can tear down many barriers. What the enemy has done and is continuing to do is to provide barriers to frustrate the man. The enemy knows the more that he can frustrate the man, he can keep him from functioning in God's image. I was not going to let the devil frustrate me when I failed the course three times.

The bible says" For a just man falleth seven times, and riseth up again: but the wicked fall into mischief. (Prov:24.16) I believed God that I am a just man and I could rise from my failure. What I knew it would take me to rise was the power God gives a man who believes. What the devil wanted me to do was to get frustrated at the system, get angry, and cry discrimination. When a man embraces the power within him from God, he knows he can have dominion. A just man has much power and the ability to rise from any setback or fall and reclaim his identity. Beloved, you have that power in you by faith, with the ability, to keep you from lockup.

I know that sometimes it gets difficult for us sometimes to want to just take care of our families. What I want you to know is God has your back, so don't let frustration shorten your future. I sometimes get emotional when I talk to some of these men who have wives and children at home. I can only imagine how difficult it is for that wife, and how much that son needs his father. My encouragement to men is, we are the world to our families, and we must stay connected with God. When we can do this, we don't have to put our families at risk by making a troubling move. God is calling you and me to say with confidence that I am not going down knowing who I am.

Sir, not only are you the world to your family, but by God, we are the light of the world. You and I as men are supposed to be able to come to this earth and set the standards. Once again, it does not matter where you come from, but it is about where you are going. What is very important for you and I to ask ourselves is, where do we desire to go from here. Now, here is what we need to know. As men, we were created to not stay the same, but to grow in knowledge. If you and I do not know that we are here to make a difference in our world, there is a problem. The problem is, we as men have a tendency to get idle, and that sets the stage for lockup.

Beloved, you do not want to get idle, because this allows the devil to present to you his plan. The devil's plan is not in alignment with the power God gave you to rise above storms. I have talked to many of these great men in lockup who for a moment became idle and trapped. Now, I want to be clear here that a lot of these men are not of gangs and uneducated. I have a lot of these gentlemen with master's degrees, and one was working on a PHD. What the enemy is particularly good at is raising his level of communication to reach the educated mind. What I am saying here is, as a man, you need to choose a path that can lead you to win. When you choose a path to win, the power from God will ignite a new strength to bring you support. God is on our side to be a blessing. when we make a choice to do good for God, the blessing shall come. The challenge is when we think that we can't, and stay where we are, the enemy goes to work. The first place that the enemy will go to work on is your mind, to get you to agree with him.

What I am looking at daily are many men who succumbed to idleness that lead to lockup. The bible says" the idle hands are the devil's workshop. (Prov:16.27tlb). The reason why this could lead to lockup is men were created to be about making things happen. I believe because man came from God's creation, he is a part of a new creation. Man is capable of doing mighty things on the earth when he comes in contact with his creator. I know that it can be tough when a man is out of a job, and desires to care for his family. Prior to start working at the prison, I was unemployed for three years with a wife and daughter.

I thank God that my wife was working, but we were really missing my income. While I was unemployed at that time, I stayed connected with God daily that I never lose focus. I believed by faith that God was doing something in me for the future. One of the things that I kept doing was saying to myself daily, that I am a man of purpose. As often as I would say that to myself, I was believing that purpose was connecting with power. When we do this as men, we are preparing ourselves for what God already knows. God knows that we are men of power, and we can rise above our circumstances as long as we believe.

I believed that I would not go down a failure because my situation around me looked dim. I knew that as often as I believed, things would get better as I gain strength for another day. What is doing this is the confidence I have in God, and in what he is doing in me. Now, sir, things may not be as you like them now, but know that God has worked it out. Now, like I was, my confidence was not paying the bills, but it kept me strong for the comeback. Let me encourage you to not let the tough times deceive you. Once the enemy again robs you of your power, he will try to lead you to a bad decision.

I had a great young man who was an inmate at the prison working with me. This was a really great guy, and he told me his story of how the enemy led him to do the worst. He committed a robbery. What he shared with me was how things became tough, and the enemy slipped in. I asked him what did he think allowed the devil to slip in, he said the moment he forgot his identity. See child of God, the devil has his way of making you forget you are a man. Now, what I mean here is, a true man made by God. What the enemy knows is if he allows you to come to yourself as a man of power, he is done. I want to encourage a man out there who the devil is trying to deceive. You are a mighty man of God with power, who has the right to go to your God for what you need. Please do not allow the enemy to deceive you to lockup, that you lockup destiny in you. You are a bigger man than that beast of a storm that might be in front of you. The beast of that storm knows that if he also grants you to commit to that , you bow to his command. God has given you and I greater than what the devil can give.

God said that you and I can have dominion on the earth, and this includes over hardship. With God and the power that is in you and I as a man, we can beat the beast that sends to bars. These are cell bars of lockup that were never intended for men of power. Sir, you are a man that God has chosen to do great and mighty things on the earth. This is not the time for you to be locked up, because God is calling you to freedom and favor. I am here to remind you that there is power residing in you that needs to be stirred up now.

The Power Of Man's Word

One of the things as a man I now understand is the power of words that comes out of me. I truly can say I have witnessed more than one can think of my words coming to pass. I have witnessed them coming to pass knowing that only God did it. What I had to understand is when God gave man dominion he said over all the earth. The bible says "Death and life are in the power of the tongue, And those who love it will eat its fruit. (Proverbs 18.21nkj). I am concerned that many men are speaking death, rather than life , which leads to lockup. Beloved, as a man your words set the stage for your entire life.

The only way that I can get you to see this I pray is to give you some examples that changed my world. The first thing we must stop saying as a man is **I CAN'T.** The devil knows the moment he gets you to think you can't, he weakens your abilities. What's important about this is he weakens your ability to create, comeback, or recover. When I was growing up in the projects the system knew that I was going nowhere. I watched the I Can't take root in some men that led to low self-esteem. This is another setup of the enemy to trap you in trouble that leads to lockup. I had to continue to speak great things in my life such as, I will be a great soldier in the Army.

I began to understand early that my words have authority in my life, and in the world. When the man believes that his words have power, he now has the ability to create a door for success. I honestly believed God allowed me great success in the military, due to the words I released. Now, even though sometimes odds were stacked against me, I never released words of defeat. I believe when we as men began to only speak words for success, we will inherit success. When I was 21 years old and single, I said to my friend Fred Horn, that at age 25 I will be married. One year later, I met the lady of my dreams, and 3 years later we were married at age 25.

What I believe made that happen is when I released those words, I released them with confidence. We have been married for thirty nine years today, and God has been faithful. Beloved, it is time for you to use only words that you believe, and expect to come to pass. When you began to believe this, you will see your world take shape to the words from your mouth. I want to first encourage men to stop saying words that disconnect you. What I mean, is there are words that disconnect you from what God intended you to be. The devil will allow you to use these words long enough for them to plant a seed in you of failure.

I used to say words like "I am just a little peon" and what I was getting was a little peon results that hinder. When I was living in darkness, these negative words were keeping me bound until I found Christ. The bible says "I can do all things through Christ who strengthens me. (Phill:4.13). You and I as a man can do all things in Christ I believe, especially when we know our words are powerful. Sir, delete out of your vocabulary" if it wasn't for bad luck I wouldn't have any at all". These are words that rob you of your destiny, that send you on the road to bad thinking and possibly to lockup. What happens is you have closed your mind to new creations, and the power of God. I promise you the moment your words get a new makeover, there will be a celebration. I know for a fact that I was looking in the eyes daily of men in this prison who are here as a result of words.

The reason I know this is true is that talking to inmates, I get a history of their words also. See here's the key, your future will come as a result of the words you speak over your life. What is also critical is the words others speak over you. Remember as a man, you were created by God who created the world by words. (Gen 1.3). Once again, the devil knows this is true therefore, he wants you to use words that destroy futures. I love telling the inmates one way that you can correct your future and your life is through your words. I want to stop right here to tell a man to watch your words. I say this because if you don't watch your words, your words will watch you all the way to lockup.

What I discovered is my words are so powerful that they are not being stopped by conditions. A man has the power to become who he desires, and they begin with the words out of his mouth. Sir, I want you to think about this. The highest position in the United States of America comes from words. The president of the United States gets elected based on what was said out of their mouth. Notice his words make the difference. Now sir, all you need to do is change your words, and watch your position change. You might not have a desire to be president, but I do pray that you desire to take authority in your life. The power of a man's word has the potential to reach heaven to move on his behalf on earth.

When I was deployed to Iraq, I heard the voice of God said, I will preach there, and I believed. I was not concerned that I was not a chaplain, I just believed what God said. Now, because I knew the power of my words, when I arrived I asked where was the church. Three months after my arrival in Baghdad Iraq, I was appointed Senior Pastor by the Chaplain staff. I was later awarded the Bronze Star Medal for exceptionally service while in combat. Sir, let me say to you that you and I as a man can fix our destiny with words. Now, the words must be what God says and what he will do. It is time for men to stop saying I come from a poor family, and I will be poor. I am here to tell you regardless of your situation start saying words that **uplift** than **tear down**. **Tear down** is very close to **lockdown** and **lockdown** is a prison term.

This is a set up again by the devil to get you to think you are nobody. This has robbed the life of too many great men that I am witnessing as I work at this prison. Men, it is time to stop saying I am too broke to pay attention. The enemy tried to really plant those words in me deeply. The reason why is he knows that my father had difficult times raising seven children in the projects. What the devil would hope was that these words would take hold because of what I saw. Beloved, you do not have to say words based upon what you saw in your past. You as a man have the power to speak blessings over your life and turn your life around now. The bible says "So {it shall be} that he who invokes a blessing on himself in the land shall do so by saying. (Isaiah 65.16 amp). Sir, all you have to do is speak blessings over yourself by faith, and watch God. Stop saying words such as I will never come out of debt, to I am on my way out of debt. If you know you need to go back to school for your diploma or degree, say I will do it. Say to yourself it will happen for me and God will do the rest.

The power of a man rests in you sir, and you do not have to go down the wrong road. You have authority over those temptations that are trying to get you to go down instead of going up. I had to start speaking blessing over my life by saying words of faith. Faith words are words from God in the mouth of a man that believes God and expect miracles. I know the devil tried hard to get me to go down with negative words that could impact my life. One of the things that were very important for me was my environment that impacted my words. Sir, I am telling you if negative words are all around you, change your environment now.

I promise you when I say many of these men are in this prison due to their words. I am here to tell you that regardless of the situation, you speak blessings over yourself. If you are out of work and need a job, start saying blessings over yourself of a job. I promise you this is what I had to do after being unemployed for three years. Now, yes it was a challenge, but I knew God was working with me for a reason of His own. I begin to speak blessing over me that would reach over a bad economy, and God sent the blessing. Now, I began to speak words of power that I knew would send me where God wanted me.

The job God sent me to was the job at the prison working at the hospital. I believe my assignment was to capture this huge problem that is robbing great men. The huge problem that I am speaking of is lockup. I believe again that a large part of the problem that is bringing great men to lockup is words and environment. Now is the time for men to invoke or say blessings over themselves. The power that is in a man by faith can knock down walls of a bad economy. I am here to say to men even if the circumstances seem to be working against you, speak a blessing. When you learn to speak blessings over yourself, you will see that your purpose is too big for lockup.

I want every man that is reading this book to know that you are a difference maker. Since God made you to make a difference, we must know that He equipped us with the tools. I believe one of the simplest tool we have to do that with is our words. Once I recognized how powerful my words were to God I immediately managed the company that I kept. What I discovered was it is too easy for me to live and believe in the words of my environment. What's even worse than that is I can take those words and watch them make me or break me. What the devil has done over the years is setup traps for men to fall by words that trap. Beloved, don't get trapped by words of defeat when you have the power in your mouth to succeed. The bible says "For verily I say unto you, that whosoever shall say to this mountain, Be thou removed, and be thou cast into the sea; and shall not doubt in his heart, but shall believe that those things which he saith shall come to pass; he shall have whatsoever he saith. (Mark 11.23).

Sir, trust me growing up in the projects I said a lot of things that didn't make a lot of since. Most of what I said then I didn't expect to come to pass. Now that I have been born again, I still say a lot of things, but with my faith in God, I expect them to come to pass. God has allowed me to see much that I said to come to pass to show His power and the power in man. When I became the first African American Chief Warrant Officer as a technician in the Alabama National Guard this came from words. They came from powerful words that tore down mountains that stood for many years. Beloved, as a man of powerful words, you can tear down that mountain that may be in front of you.

You may have a financial mountain, educational mountain; health mountain, job etc… say something. Trust me when I say it is in your genes by faith as a man to say what you believe to come to pass. Now, stop saying or thinking that nothing good will work out for you because it is in your words. Sir, I want you to notice the scripture above that says "whosoever shall say". It doesn't matter where you come from or how bad your situation may look you are a part of whosoever. This means you as well can say to your mountain to be moved and it can get out of your way. I believe many great men right now needs to say to their mountain move right now or lockup is waiting.

Beloved, what I am trying to say to you as a man is you are made for your words to set the stage. Whether we like it or not, our words that come out of our mouth paints a picture of where we end up. I believe that if most men words were for good, we would not have prison overcrowding. God revealed this to me that if this simple principle change, there would be change. I believe change would be in homes, communities, and our entire world if men would change their words. As long as men are saying things such as I can't win for losing, defeat is at your doorstep. This is all the devil needs to plant bad decisions that leads to trouble and lockup.

You and I as a man were placed on the earth to say words of empowerment without doubt. God made us that we can rearrange what the world has setup for us by saying them with faith. I believe what God did for me was to allow me to see rough times first, then to use the right words. I now do not give the enemy any room to allow negative words to come out of my mouth. The power of words in a man do not know that I don't really mean what I say. What is important is that they came out of my mouth with power. This is why I tell men to stop saying **"My Feet Is Killing Me"** because your words you say are meant to come to pass. We know your feet may not bring physical death, but they can cause death to your dreams. This comes by walking in the wrong direction. I believe that wrong direction can lead me to trouble that is **killing** my dreams. Beloved, the power of a man's word can go much farther than the average man's thinking. What I want to encourage you with is you are not just average, but a man made with destiny. What will get you on that road to your destiny is words of success that you win the race.

Let's begin this new journey by saying that you are a man who are days away from your breakthrough. I want you to begin to say daily that you are a prosperous man, and it is about to be seen. I want to speak now to men that are truly ready to see your life make a turnaround. Beloved, let us start the fresh journey off by eliminating the cussing in your vocabulary. Now, I know this might seem not so important, but sir, please note that when I did my whole world changed. Again, growing up in the projects I said every cuss word imaginable in my days. What God revealed to me was with my **cussing** I was **cursing** my future and **contaminating** my vision.

When I made a recommitment to Christ and stopped the cussing, God began to reveal to me His plan. What I began to see was while God was speaking to me, my cussing was keeping it from me. What I see in most men with the cussing is, it supposed to make their statement more meaningful and powerful. When I came to myself as a man made from God, I realized all I say in faith is powerful. I now can speak to those mountains with words of faith, and see God move. God gave my life a new makeover and meaning when I changed my words, and stopped the cussing. I desire to see this in all men that they may win the race of life, that lockup has no place in them.

Most men that I hear cussing also appear to make them more of a man. Knowing what I know now, it is really destroying their entire inside where greatness begins. When I was cussing like I hear most men now, I felt really good about being heard for my foul language. When I began to grow in the knowledge of God, I realized I was headed nowhere. I knew that whatever was in me, would come out of me at some point in my life. Beloved, as soon as you cease the cussing out of your mouth, destiny will sign you up. The bible says "Not that which goeth into the mouth defileth a man; but that which cometh out of the mouth, defileth a man. (Matt:15.11).

I believe there is much in you sir of greatness that has great words that will define you. God has a work for you to do that demands sound knowledge with sound words. I believe you are about to come into new life now with meaningful words.. The bible says "Let your speech be always with grace, seasoned with salt, that you may know how ye ought to answer every man. (Coloss: 4.6). When the words out of our mouth are clean and pure, they can touch heaven. The power of man's words sets a high standard on the earth that is of God. Let us walk in faith as men, that our words set us free, that the world cannot bind us in chains. We as men can only bind ourselves in chains, and they begin with words. I believe this is the hour where God is about to set many great men free. The men that are touched by God and delivered in this hour, will witness miracles. I believe healing will take place in hearts and minds of men that lockup take a back seat.

Understanding The Old And New Man

I believe it is critical that a man understands the importance of in Christ, he is a new man right now. This is important for man to know, because the devil's goal is to keep you in the old man's way of life. The old man is where the man is constantly being defeated with sin, and darkness is ever present. The problem with the man walking in sin and darkness, he is very likely to find himself in bound. Darkness and sin when it have taken the best of man, can allow him to function with an unstable mind. God intended for the man to become new in him that he may be great in the earth. When we put on this new man we have the power to take authority over darkness and walk in light.

The bible says "Lie not one to another, seeing that ye have put off the old man with his deeds; And have put on the new man, which is renewed in knowledge after the image of him that created him. (Coloss: 3:9-10). Beloved, with this new man in you and me, we can overtake temptation in faith and power. The new man in us as men by faith drives us away from the natural to the supernatural. When it appears that we can't make it, the new man reminds us that we have unseen provisions. These are the provisions that keep us from lockup that the enemy can't see. What the new man has done by faith is received knowledge from God, that gives him hope. In the old man, it still appears that he is without, and must take what is not his.

I am confident that the devil is at war with man, to keep him in the old man, at any cost. The reason the devil desires this is because, he knows he can control his life. In my old ways as a man, I am living with old habits, old thoughts, and old lifestyles. When man is in this state of mind and living, he is on his own because he believes he is in control. I discovered that this is a dangerous place to be, because with this lifestyle, to you there are no laws. This is a great place to plant a seed for lockup. Beloved, God has a master plan for your life that is worth living. What will be required is to believe that new life is awaiting you.

With this new life that is waiting comes a complete new way of thinking. This is where you will find the life that Jesus died for, that you have life and life more abundantly (John 10.10). I know that I look in the eyes of many young men at the prison that came in the old man. Now, what is good for them is that they know they were in the old man, because they said so. I thank God that many have been delivered from that old man, and will return home new. God has a plan for you, and it requires getting to know Him, that the old man becomes new. Beloved, I am here to tell you that there are major benefits when you become a new man. I believe upon getting saved, and knowing God, my new man in me took major leaps and bounds.

When I received the new man in me, the first thing I remember changed immediately was my thoughts. I no longer thought that I had to settle with being average and ordinary. I began to believe that in the new man, I could have new dreams that can come true when I believe. The advantage that I have with the new man is my new identity out weights my old status. I can now by faith see myself as God sees me, and get a new perspective on purpose and position. When I can believe I am the new man God called me to be, I can function great in my calling. What the devil has done and is doing daily is capitalizing on man's inability to walk in his newness. The old man delights in his old ways because his accountability requires no discipline or determination.

What I have discovered is when determination and discipline in man have no place, evil has a place. The evil that can arise in the man can send him to lockup. When I talk to a lot of these young men in lockup, I see and hear these two missing essentials. Beloved, in the time in which we live right now, you must embrace these two to recover. I say recover because in the old man, you will constantly get knocked down in your own strength. The new man in you by faith in God links you to the discipline you need to win every battle. In the new man you are led by God to have success in everything you put your hands on. I knew when I met the woman of my dreams that I wanted the new man.

I wanted the new man because after being the old man in darkness, I knew I was not fit for marriage. When I gave my life to Christ, I was overwhelmed with a new spirit that set my feet on solid ground. Now, I knew I had the right chemistry to be the husband God called me to be with determination. I am here to tell somebody that there is a new man deeply rooted in you that you need to meet. I also need to say that whatever is on your mind to do that is not of God, that's the old man. I come by to tell you to call on God to deliver you of that man before your address is lockup. Beloved, I promise you that lockup is not for you neither is that old man.

I know that you are the right one for the new man because I believe God has been speaking to you in silence. What I am here to say to you is, don't ignore God's voice because He is trying to tell you something. I believe God is trying to tell you that He cares for you, and desire you to know Him. When you get to know God,

He will make you that wonderful man you can be as a father and husband. One thing that is amazing about the new man is, for me every giant has fallen since my new identity. I am not saying that there were no rough places, but I never had to fight on my own. God has made a promise to His children that he will never leave us nor forsake us. (Hebrews 13.5).

Beloved, when you get to know God by faith in the new man, every giant must fall at the hand of God. I spoke with a young man in lockup that had such a wonderful story that gave in to a giant. This was a giant that many young men are facing today without a chance in the old man. Sir, if you think you have the system tricked while you are enjoying the darkness, lockup will find you. What my prayer is for you is that you find Jesus, before lockup finds you in the old man. Here is what I have learned in my six-year study working at the prison. Lockup has an invisible range and distance that captures the greatest minds of darkness. Now, we must understand darkness is a product of the old man walking in the wisdom of man. What is important to note here is the new man is walking in the wisdom of God. I have talked to brilliant men in this six-year study who was walking in the old man unknowingly.

What is important to note about the old man is he wears a mask of denial, that ruins the greatest. The enemy has such a tight grip on the old man that he can forget his last footstep. This can happen because the devil knows what type of food of temptation to feed man's emotion. God desires you to come to know Him in the new man that you never have to fight this fight. When we are in the new man, the only fight that we fight is the good fight of faith and avoiding lockup. The bible says " Fight the good fight of faith, lay hold on eternal life, whereunto thou art also called, and hast professed a good profession before many witnesses. (1Tim:6.12). The problem for the old man is he is not able to profess a good profession, and lockup is at his fingertip.

What happens in the old man is he fights against the giant that holds his destiny, because he has no voice. This giant is the devil, who takes the man, and leads him astray where there is no turning accept to Christ. Beloved, God has a master plan for you that has the master's reward who is Christ. I listen to young men at the prison daily who are still fighting the wrong fight that has lockup make-up. I believe a lockup make-up can be imprinted all over the man if he is not careful in the old man. The old man is walking without faith, and sees no hope, and walks with insecurity. What insecurity does for the old man strips him of a comeback, and plants in him go back.

What the old man decides in most cases from here is, there is no way out under pressure. Now, the enemy knows what he is doing to the old man in this case, and he works it day by day. The enemy knows that once the old man comes to Christ, he is that new man of faith. The new man comes into a man of faith who knows how to fight the good fight and watch God. When I came into my new man, I found that this is where I must help every man I know get here. I discovered in my new man; I can see God in faith that I never stumble. This does not mean I will not have any challenges, but every challenge dials up great faith in me.

In the new man, we have a measure of faith that can bring us to a point of victory. The battle gets the best of my faith when I know that the new man has overtaken me. Beloved, now is the time to let the new man overtake you by the word of God and bury lockup potential. When we look at the world today, it is no question that many men are living in the old man. I watched on the news the other day where a 35-year-old man kills a 12-year-old girl. Now, humanly thinking one would say, this little girl is young enough to be his daughter. Here is the catch, the old man functions totally in the flesh and has no feelings for consequences. This is why as I minister to the men in lockup now, my goal is to lead them to Christ. The reason for this is, I know that the new man will turn their hearts into a new place of light. Beloved, it doesn't matter where you are or what you may have done, God can change you. When God changes you, He will make you new, that your life is in His hand and free from lockup. Free because of the discipline that comes with salvation.

I am a witness that God can shield you far from lockup, even though you make think you deserve it. This is where God's mercy comes in you, and makes you new with a new mind. The new man in you brings a transformation that commands trouble to get under your feet. With this new man, you are in control of your destiny, with God opening every door. Sir, I am here to tell you that the moment that you are waiting for is a step away. The way to that step you need comes through knowing God, that you enter new territory. Yes, you come into some territory that you may not have experienced due to troubled waters.

God is on your side now and is inviting you to new territory that you desperately need to be. I believe you can, with this new man upon you can really show a wife, how a true husband functions. Now, the devil doesn't want you to hear this, because he desires to keep you deceived. I believe sir, that there is something in you that is reaching at the real you, that money can't buy. What I know for a fact is the world's outside system of deception Now, notice I said many men were bought by something from the outside that led to lockup. I know this because as I look at these men daily in lockup, I see the negative forces from outside interventions. Some of these interventions were lack of education, lack of hope, and the inability to establish confidence.

This is what the old man does when the new man has been shut out by these forces. Beloved, you have the abilities and now the information that you need to recover and respond. God is calling you to rise up and get moving to where He desires you to be. By faith, you have dominion over your world to give God glory. You can have this done first by making a decision that you will no longer live in the old man. Now is the time to call on God for the new man that no devil can lead you to the road of lockup. I promise you that there is no room in these dorms at lockup for you in the new man.

The old man forces the hand on the system to keep him a bed ready, even as overcrowding is massive. I witness the old man brought in daily by men of all status, who allowed lack of knowledge to bind him. I am declaring that you are on your way to greater achievements that is far greater than chains. This is the day I believe that can change your entire future with one thought and decision. In this decision, I believe your every dream can make a new entry into a new man. Beloved, let's allow this new man to make his way to your address that you stay there with anticipation. I believe you are about to come into a place that will allow you to discover the new you. With this new you living inside of you, many will come to know Christ and be delivered from lockup. Beloved, lockup is taking the best of men by storm, one bad decision at a time. I pray that you would make the right decision and get to know God that lockup is far under your feet.

The Man as God's Masterpiece

I believe when God made man, He made him a masterpiece designed to work on the earth with superiority. Now, I say this because God made man just like Him, that he can master whatever he chooses. This is because he is by faith functioning like God with His image that he be a success in the earth. What the man must understand is the devil desires to strip this opportunity from him. In this hour, man must know that God has equipped him with masterpiece quality. The bible says "For we are God's masterpiece. He has created us anew in Christ Jesus, so we can do the good things he planned for us long ago. (Ephes: 2.10 NLT) When I think about this, I get excited and determined to remind the man who he is.

I am committed to reminding him of what God thinks of him, that he can overcome the world's potholes. The enemy has set things up for man to fall into the pit, and he loses sight of his calling. The problem is when the man loses sight of who he is, he also loses his ability to be God's masterpiece. The setup that the devil has is the moment he loses these gifts and abilities, lockup is his relief. I believe what has happened is the enemy continues to find that weak link in man to target his attack. Now, the devil's goal is to get him at work for him through any means, then drop the bomb. I hear this daily while working at the prison and I can see how the trend can continue.

What I want to do here is to remind you sir wherever you may be, that to God you are his masterpiece. By faith whatever you may be facing, you have God's makeup and design in you to be great now. I want to share with men that as God's masterpiece, you have no right to settle for less than amazing. This special connection you and I have with God allows us to shake off trouble with assurance. The only way that trouble takes authority over us is we surrender our rights to kingdom privileges. Beloved, with kingdom privileges, and a masterpiece for God, you are **The Man.** Regardless of what you have or do not have, if you are breathing there is a seed of recovery in you.

God has placed a special anointing on you as a man, and God's masterpiece to come out of any dark place. You no longer have to submit to the wiles of the devil and his tricks to find you in lockup. I submit to you, to study the word of God now that you regain your strength and master your every footstep. This is all I believe man needs right now to recover from what the devil has done. The devil knows that once you reclaim your masterpiece rights, he is through and is totally defeated. I want to share with young men today, that the enemy is after great men to deceive him that he falls. The great thing is that men know that they do not have to go down unless their masterpiece guards go down.

I was speaking to a young man in lockup with his story and he agreed with me about what the enemy is doing. The young man spoke to me about the fact that he was charged with that he did not commit. I spoke with this young man and he was telling me about his wife at home who he loves so much. Now, I told him that he looks like a college professor with much potential. This young man said I really feel like that's where I'm supposed to be, but the enemy led me with the wrong company. I really was hurt when this young man told me that he had been stabbed several times in prison. My heart hurts for him, and his wife, how the enemy has temporarily robbed their home. As I try with everything in me to convince men today, I do it with conviction. Beloved, I am here to tell you as a man, that is God's masterpiece, you have power over the enemy.

Now, what is serious is if you do not know you are God's masterpiece, the enemy will come after you and me. This young man realizes that the enemy has robbed him of his destiny as he faces life in prison. I want to remind a man out there, that this is the day that you make a decision in identity. I say this because I have discovered in this assignment, that there is a thin line in greatness. What I want to point out here is there is a thin line between a great man free, and a great man locked up. I believe what separates the two is the great man free knows he is God's masterpiece. When the discovery is made, you are his masterpiece, a wedge of protection is all around you.

This man has established a new walk on the earth and connects with God daily for his course of direction. Beloved, when we look at the world today, and the trouble that surrounds us, why not join God's elect. This requires you to get to know God, and allow him to change and lead you. When you give your life to Christ, he will embrace you and receive you as His and make you new. Now, at this point, you have made a major decision in your life that sets you high above your trouble. God by faith began to work wonders in your life that He begins to hide you in his pavilion (Psalm 27.5).

When the word of God revealed this to me in my life, I saw all things new.

I began to gain confidence that even though I came from the projects, I can be the man God desires of me. When I accepted by faith that I was God's masterpiece, God placed my feet on solid ground. I was able to make a complete turn from uncertainty to most definite when I believed in the word. What God wants in this hour is for man to believe that he can be God's masterpiece for His glory. Sir, what I am learning daily as I speak to these men in lockup is trouble has double vision. What this means is trouble can sniff you out on your good day, as well as your bad day. What is important to note is, you can't stop it. The reason why you can't stop it is because you will never outweigh the devil alone.

When you accept Christ Jesus as Lord, and now you are His masterpiece, you have the strength to overcome the devil. This is because you have the kingdom living in you, that is capable of moving any mountain. Your life can turn around and your world will know that you are a new creature. When I began to believe that God had chosen me as his masterpiece, new dreams began to take shape. I now know exactly what my calling is which came through understanding. I can be the greatest husband on the earth when I walk in the calling of God. Beloved, you too can be the greatest husband, business person, teacher, athlete, etc.. when you believe. Again, this has nothing to do with where you come from, but what you can believe. The reason I believe some men end up in lockup is the enemy caught them sleeping and blinded them. The way the enemy did this was while the man is suffering, he reaches in and binds his belief. The enemy knows that unbelief takes the legs out of your ability to succeed.

Beloved, please don't be deceived by the devil that you are nobody, because in God you are a mighty man. You are by faith a mighty man under a master plan that desires you to believe that you are. I promise you that the moment you believe you are his masterpiece by faith, mercy fills the gaps of your past. I believe your past goes into the sea of forgetfulness by God and sits you at the king's table. I felt this by God when I was called all the way from the projects of Trenholm Court, Montgomery, Al. to Baghdad, Iraq as Senior Pastor. I was honored by God to pastor these great soldiers from across the country. There were also civilian members from 5 nations. What I was able to do quickly as a man as God's masterpiece was develop a mastermind for Christ. I did this by believing that God had renewed my mind for this plan for my life.

I am in the presence of great men in the prison where I work that carries seeds of ambassadors. What really concerns me about it is the devil went in when they lost sight of the master of all. Now, how I believe they lost sight was through the fiery darts the enemy threw. When the man turns back to God by recommitting his life to Christ, he is reintroduced to his royal place. The moment the man gets his royal place by faith, his power is revealed that floors the devil. Sir, I want you to know that you are in a great place that can steer you from that unwanted place. The unwanted place for you is lockup which is screaming loud in the face of great young men.

What the enemy is screaming is go ahead and do what you need to do. Now, what the devil is trying to do in this becomes your master that you may obey him. What the devil is also doing is trying to rob you of the gift God gave you as his masterpiece. Beloved, you are too sharp of a man to fall for what the devil is trying to accomplish. Here's what's important to know. The bible says"No man can serve two masters: for either he will hate the one, and love the other; or else he will hold to the one, and despise the other. (Matt:6.24). Beloved, here is where the devil is trying to rob you of being God's masterpiece.

The devil knows that you learn to love God who is the creator of the world.. What the devil desires for man is to hate on God, that the devil is your master. I am here to tell you that once the devil becomes your master, he masterminds your mind for lockup. Sir, this is your opportunity to pull away from trouble and push your way to the true master. When I say push your way I mean **Pray Until Something Happens** that you become God's masterpiece. I believe you are the man that God is willing to do great things with now. The reason I believe this is because I sense a moment in the spirit for men of your character. What I would like to do is to ask you to think outside of your environment for a moment. I believe what is going on with potentially great men is environmental trauma that yields bad decisions. Beloved, God is a good God and you are precious to Him, and He is able to purge men greatly. I must say that I went through a purging by God, that pulled me out of a dark pit. I wasn't sure at one time I would be able to climb from where I once was in uncertainty.

I began to pray and rely on God, that He would cleanse me from where I was. God answered my prayers, and He took me in and made me new. When this began to take root in me I began to study the word of God and discovered I was by faith His masterpiece. Beloved, hear me out. God can cleanse you just like He cleansed me, and make you whole. God can put you in a place of rest and restore you, that you will know that you are His. I Believe God is calling you right now to be His man of a masterpiece for Him. You are on the verge by faith of coming out of that world that may be prone to lockup.

I believe it is not by choice that many great men are reading this book today. God is about to turn things around for men that were soon to make difficult choices. In these choices, some were headed for lockup, but God has a different agenda to change your life. Sir, you may be out of work right now, but God is about to change that for you right away. I believe there are some men out there that are anticipating bad choices, but a good God has shown up. God is even speaking to someone who has already been in lockup and saying I 'm watching. The reason God is saying He is watching is that He is also watching your back. God has a plan for you to stay out of lockup.

God is watching a nation of men to do great work and make great role models for change. I believe sir, you have the breastplate for God's masterpiece if you would hold on a minute longer. If you would call on God, and let him give you rest, heavy forces from heaven will show up. You will be able to be that man that you always wanted to be your son. I believe there are men out there right now that have a son that is watching every move you make. I want to encourage you to make greater moves for your son or your son will follow you. I have looked into the eyes of enough men and their sons at this prison that hurts me dearly.

Beloved, this can be the greatest decision of your life to get to know God. It doesn't matter how close you are to the fire, or the trouble, there is room for you. Again, there is no room for you here at lockup, but there is plenty of room for a bad choice. I promise you the room in lockup is nothing to write home about because there is no celebration. When you come to know Christ as God's masterpiece, we all celebrate because one man has been saved. One man like you has been saved from coming to lockup and training up his child. I believe the time has come for great men like you to make the decision that you will become great. You will have the capacity by faith, and the work of God in you to move the mountain of not enough. As a man of God's masterpiece, He will enable us to look to heaven for all our needs. Heaven is not running out of provisions for God's people and especially those that are His masterpiece.

Chapter 2

THE MIND OF MAN

I believe that the moment the man can discover the depth and height of his mind he soars. **I** believe he soars to new heights with the revelation he can have access to. What strips him of bearing such revelation is a lack of knowledge of himself and of God. What I have discovered is the devil uses men to poison their mind with their own hands and not know it. I have watched the devil do this all of my life through the use of alcohol and drugs on others. Now, for me, whether it is proven medically or not, I have watched enough great minds stripped from their destiny. This was one of the devil's tools that would begin the road to lockup. One of the sharpest gentlemen ever walked through our prison was there for vehicular manslaughter. This young man allowed alcohol to overtake his mind to drive a vehicle while heavily intoxicated.

Beloved, as a man you can be all that you desire to be and do great things for God. The bible says "Let this mind be in you which is also in Christ Jesus (Phill:2.5). Sir, the state of your situation is not dependent upon your economics or your education, but the state of your mind. What the enemy along with this world wants to do is to ruin your mind however possible. The reason why the devil desires to do this is he know if you tap into your mind, you are coming out. You are coming out of the poverty mindset; the I am nobody mindset, into I have Christ's mind. Sir, this does not take knowing a lot about bible, but knowing a lot about being a man.

When God made man, He put a mind in him that would allow him to be the best at what he desired. What the enemy hopes is that the man underestimates his mind and succumbs to the opinion of others. You have been called by God with His mind in you by faith to conquer on every hand. Now, what is significant for you to know is God has already qualified you and called you more than a conquer. (Roman 8.37). The mind that we have as men when we believe can pull us from the debt of despair. The reason we have these abilities is to demonstrate God's power that rests with man. I am confident that as long as I can keep my mind right, I can make the devil a liar.

When I keep my mind right for what I was placed on the earth for, I can stay in the game and win. Here's what I have discovered. Every defeat, setback, or disappointment desires my mind first. When I have settled in my mind that I can't come out of darkness, my heart stands to agree. After years of this kind of mindset, acceptance begins to set in and my ways grow dim. By faith, you have the mind of Christ to take authority and watch darkness take a hike. When you embrace the mind of Christ in you as a man, all the forces of darkness bow to you. This includes those forces that the enemy sends your way that land you a seat in lockup.

Beloved, I am here to tell you to spend some time with God and discover His mind in you by faith. Since knowing that God has trusted me with His mind in me, I have experienced many impossibilities. The reason these were accomplished was with Christ's mind operating in me, I had the advantage. I am here to tell you that you have the mind of Christ to rise from where you may have fallen. One of the reasons you can rise with the mind of Christ in you is because He rose from the grave. What you need to remember is you have resurrection power in you that begins in your mind. The only way that you never get up from your fallen state is Satan has tagged you for trouble.

You do not have to accept his tag now, because you have this knowledge that you have the mind of Christ. All you have to do is say it and believe it in your mind, and you can turn it all around. Beloved, the mind that was placed in you by God was not to be locked up but grown up, for greatness. I am here today to encourage you to stop thinking and stop saying that your mind is bad. I believe I am speaking to someone who knows that I am telling the truth, that you have spoken negatively about your mind. God sent me to you through these pages to tell you to get to know Him. When you get to know God, you will witness a restored mind that will do wonders for Him.

I believe a man is capable enough to go from a janitor to an astronaut once he discovers the mind of man. Sir, your trouble that may be haunting you can be overturned by the discovery of who you are. You are a man of power, and by the faith of a sound mind when the power of God is upon your mind. In this hour, the devil desires your great mind that he can torture your mind in route to lockup. I declare today, that you are putting away that way of thinking, and coming back to the real you. The real you is that man that God made and gave His mind that you get your name back. Once you can connect your name to the mind God gave you to dominate, your glory shall return.

What this will take is a renewed mind to the things of God, that the enemy can't force you to lockup. The reason why he can no longer line you up for lockup is your mind shall be renewed to promise. The bible says "And do not be conformed to this world, but be ye transformed by the renewing of your mind, that you may prove what is that good and acceptable and perfect will of God. (Rom:12.2). Beloved it is with a renewed mind that you will prove to be good for society. I know how it is coming from the projects when you are labeled not to be good. What is important for me was having a strong foundation that I did not conform to the world.

I want to encourage other men that if your mind does not get renewed now, later might be too late. The world has its way of getting into the mind of great men, and putting a damper on dreams. I have talked to many inmates that shared with me their dreams before lockup. What I discovered was the devil had programmed his mind that he conforms to him. I am confident that when a man renews his mind through the word, much come to light. I believe behind the man's worst nightmares is a hidden mind that's made for wonders. The reason I believe this is we were made by a God who knew no flaws when He made man. Sir, now is the time for renewing your mind with Christ. When your mind gets renewed, there will be no thoughts of violence to lock you down. In your renewed mind shall be made that gentlemen's spirit ready to be used by God. This is a man that is ready to be who he desires because of the wisdom of God.

Beloved, you are a prime candidate the moment your mind is renewed from the way you were until now. Greatness resides in you as a man that requires a renewed mind to get revealed knowledge. When I gave my life to Christ, I began to study the word that I might have my mind renewed. The reason I was concerned about this was I couldn't see myself as a Christian with my state of mind. I'm just being real as I can be because when I was in the world, I was in the world as a chartered member. When you are in this world as a man with his natural mind, you are a breath away from trouble. I am for certain now that this applies to the greatest family men on earth.

I was excited for a week for seeing one of my greatest inmates end his time in lockup. This is because he is not only a great family man but is a great pilot who flew Blackhawks in combat. Now, certainly, he and I shared a bond because of military men who served in combat. What he demonstrated is the amazing ability to endure the worst with a renewed mind. God allowed him to capture the heart of many inmates and staff with his wonderful spirit. I am grateful to God for allowing me to meet him and I am sure he will bless many with his story. This is a man I believe that God allowed come through his test to touch lives greatly. Beloved, when you get a renewed mind through the word of God lives shall be touched.

The mind of man when it has been renewed is capable of affecting all those around them. This is possible because the spirit of God can rest in you in a way that will be noticeable. We are living in a time now where men need to see the reflection of a true God on man. I have discovered that this is impossible for a man to do in his natural state of mind. What the devil will do while man is living out his flesh is keep blinders on him that he stays bound.

How Satan Blinded The Mind

When we look at our world today along with the trouble, something has affected the mind of man. What I have witnessed over many years is how the devil has put his covering over man's mind. Now, he did this undercover in a way that man cannot see what he has done in the natural. Here's the key, the answer to most of our problems will not be found in the textbook. The devil knows this; therefore, he doesn't mind the man getting super smart through secular education. Now, again I am for getting all the education that you can. You do need to know that while family and friends are celebrating your degrees. the devil have no problem with that. I say this because the devil does not mind me with world knowledge. What the devil is overly concerned with is my bible knowledge.

The bible says " But if our gospel be hid, it is hid to them that are lost: In whom the god of this world hath blinded the minds of them which believe not, lest the light of the glorious gospel of Christ, who is the image of God, should shine unto them. (2Corr:4.3-4). Beloved, it is very important that you get this or trouble will get you to lockup. The god of this world is the devil and has blinded the mind of the man that he has no vision. What I am saying here is he has no vision for overcoming therefore, he can easily resolve to trouble. Since the mind of the man has been blinded, he can no longer imagine himself successful. The devil also knows that since he has blinded the mind of man, he can push him to the limit of frustration. Once frustration sets in on the mind with no outlet the war begins.

What I saw daily in lockup where I worked are the results of frustration due to blinded minds. Here's what serious, when the devil blinds the mind he can control our minds for his kingdom. When I look at most of these guys daily I see war going on in them and minds that are wounded. This is what I see now when I see all the violence on the news from one killing to another. What I am confident in with this is the word of God is the only hope to restore the mind. As I look at these wounded minds in prison in the spirit I see them wounded by circumstances. Now, most of these circumstances were by choice, but I see some wounded by the enemy's setup.

The men that I see minds that were wounded by choice were those that never saw the enemy coming. The devil blinded their mind that they can get away breaking the law and never getting caught. This was a snapshot of the way the devil enticed Adam and Eve to eat of the forbidden fruit. Adam and Eve didn't think that they would be caught, but God saw them. (Gen.3). I said thank you Lord for revealing this to me in the spirit. The devil is up to his same tricks on the earth now causing men to fall. I am a living witness that when the mind is saturated with the word of

God we defeat the devil. Beloved, it doesn't matter where you are right now in your walk with God, the devil is after your mind. The devil is after the mind of man that he can destroy all of his seeds of greatness.

The devil is after all of our minds as men that he may blind all our minds that we are of no effect. Those of us that are confident that we have the mind of Christ (1Corr:2.16) do not fear. Our jobs as men with the mind of Christ are to help others become like Christ and stay free. The devil is also trying to get men to have a mind like him that they can do what he does. The bible says "The thief does not come except to steal, and to kill, and to destroy. (John 10.10). This is where the devil really blinds the minds of men that they do what he does. My prayer is to get the word of God with much hope in young men that they shake the devil out of their minds. The only way this happens is their minds get renewed that they know God.

When I look again at the news and I see all the killings among young men, what I see are blinded minds. Since the devil knows scripture and he knows Jesus says the things that I do you do (John:14.12), this is what he wants also. When I look at some of the men that are in lockup for murder it hurts. What it also does in me is to go beyond the call to let men know that they are called to be kings. Beloved, your mind was made to be a master of choice rather than to kill and destroy. The enemy has done this by way of trickery to steal your destiny that you make your way to lockup. What the devil is doing now with his kill mindset is releasing a double dose on our men.

As I look at the alarming rates of killings with guns in our communities it is staggering to just witness the acts. What the devil has done is put the blinders so deep on the minds of men that they see no value in themselves. When the mind has been blinded on man, he sees no value in him or another man. This is where we are in the world today and I see it daily in the eyes of men in lockup. The double dose of the killing nature on men is reaching to our little children. Not long ago in our city, as schools were letting out for the summer, a 16-year-old male was charged with murder. The 16-year-old shot and killed a beautiful 14-year-old female as she was walking home from school.

Today, as I am writing an 11-year-old male, has been charged with murder for shooting and killing a 9-year-old male. We all later discovered this was his little brother. Now, here's what I see, the devil is having his way in the mind of even children to cause destruction. All Satan is up to right now is robbing America of potentially great minds and ruining their lives. Beloved, it is up to you and me to take a stand and say what can I do to save one mind. This is beginning to get out of hand, and it is now time for true men who know God to act. What is critical is that if we don't begin to act and be a witness for Christ, this could be at our doorstep. The first thing that we have to do as men are to be sure that our minds are right with God.

The time is out now for men to live as though we know God, but our minds are as corrupt as the world. I promise you that in the last six years working at the prison, I have discovered that this lifestyle is a hot- bed for lockup. This is because the devil has blinded the minds of the men that they can play church and be corrupt. What the devil wants is for you as a man to say you love God and live a double life. This is the nature of the devil and he is seeking new men daily and I see them coming. What I see with all the killings is the devil is steadily wrecking great minds to die in prison. Our job is to be men like Christ with His mind that we can bring peace to our neighborhoods. The bible says "When our oxen are well loaded; when there is no invasion {of hostile armies} and no going forth {against besiegers when there is no murder or manslaughter} and no outcry in our streets. (Psalms 144.14amp.) When we come together as men for Christ with His mind we can accomplish this.

When we walk by faith and walk with the mind of Christ, we can have peace on our streets without the murders. In the city of Montgomery Alabama, our city is called **The City Of Dreams.** What the devil is trying to do with blinded minds and all the murders in our city is make us **The City Of Nightmares.** The devil is a liar because we have great leaders in our city that is committed to keeping us safe. We have an outstanding police force that you are caught in a **short time** in most cases. We have a district attorney who is serious about making you pay maximum time for your crime. We will continue to be a city of dreams, and we desire every man to dream big. When great minds come together for one cause, we can make our communities great. Beloved, as a man, we need you to be committed to being an example for Christ and other men. When you do this you will be amazed at the impact that you have on keeping others from lockup.

Some of these men that I see daily had no man in front of them that demonstrated a man of excellence. What I mean here is the men that were in their life's minds were blinded due to their words. Beloved God is depending on you to get to know Him that you can be His light for your circle. There are many young men in this prison that were so close to being the greatest. Unfortunately, close in the devil's eyes doesn't count, because if you don't know who you are your mind is his. The moment the man comes to himself that in God's eyes he has his mind, change can come. God is calling for the man to stand strong and wait on Him and He will come through.

When man is able to keep his mind on Christ, he can believe in Christ, and the devil is defeated. This is what I witnessed as the devil was after my mind while I was in combat in Baghdad Iraq. What the devil wanted to do here was to blind my mind that I had no hope, and death was imminent. My job was to stand strong for Christ because there was a calling in my life. The calling was for me to trust God in the worst and stay focused on the mission. What was significant was I didn't lose heart for what I was seeing going on around me. The enemy really tried me shortly after I arrived in Iraq by having 25 U.S. soldiers killed in the dining facility. This was done by an interpreter for us that was a suicide bomber that wore a vest that exploded.

The enemy knew that this could take a toll on your mind and bring you captivity to his ways in a battle. What I had to do immediately was confess to Christ that I needed Him. I needed Him to keep my mind that I do the work He desired of me. I was blessed by God the entire twelve months journey in Iraq to do His will. Beloved, God has a plan and work for you that requires your mind and His will at work. Your community and your family need your mind that it can be a model of success for others. I knew God needed me to be effective in the midst of all the killings at war for His glory. Beloved, God has a need for you to be a true man for Him in the midst of all the killings in the world. What is critical is not allowing your mind to get blinded by the devil that you succumb to lockup. Here are some keys to keep your mind covered and protected from lockup.

One of the ways I discovered that I can keep my mind for Christ and from lockup is having great faith. The bible says "When Jesus heard it, he marveled, and said to them that followed, Verily I say unto you, I have not found such great faith, no not in Israel. (Matt:8.10). I believe when a man establishes great faith he has a made-up mind that can't be shaken. All this take is knowing that your God will not let you down. Most men are so close to great discovery when a major challenge comes to their mind. Beloved, you do not have to fall to that temptation of trouble when great faith is in you. Great faith can be anchored in your bloodstream if you just hold out. While you are holding out, God is making provisions for you because you trusted that He will be there.

I am here to tell your sir, that faith can keep you upright that you are not upside down in lockup. I submit to every man right now that you are called by God to Man Up to the faith in you. I believe the moment you Man up to the great faith in you, there may be found no such great faith than yours. I believe during my worst moments in life such as my three years of unemployment, and war, great faith showed up. What was required of me to make it through was to say, I had great faith. When I said this often my mind was reset when negative thoughts would come. Beloved, in this hour, you need a reset button in your mind when the enemy comes in to devour. The reset button restores in you the mind of Christ that overcomes.

I am here to tell you, I witnessed many men in lockup that did not have a reset button in their minds. Having great faith in God produces great faith in yourself and your mind that you stand the test. I want you to know beloved that you can't win that battle in your own strength and knowledge. Great faith sets you high above the wisdom of Satan, that your destiny is never tampered with. This is due to the full trust that you have established in God by faith that you can make it. God knows exactly where you are and what you are going through, and wants you to know Him. When you get to know God and rely on Him, your great faith brings out the best of His provisions.

I discovered this when all signs were I was going down, but great faith said I was coming up. I believe by faith that you are coming up even though the devil desire you to go down. I pray right now that if you know that I am speaking to you, that you declare you are a man of great faith. The moment you declare this, I believe the God of hope is moving upon your mind right now. I believe God is pouring down great wisdom and power from heaven to restore the minds of men. What it will take from the man is a heart that knows he needs a savior to rescue him.

Beloved, today is the day, not tomorrow, that you decide that you need a savior that your mind is in Christ. According to the scripture that we started in this section, there is no other hope but the word. Now, again I have seen enough brilliant men come through these cells of lockup. What I have discovered is with all of their worldly knowledge and influence it was not enough. What I am saying here is their minds with all their knowledge and skills were blinded by the enemy. You and I are not immune from the enemy's trap but can be covered only by the word. God is calling us as men to be the hope for this world, but the hope must be with the mind of Christ.

As A man Thinks

I believe we are living in a time now where the thinking of man will set the stage in our world. The way that we think as men could have a major effect on the totality of our well-being. I believe when I say I can't, I lose strength in my motivation to become much greater than my natural resume says. By faith as men, we were given the thinking abilities by God to dominate in the earth. I say this because we were given the image of God to think it and watch it come to pass. What is critical is that we must believe the word of God, and what the word says we can do. The bible says "For as he thinks in his heart, so is he. (Proverbs 23.7). Notice as he thinks it he can be it.

This is what I stood on in my weakest and worst moments in my life because in my heart I said yes. Beloved, you can be in control of your thinking the moment you seek God for His guidance. What the devil wants for you and me is to think that we will always fall short of the best in life. Once this is set in stone in your thinking, you become settled with average and below conditions. What generally happens is this man's thinking becomes distorted by current events and conditions. Man was made by God to rule and have dominion and the devil knows how to tamper with the mind.

The moment the man thinks that he cannot rule, his condition is in question.

Now, the devil knows that he is made by God and if his thinking is superior he also can be superior. What the enemy is doing in this hour is tampering with man's thinking that keeps him in lockup. Beloved, let me tell you if you think that you can, I am here to tell you that you will and you shall. I believe every man's success and ability to succeed is at the tip of his thinking abilities. The moment that the man can set his mind on Christ, his thinking can be reset that nothing is impossible. This is where God desires the man to be that he totally relies on Him for all his needs. What man is fighting right now is his place in the earth without the knowledge of God.

What I am confident about is a man will soon deplete his own strength for his greatest desire and reward. Once his strength is gone, he is on an uphill journey to satisfy the flesh which will tap into his thinking. What the devil can now do is force him into a battle with himself knowing that he sees no way out. This is how he began to think that **It Is What It Is,** and he becomes a slave to his environment. Beloved, you are by faith a picture of restoration when you can believe God. The enemy wants to drive you to do the things the average man will do under pressure. When the pressure overwhelms the man, it can drive him to the highway that leads to lockup.

God has given you and I beloved the hope of His glory, and we can step into the field of play of recovery. What we must do in this hour as men with purpose is to fix our eyes on the word of God. When we do this our thinking becomes a new element of discovery as to who we are. The world told me because I grew up in the projects that I belong in the rear and be happy. When I can be happy by way of the word of God, I began to think I can do all things. (Phill:4.13). Now, this thinking bothered the devil because he expects me to think it's just good to be here. I discovered that my thinking shall usher me directly into my purpose. This is where I am trying to get young men to embrace immediately because this is their platform for success. If a man thinks that success is not attainable, it robs him of his ability to reach for the highest mountain.

Beloved, what you think of about yourself is a breath away from the finish line, that is finishing the thought. If you think that you are going to fail, failure has already started the welcome party. If you believe that you will end up in poverty, your local feed shelter has a special seating arrangement for you. It is time for true men to stop thinking the worst and know that they were made for the best. The enemy has set up a base shop for men who really just think that they have no future. I am here to tell you that God has a future for you that is designed for you to be head. Your job as a man is to think the way God has purposed for you to think. Stop thinking that you are not good enough when you were made by a God who is good and who cares.

This is a time I believe for every man to think that if you don't do it, nobody else will. Sir, there are more watching you than you think who need you to make the change in your thinking. I discovered that if I think that I can be great as a husband, I can take authority over a troubled marriage. We as men have been given this authority by God to be the head of our wife. (Epes:5.22). I believe since I am the head of my wife, if my thinking is right with God, I can have a successful marriage. The reason why I believe many marriages end in divorce is the head thinker is out of control. See, I began to say two years into my marriage that on our twentieth anniversary we will upgrade our wedding rings.

Now, I said that in faith, but also with thinking abilities that go beyond natural abilities and statistics. When we as men began to think the way God desires, we can have everything God has given us. Now 39 years in my marriage, I think that every man by faith must think in his heart that his marriage can succeed. Not saying that my wife and I have arrived, but we think together with God we have the victory. Beloved, if you don't begin to think in your heart that you are victorious the devil has a plan. The devil will send your thinking down the road of I can't and find you in lockup. It is important for a man with a mind like Christ to know that your thinking makes a difference.

Beloved, from this day forward let's start thinking that there is no valley that we cannot climb to achieve. We serve a God that is able to take you and I higher than we have ever been. Start thinking right now that this is the year that you will go higher in God than you have ever been. I promise you that this is the beginning of your next level to a new life forever.

Now, start thinking this way right now because tomorrow may be too late, and the devil is on the attack. It is important for every man to start a new way of thinking now because the old was in the natural. By faith know that you are a new man in the spirit and things will begin to change. I am on a mission to get men to think kingdom-minded now and the chains will come off. The chains will come off that have many men bound that they cannot come out of bondage. Beloved, bondage in any area of life on a man is a symbol of lockup in his mind that holds him hostage.

As I am on this mission to free the man from being bound I am consistent in encouraging him that a king is in him. Once again the system has robbed us of this in our mind that our environment is our gage. I stepped out of my office one day at the prison and one inmate said, don't I know you. Now, when I looked at him, he did look familiar, but I could not quite remember. Once we kept talking and I kept looking at him I remembered we grew up together in the projects. As we begin to talk for a minute I picked up immediately that the system had affected his thinking. This gentleman and I finished high school together and I was hurt that his thinking has him in lockup.

My high school classmate then said to me all of these five guys on the bench are all from Montgomery. I said to all guys this is just a pothole, but you must begin to start a new way of thinking. I am only here as a light of hope for you to take a look at me and know that there is hope. I said to them that your fellow inmate here on the bench with you, yes, we grew up together in the projects. My goal here I mentioned has a few objectives, and one is to get men to manage their thinking. I want all men that are in lockup to know that the only difference between me and you is our thinking. Here is what is clear to me in the bible, as a man thinks in his heart, so will he end up.

Beloved, the system has fixed it that your thinking will put you in the path of your environment. Now, your aim must be on target. Unfortunately, what I have seen in many of the young men in lockup is they are hitting bullseye. Parents, what you and I must do now is a better job of influencing the thinking of our children. Now, what is important about this is there is a way I have discovered this and will discuss it in a later chapter. What I am passionate about now is the thinking of our men and the consequences. I know what saved me while in the projects was learning how to apply thinking against pressure.

What this takes is a moment of measuring the act against what I believed was waiting for me and my future. I knew what my goal was which was going into the military, therefore I began to think like a soldier. Now, I knew that I could not continue to hang with the wrong crowd because that could spell lockup. I had every opportunity to do that, but my mind and heart were set in stone for good. The enemy is still working now as he was then on men when I was living in the projects. One way I know that for certain is how my classmate I mentioned was attacked by the enemy in 2017. This is forty years after we graduated and how a man can still be wondering in the wilderness. Beloved, you can be wondering in this world until you obey God and get to know him. When you get to know God, you may still experience some wilderness, but are amazed at his wonders. The bible says "Behold, I and the children whom the Lord hath given me are for signs and wonders in Israel from the Lord of hosts, which dwelleth in mount Zion. (Isaiah 8.18).

Beloved, yes, you and I as men were made for signs and wonders that we may do the impossible. Once we can have our thinking adjusted to the ways of God, these shall come to pass. I pray now that you begin to think that you can be world changers that you may do great things now. God is holding us accountable as men who have been given His image to do these wonders now. You as a man were made to turn every situation around that God be glorified. I believe one moment of your thinking about the power of God shall adjust your thinking. I am believing for you right now that the true man in you is taking place for God's wonders.

By faith, these wonders are about to lose you from the grip of troubles that could find many in lockup. The enemy has been trying to sway you away to his house, but I am believing you are coming to God's house. In God's house, you will find evidence that God's glory can overtake you and change you. I believe through God's glory you will walk out His goodness and find your way back to Him. When I found my way back to God I saw something in me that I never saw while I was spiritually blind. What blinded me was thinking that I had to be what the world wanted me to be that had me bound. Beloved, I come to tell you that when your thinking is bound, your life is not far from being bound. When you are bound the doors are shut tight in lockup.

Here's the good news, this is a new day and God desires to give you new light and new hope to win. Your first step into this new light and new hope are to trust God that you will not be bound but free. In order to secure this as a man, you must be willing to be different than you were with natural thinking. God has called you to be His chosen man to do some things that must be done with a new mind. Once again, don't be concerned about what has happened in the past, we are moving to the future. I want to encourage you sir to get into the word of God that you may see His plan unfold. I have seen far too many men miss their future because they were stuck in their past.

I believe once you get in the word of God and learn of him your new way of thinking shall propel you to new creations. This is what I watched the word of God do in me and in my thinking about how far I can go. The system did this to me by making me think that there was a limit on how much money I can make. Now, it's not always about money but is always about your thinking about what to do with it. Beloved, it is no different if you said to me that you have four master's degrees. The issue will be in your thinking as to what can you do with them and are you doing anything. I believe as a man in God's image your thinking and how you think set the platform for greatness. I want to encourage every man that you can be everything that you think you can be. You have God standing by you to support you in your endeavors that will bring him glory. Trust me when I say you can think your way out of your every pitfall by thinking. This made a difference in me when I believed that I could be all that God said I could be. Sir, the moment you began to think that you are all God said you are the game is over for lockup.

I believe you will discover as I did that your life is designed to bring others hope than shackled with no hope. What I have witnessed in many young men is how in a short time their cell drains their hope. What I do is pour out everything in me and ask God to give me the right words to restore this soul. One day one young man in our hospital at the prison said to me you would not believe what I have been thinking. I said to him why are you thinking like that and he said because of my condition. Beloved, we are living in a world today where your condition can alter your way of thinking. I have a question for you sir, have you allowed the condition that you are in to alter your thinking. Let me say to you that if you are not careful that thinking can change your position. For many men unfortunately that position has been lockup for a long time.

Let me encourage you now that God is the only way that you can get your thinking above your condition. By the grace of God, you can override what the condition has the tendency of doing in the natural. We serve a God who can fix anything including your thinking and your condition and set you free. Know that God cares for you and He desires your thinking to be far above this world's ways. Then you will know that there is a God who can do exceedingly above all that we can ask or **think.** (Ephes:3.20).

The Mind Of Overcoming

I believe one of the greatest gifts God has given to me and to men is a mind to overcome all things. One of the important things about this is when you master this nothing can keep you bound. The reason I believe this is the enemy sets the trap in the mind that takes away our energy. What I believe happens in the mind of man when he knows he is an overcomer is life-changing. Some of man's greatest challenges are conquered the moment he realizes his abilities to overcome. Once overcoming rests in our minds, we get a new burst of energy that is second to none. I believe God gave this power to man that he never stays down but conquers the fall.

The bible says "Yet amid all these things we are more than conquerors and gain a surpassing victory through him who loved us. (Romans 8.37amp). Beloved, no matter what your situation may look like you can conquer it. All this requires is you having the mind of Christ in you that gives you overcoming power. God gives power to the man who believes he has the mind of Christ that sets the boundaries. Now, the problem comes when man has no knowledge of God's power in him. This is where he takes the wrong turn and trusts in his abilities and the world's that leads to lockup. This happens because all of us are going to face adversities that attempt to take the breath out of us.

When we are walking in faith with a mind of Christ we are not moved about our condition but the promise. The promise is we have the victory in Christ Jesus and the mind of overcoming all obstacles. Here's an important note for my believers. The promises are **true** even though your conditions may appear they are **false.** I want to encourage every man, do not be persuaded by the devil's lies. You can overcome that financial setback, job setback, sickness setback, marriage setback, etc.. right now. The reason why you can is that God has your back that puts you over every setback. You have the victory, don't give in to the lies especially when they have lockup all over them.

Many of the young men in lockup tell me that they gave in to the devil's lie quickly. I tell them that I almost gave in to the big lie also while living in the projects, but took a different path. The only way that occurred for me was I had a father that demonstrated a mind for overcoming. As my father gave an example of overcoming, I was introduced to my spiritual father. Living by faith while enduring tough times I got a word from God of overcoming. When I gave my life to Christ, His spirit began to live in me and changed my course of travel. I began to think on the level of who I was converted to and overcoming rested in me.

Beloved, you are not the person like a man that might be fighting a painful path. God has made a way possible for those who can endure until His power shows up. When you learn through the word to live by faith, overcoming will get fixed on your heart. I promise you that you do not have to give in to trouble that might be coming from your past. Now, I say past because I believe that you are growing into that man that is not who he once was. God is guiding your footsteps to a place of healing and deliverance that will free you. Once again, your past may be trying to mislead you, but by faith, I call you a changed man. God is right now looking down on you by faith as I pray for you, that your greatest days are in front of you. You are not that man that once did not know who he was that the enemy could send to lockup. You are that new man that God has placed His hand on and is calling you overcomer.

Beloved, I declare that you are the man that God has called for such a time like this to be his man of change. I believe in doing this if you only believe God is about to change your entire world for His glory. Now, you can't get into doubt because this is what has caused enough men to fall hard. I want you sir to begin to call on God now in prayer, and on this day, I declare a mind of overcoming in you. You are about to overcome those thoughts that have very crushing blows in them. The enemy has a tendency of reaching great men like you and delivering blows to kill a man's future. What is crucial he is doing it at an alarming rate that is causing great men to do bad things.

I believe you are one of the men like I was who had experienced enough hardship that winning seemed impossible. What I discovered God was doing was preparing me through the hardships for my greatest moments. As I began to seek God daily through his word, I began to examine my hardships with a new lens. I began to look through the lens of a man with a mind of overcoming to turn it around. God has sent me through these pages to tell a man somewhere that you must turn around now. The enemy knows that there is a man that is reading this that only may have one more chance to get it right. What I mean here is someone is on the verge of trouble that is straight lockup for you. God is standing by to let you know that He is able and you are a candidate for a mind of overcoming.

As a man, you can make this change in record time when you only believe in and know God. Once you develop and receive this mind of overcoming, there are no tough times that you can't endure. What makes the difference in you now when you receive this mind, the pain is not as severe. I am not saying that everything is now perfect, but I am saying that you have the capacity to recover. I was able to recover from my hardship of being unemployed for three years with a different mind. I knew I needed to provide for my family and having no job was a painful blow. What my mind of overcoming was doing was holding back the **abnormal reaction** from a trauma.

Here's what's worth important to note, your mind and body have a tendency of presenting an **abnormal reaction** to a physical need. For instance, my head gets an abnormal reaction to when I am hungry, and pain/trauma sets in or a headache. I have a need to eat right away. Now, when I am fasting for God I have a mind to overcome this pain, and patience sets in and I endure. What the enemy has done in man is when a need/desire shows up and he is not able to hold back **abnormal reaction** trouble comes. This need or desire will register in the man as trauma and he knows not where to turn. Unfortunately, this trauma brings hardship and in the worst cases lockup for the greatest men without hope. Working at the prison and listening to inmates' testimonies, these **abnormal reactions** can bring disturbing results. Unfortunately for some of them, they resulted in rape, robbery, drugs, and even murder.

Sir, when you get a mind of an overcomer for Christ, His power works in your behalf in all things. You do not have to be in fear because as a man with a mind for overcoming, you defeat every challenge. The way this happens is your mind moves to a new dimension that brings a wall of confidence. With this confidence, the mind recognizes the need and it feeds in the spirit realm of possibilities. Even when I had no money to support my family while unemployed heaven made away. My household was missing a large part of my **income,** but provisions from God were **coming in**. Beloved, as a man, all God wants from you is trust that He will provide and you will overcome.

I believe many of the men that are here in lockup never believed they could overcome their present state. Many just could not handle those abnormal reactions that were testing their faith in God. I believe God is searching for men of faith with the mind to overcome that he may forever be free. This is not only being free from lockup but being free that he can be all that he can for God. I thank God that He has shown me how powerful He is when I trust and lean on Him in confidence. This is an element that brings your mind to the place to be an overcomer in every area. I believe there are two major factors needed for the overcoming man that endures abnormal reactions.

The first factor in the man is he must be a man that will not accept defeat, and get the devil under his feet. This is what it took for me when the heat was getting hot in every area where I could have quit. I was not going to accept defeat at the warrant officer academy even though circumstances said to give up. I knew that I could make a difference just by enduring and waiting for God's timing. Beloved, defeat is nowhere in you as a man but maybe near you in your environment. If you trust God, He will hold you up and keep you but you need to know He is well able. When you get this inside of you in faith there will be no need to attempt roads that can present trouble. This is your season to stand strong and know that God is with you.

The second factor needed to be a man of overcoming is to know that you are not in the fight alone. The war in Iraq was a heated battle every day of my twelve months in combat and death was near. When I would rise each day, I prayed to God and in the spirit, I knew that I was not in the fight alone. When I knew with confidence that God was with me daily, I developed a mind of an overcoming man to win. This was to win my life back that the enemy thought that he had stolen in combat. What the enemy believed was he would get me all out of synch with my future. I believed God for what He had promised and came back home the same way I went with greater faith. Beloved, whatever struggle you may be in as a man it is important to know you are not alone. The moment I knew that God was with me in the fire in Iraq it raised my level of anticipation in battle. Even when it looked like I was going down some days I had anticipated victory living in me. This is the kind of mindset that puts fear out of the equation for the opportunity.

Beloved, when you get into this kind of thinking a mind for overcoming unlocks the doors of possibilities. Now, you are on the road to a victory that allows the hand of God to do mighty works for you. What happens with this is as your mind for overcoming unlocks doors they keep you clear from lockup. This also raises the man's level of anticipation to do things for God that keep him far from trouble. Sir, I believe you truly are next in line for the hand of God to do the best yet in a man. This work that God wants to do with you comes as a result of you being faithful to His promises. What is also important for you as a man to know is you can change a whole family's make-up.

I know for certain that my mind for overcoming made a difference in defeating the hurdles of life. With my mind in this position, I never saw myself stuck in a place of no return no results. What I discovered happens to most men who fall into trouble is they get stuck in a place of no return no results. This is a place where men get stuck and in their minds, they can never get their desires met. In this place, men also think they can never return to where they started due to pride. What the enemy does with this thinking is plant seeds of underhand recovery which leads to lockup. Beloved, as a man you are born by faith to ride the waves of patience while God speaks to the waves.

I believe when we as men learn to wait on God in the tough times our minds are being conformed for righteousness. This is shaping our thinking that we become overcomers that we can be a witness. What the enemy does is pushes the man to overreact when temptation is at its best. When we stay in the word of God and pray daily our minds stays in overcoming mode to defeat the test. A mind for overcoming in the man can truly be his spiritual radar on how he navigates in trouble. Each time that we would get the words in combat "INCOMING" this was a time you are being attacked. You are about to be hit by a rocket or a mortar round on your base which could mean death.

For me, it was important while the attacks were coming that my mind was positioned right that I live. I knew that if my mind was in the overcoming mode I would be shielded properly that my life is not taken. Beloved, as a man we are living in a time where I must say to you "INCOMING" because the war is on. The enemy is firing many rockets of financial problems, marriage and relationship problems to cause you some domestic violence. The enemy is also finding ways to connect great men with bad company in any way possible that leads to lockup. Domestic violence sir is a fixed lockup. Beloved, don't fall for that, God desires you to trust him with a mind for overcoming and He will bless you abundantly. This is what God has done in me and He wants to do in you as long as you allow Him. I was looking in the eyes daily at the prison of too many men that should be leaders in the community. These are great men that were just not prepared when the fiery darts of the enemy came. What is required in this hour of men is a mind for overcoming that he can be God's man.

The Purpose Minded Man

I believe what really makes man significant is when he develops a mind for purpose on earth. This places I have discovered a strong determination in his beliefs that he must succeed due to his calling.

What changed my entire perception of my struggles was I found purpose in being God's child. Now, each day I rise the circumstances that surround my world have no effect on my purpose. I believe the moment I believed that I belonged to Christ I embraced a new mind for purpose. A purpose-minded man I discovered realigns his footsteps on the earth that his life demands attention. This is because he has established a connection with God that connects him to detailed life.

Beloved, I believe what will be a major difference in you winning the race of life is understanding purpose. What I must say here is it is critical that your mind is renewed and that there are no hindrances. The devil knows that once a man comes in connection with his purpose there are no limits. The reason why there are no limits is that this is a man who knows God. When I speak to a lot of my inmates after a few moments I can determine if he was purpose minded. The reason why I know this is I have discovered that a purpose minded man has distinct vocabulary. What I mean here is his words are clear of destiny. Now, what the enemy has done over the years with a man without a purpose is robbed his confidence and assurance.

Sir, right now is the time for you to learn how to become a purpose minded man that you reach your full potential. A purpose minded man is a man who is determined to discover his purpose on the earth and **do it**. This is a man who will not give in to the world's darts of identity destruction. What I believe that has kept me alive in every death trap I have witnessed is purposed propelled me. I pray daily each day I rise that I do not miss my daily moment of purpose recognition. See, I believe every day of my life there is a purpose moment loaded in my day. The reason I believe this is I know Christ lives in me and daily I am to focus on Him living in me.

The only way that I focus on my purpose is my mind is stayed on him that I never lose focus of why I am here. What I see men stumbling over daily is a lack of being purposed minded for right now. The devil knows that he can throw a new dart at a man daily and confuse him on who he is and where he belongs. I thank God that studying His word kept me engaged and where I suppose to be. Beloved, God desires for you to stay engaged in His word that you are not lost but found. The word of God does wonders in us when we trust Him and unknown gifts comes out of us. The purpose minded man shall always rise above his fall because he knows purpose must be fulfilled.

Joseph I believe was a purpose minded man who had a dream inside of him and even though trouble came victory also came. (Gen: 37.2). The moment the man believes in God and allow God to lead, purpose is revealed. Purpose is revealed that the man knows that he is capable of following God. I believe when the purpose minded man follows God, he set a new mark on the earth. Joseph reset his family's future even when a famine was in the land due to being purpose minded. Beloved, you can change your world and make room for others with this new mind. The world could not set a trap for you of lockup because your mind is made up as a purpose minded man. God makes a way for this man and through Him the world gets a glimpse of God's glory. The bible says "Arise, shine for thy light is come, and the glory of the Lord is risen upon thee. (Isaiah 60.1).

The purpose minded man has embraced the glory that is upon him and walks out every moment with intensity. This is because this man realizes that time is critical for him to display God in him now. Beloved, there is a light that is shining bright in you that needs to reflect over your life and your surroundings. Now, by faith it is already in you, but your condition is trying to dim that light with setbacks. What must take place is for you to get in the word of God that your mind is reconnected with the plan. The plan is for you to mirror God right where you are that purpose overtakes you. I know it may seem impossible to mirror God due to your situation, but God is backing you and your past.

What is important to note is your past is what is always trying to confuse your mind as a man to cause you to stumble. The enemy knows that stumbling consistently in his world can weaken your ability to hold glory. What I am seeing daily as I watch the news are men weakened by stumbling blocks and invade their glory. These stumbling blocks lead to sin then possibly to danger and much trouble. The enemy is not satisfied until he sees another great man leave his purpose and get to lockup. The good news is there is hope and that hope is found in Jesus Christ who causes man to rise. Upon the man's repentance and getting to know Jesus, he can get his glory back.

I have made a few mistakes in my life and growing up in the projects I had the opportunity to settle in my mistakes. I discovered if I settled in my mistakes, my purpose would be covered up and never realized. The purposed minded man understands what his defined role is in the earth and never began to doubt it. The first thing that is significant in the purposed minded man is he has discovered his purpose. I believe unfortunately many men has passed on and never discovered their true purpose. When I discovered my purpose in the earth, my every breath agreed that it must be fulfilled. My mind at that point was transformed that purpose takes a stand in my every thought.

Now, I am not moved by my disappointments or my setbacks because a transformed mind is a newborn mind. I only stay focused on the newness of God where a purposed minded man finds new hope. The reason why the devil can manipulate many men is that their purpose has no meaning and no agenda. What the devil can do with that is send him in the circles of the unknown. What I was witnessing at the prison where I worked was the unknown purpose with a man can lead to lockup. In the Bible, Adam was placed in the earth with purpose and an agenda which was to keep the Garden of Eden. (Gen:2.25). When the devil came and caused Adam to sin, his purpose was compromised, and the ground was cursed. (Gen:3.17). Jesus the last Adam (1 corr:15.45-47) came I believe that man might have life and know his purpose. When man put his trust in God he can become purpose minded and do mighty works for God. What the enemy wants to do is cause him to not know purpose that he relies on the world for all provisions.

The purpose minded man realizes that he serves a big God who created the earth with him in mind. Beloved, you need to know as a man that you serve a big God and you should not allow big problems to move you. I know how it is being financially troubled can sometimes try to steal your joy. Truly the joy is that you are loved by God and He wants you to stay in faith that the joy is coming back. Whatever the test is for man can really be troubling, but the joy of the Lord can overwhelm your trouble. Here's the key, in this hour it is only the joy of the Lord that can calm your troubles. The enemy knows that if the Lord does not calm your troubles, your troubles lead to lockup.

The second thing that is significant for the purpose minded man is being passionate about his purpose. When I went to Iraq in as dangerous as it was I had a passion about reaching souls for Christ through the gospel. Again, I had no idea how this would happen not being a chaplain, but I trusted God. In my passion to reach souls, I watched God shut down and rearrange our chain of command ceremony. In my passion to reach souls, I was asked to preach the next Sunday after my arrival. The problem was our service time was the same time as the change of command ceremony. I asked the battalion commander if I could be a little late due to preaching at the service.

My purpose-mindedness and my passion expected a breakthrough that the word of God was not hindered. The battalion commander asked me how much time I needed, and I said to him about thirty minutes. My battalion commander called the outgoing commander and told him we were changing the time. The change of command ceremony was moved thirty minutes later that I might preach the gospel. Beloved, when you are passionate about your purpose on earth God will do wonders for you. This is why you as a man do not have to any longer live below the bar of greatness for God. I have watched God do some things that only He could do even when I was overtaken by darkness.

God did this mighty work in me as a purpose minded man while I was in a battle bigger than me. Here's the key, The bible says " Who is the King of glory? the Lord strong and mighty, the Lord mighty in battle. (Psalm 24.8). Beloved, I saw the Lord mighty in a heated battle while I was in combat work miracles for me. When you get to know God personally the spirit of God will show you new life. As you grow daily in him the purpose minded man will come out in you upon the earth. This is where real change will show up in your life that shall keep you in him and from lockup. What the enemy is doing in the life of great men is presenting darkness of all manners to bring down a man. This is being done in various ways just to get the man off the scene and into lockup. Beloved, allow me to pray for you as I am that you become a purpose minded man that you find your passion. I truly believe when you find that passion with God he will bring power as you are passionate in your gift. Just like God showed me his power in Iraq in my passion for his people he will do it for you.

I am a believer that when a man gets his purpose mindedness back God will reward him. This reward will come in a way that you will know that God is mighty and he will come through. Sir, now is the time for you to put down the anger, put away the thoughts that breed trouble. What I pray that you pick up is the word of

God as he reveals to you the purpose minded man in you. Once you find that man in you that I believe is there you will need an introduction. What I mean here is you will by faith be introduced to the real man in you that was never discovered. I am talking daily to men in lockup that have really never been introduced to the real man in the mirror.

The person that they have only identified with is the old man of trouble and fault that shields the new man. I was speaking just today with a retired Vietnam veteran in lockup who confirmed this condition of man. Now, this is his second trip back to lockup within a two year period. I asked him how was things going and he said "well things are just fine as they should be all is well" I said to him you must be getting out soon and he said yes next year before I have to go to Georgia on my next case. Now, he was sounding excited about going to Georgia to do more time in lockup. What's happening here? This is a man only identifying with the old man of trouble never knowing the new man of purpose. I must point out here this man is approaching 70 years of age.

What am I saying here, beloved the enemy can trap a good mind of a man and set him back years from his purpose. I have good news for the man that is ready for the turnaround to get to his place with greatness. God is standing and waiting for you to call on Him that you get the years restored. (Joel:2.25). God by faith is ready to restore everything that you might have missed as a purpose minded man. I believe you shall get your passion back that you know that you once had to be great. I know that you may have had a rough road like many of us has and the enemy tried to destroy you. I am here by the grace of God to be a fisherman of great men like you to bring you hope.

God is calling you to purpose with all of his provisions in mind to bring you all the support you need to win. You do not have to think that you will run out of provisions because God has a storehouse full for you. Now is the time to pull away from the things that are close in nature to lockup. There shall be great joy in your house for the new man that God is about to restore in you. As the days and months pass I believe there will be much coming back your way that will bring joy to your life. Now, let's stay focused on God and what he is now doing and shall continue to do in you. The enemy will turn up his attacks due to you having decided that the pathway to lockup is not you. Beloved, I am believing God for you that you are dedicating yourself to understanding purpose. The purpose minded man in you shall not settle for the trouble that once was. You are moving to a new height with God that your future is much brighter than your past.

This is the day that God has been waiting on with you my brother that you surrender to his plan for your life. This is a great plan that you can get abundant blessing falling fresh upon your life now and forever. Sir, it doesn't matter what state of mind you were in yesterday, it does matter today. It does matter today because with as a purpose minded man you can turn it all around in one day. Let today be that day that you be the man God created you for.

Chapter 3

THE COMMON DENOMINATOR OF TROUBLED MEN

In this six-year study of inmates, God revealed to me a common denominator for troubled men. What has been simply amazing is how the devil has created a monster for troubled men. What I simply asked God was to give me the wisdom and knowledge I need to expose the enemy. I knew that God is well able to give me all I needed when I need it and to just trust him. Now, it is important for men to note that I am only making a comparison based on my insight and experience. I can think of all the times in my life of hardship and recall praying for the hope in me. When I did that something came alive in me and said you can call on Jesus and He will come.

What I believe is the enemy knows that the moment hope is not realized a man's entire being is lost. As men, we strive on our hope because when we stand on this hope we are free from giving in to pressure. We can now know that our lives are turning around and our hope is our foundation for recovery. The bible says" Blessed is the man who trusts in the Lord and whose hope is the Lord. (Jeremiah 17.5). When you know where your hope is coming from you now know where you are going. One of the places you know you are not going due to the grace on you is lockup. God has a plan for you and that is much too big to be contained inside walls of incarceration.

In the six years that I have studied men in lockup and looked into their eyes, I am confident of the common denominator. This common denominator I have discovered in troubled men is on the rise. I know that it is on the rise when I watch the daily news and see the deceiver (the devil) in control. What the devil has done is taken this common denominator and maximized it's potential in men. What I am confident in is there is a way out for a man that brings this stronghold down quickly. What this will take on the part of men is the willingness to see the doctor of doctors. The doctor that I am referring to is Dr. Jesus who can free all men from this undiagnosed disease.

This undiagnosed disease and common denominator I have discovered in men of trouble is what I call **Chronic Poison Hope Dysfunction or (CPHD).** I define this as **deception** of the **mind that all hope is gone and recovery is impossible.** This is also **a dysfunction** that can cause a **malfunction** in **abilities and knowledge.** This dysfunction is designed to limit man from the knowledge of God that he dominates. The act with this disorder can even be deadly. This disorder has caused a person to inflict poison on dreams and on the lives of others. I have found this in my six year study talking with inmates of most serious crimes. What has happened in most cases is their hope in their act played tricks in their mind to deceive. Here's what's interesting, most knew that in their hope they would succeed in their trouble and never get caught. We are living in a time I believe where this disorder is playing out real in many lives. When I turn on the news now and hear the violence I see much of this disorder in the lives of men.

When the pandemic hit our world, I watched how this dysfunction I discovered robbed many marriages. When I saw on the news that a man killed his wife over a stimulus check, I knew all hope in his marriage was gone. The results during the pandemic in marriages were skyrocketed divorces and a large increase in domestic violence. What am I saying? When the man allows his hope to get poisoned, the enemy is after the best of him, particularly his family if he has one. God empowered Adam in the Garden of Eden and he was designed to function like God with the hope of God. I believe this is the same empowerment that is on the man today who can function in the hope of God. What the enemy has done across the globe in men is dropped a stronghold with (CPHD).

What I have found is that Chronic Poison Hope Dysfunction can be on a small or large scale in our world. There are many cases I can think of that you would easily remember that I connect to this disorder. When I think about the shooting at the church in Charleston South Carolina on June 17, 2015, I see this disorder. When I listen to this young shooter on the live video it is clear that his hope was infected with poison. What I also see and hear is his mindset was poisoned and led him to the destruction of lives. This was part of the bad decision-making that is associated with this disease. Beloved, what I am saying here is the world can give you hope that is misleading. The world can give you hope that can lead you to lock up or death.

This common denominator in trouble men that God revealed to me discriminates against no one or economic status. On June 30, 2017, a doctor in New York killed one woman and wounded six others before killing himself. It was stated that the doctor was troubled with sexual harassment charges. I also read that he was charged years earlier with the same charges that were recorded. What I see in this situation is poison hope dysfunction deceived him that there was no hope for his practice. Beloved, it is vital that as a man you learn of the God of hope that can bring true hope. When you get to know God, He will equip you with bible knowledge that will shield you from destruction.

The bible says "Now may the God of hope fill you with all joy and peace in believing, that you may abound in hope by the power of the Holy Spirit. (Romans 15.13). What I discovered in my worst days of struggle and setback is the God of hope shields me from losing hope. There is a peace that God gives when it looks like no way out. The world's hope can't provide this due to the flesh provides false hope. When the man is walking in false hope at the moment of pressure disaster can strike. Poison hope dysfunction brings the man this false hope that robs him of everlasting hope in Christ. Now, at this point, the man is left with him and his own strength mixed with a hope that blinds.

On May 28, 2017, a man was arrested in Mississippi and charged with killing eight people including a deputy. It was reported that it all started over child custody from his estranged wife before the shooting. What I saw was how CPHD deceived him that there was no hope of being a family again. The shooter stated that he hoped for death or suicide by cops after what he had done. I am convinced that when a man's hope is not from the God of hope it will always be suspect for violence. I have witnessed this through much communication with these inmates that release their thoughts. When I connect their thoughts to what we witness on the news daily I see the root of the problems.

On August 11, 2018, in Seattle, an employee steals an airplane from the airport and crashed and kills himself. Now, what I am personally sure of is all of this man's hope was gone and he was deceived. Now as if this was not enough, less than a week later another man in Utah crashed his plane into his house. It was reported this man was having domestic violence issues at home and tried to kill his family. Sir, listen to me, heaven has revealed something to me that is worth your ear of hope. This common denominator cares less about how high you can fly in the air or on the earth. Now is the time for men to know where to look when it appears all hope is gone and no way out.

In August 2019 a Michigan man was sentenced to 60 weekend days for putting **poison** in his wife's coffee. Now, notice here that he used **poison** to cause harm to his wife. According to the news report they had filed for divorce two months earlier. What do I see here? I see CPHD which I stated in my definition of thinking all hope is gone. This man apparently had lost hope in marriage and possibly of anyone wanting to marry him again. Upon hearing of this act, the Holy Spirit confirmed to me that I had made the right discovery about poison. My mission from God is to release this to His people so that lives might be saved.

The devil cares less about what is going on in the world, as long as the man's mind sees no hope. Even while the pandemic with the coronavirus was going on, in our cities, men were still shooting and killing. Now, they were supposed to be at home under the stay-at-home order, but still shooting day and night. Why? When the devil has caused this dysfunction in the mind, he can poison the mind so that it listens to no orders, rules, or curfews.

The devil is doing a historic job on the minds of men when he can take away the hope that strengthens man. I am confident that in this hour the only hope that can sustain man is the hope of God. I believe and it is evident when we look at just a few of these cases mentioned that poison hope is no hope. What I am on a mission to do for men is to impress upon them the importance of real hope. Beloved, in as much as poison hope disfunction, is alive and **well** God is **well** able. The good news is poison hope dysfunction must bow down to the God of hope that is in you and me by faith. I am here once again to tell men that you can't get high enough in the world to escape this. I watched this for 6 years working in the prison and it is still widespread today. Again, your title means nothing to the devil as long as he can poison your hope. In December 2020, an Alabama judge was sentenced to prison for theft of funds and placed in custody. Yes, you heard me right, I know what you want to say. You want to say the man that sends people to prison is being sent himself? Yes, here's the key, even the judge himself must know that the bible says "But God is the judge. (Psalm 75.7). Even the judge in the courtroom must know the judge of all judges in heaven that he may never lose hope. This chronic poison hope dysfunction can take you along with your title and education to a place of horror. On Christmas day of 2020, a suicide bomber sent explosions through Nashville Tennessee doing major damage to the city. No one knows of any motives, but let me assure you when suicide is committed, all hope was gone.

Just when you think these kinds of disasters will never happen again it happens. On May 26, 2021, a former coworker killed 8 people in San Jose, California. The man also killed himself according to reports. Now, at that time authorities knew of no motives for the shooting. What I am confident in about CPHD is this dysfunction plays on the mind and needs no motive for its actions. What I do believe is the man that killed those 8 people watched his hope take its last breath of possibilities. Unfortunately, this is the pathway that many CPHD cases lead including suicide.

Chronic Poison hope dysfunction tried its best to overtake me in the war in Iraq but fell short of the authority in me. Now, what it tried to do to me was to lose hope that I was going to die and never see my wife again. Now, this is the trick to this disorder that is to show you that your storm is bigger than you. See, if I am unemployed as I was with no money to feed my family, that is bigger than I am. Many of us have seen on the news when a fired employee comes back to the company shooting the supervisor or others.

Beloved, in my eyes this is a clear case of poison hope dysfunction that tells the man that he can't get another job. When we are in faith and serve the God of hope we can say my God is bigger than all of my problems. This is what kept me strong in faith and hope in the war while I was unemployed for three years. Poison hope dysfunction had to take a back seat to my hope that was in the front seat. Beloved, you too can walk in this kind of hope when you get to know God and serve Him. God will be your hope for you for your every need that you will never have to worry about no more. I am continuing to witness this common denominator on a daily basis that is destroying families.

It is my job to speak and witness to as many men as possible that we get our place back in the God of hope. Now is the time for the true man to rise up and believe God that He is our hope for today and tomorrow. Poison hope dysfunction showed up among every inmate I spoke with no matter what was his charge. The charges ranged from drug cases, murder, sex offender, robbery, domestic violence etc. Now, I must say many of these men I found were really great men throughout my six years of study. What I found was the pressures of the offense overpowered the moment of occurrence. Beloved, what is shocking is how often this painful disorder is ripping men daily. My main concern is not many men will win in that moment except his mind is renewed and trained of real hope.

What I believe I have been given by God is what I call **Treatment Objectives** as preventive measures for Poison Hope Dysfunction. What I do know is this worked for me and I am blessed to have no **PTSD** and blocked (CPHD) and taking no medication. I thank God in 2020 it has been 15 years since my deployment. The treatment objectives are with no **medication** but much **dedication** to have life and have it more abundantly. (John:10.10). What the spirit has revealed to me about my discovery of CPHD is shocking. What the spirit revealed is if **PTSD** is not properly treated, it can move to a phase of **CPHD.** Unfortunately, this poison again could lead to a bad decision of even suicide.

I was really stunned when I read in an article that the Department Of Veteran Affairs released that 60,000 veterans died of suicide from 2008 to 2017. Here is a revelation God gave me. To be delivered from CPHD, one must become a **Prisoner of Hope.** The bible says "Return to the stronghold {of security and prosperity}, you prisoners of hope: even today do I declare that I will restore double your former prosperity to you. (Zechariah 9:12amp). Here's what I believe. A prisoner of no hope is subject to give up, but a prisoner of hope is empowered to **rise up.** As a prisoner of hope, I am locked up in the hope to fulfil my purpose on earth.

What God has also revealed to me are treatments to help steer the man so that he may get his hope back . The first treatment is man must **Refocus.** Yes, the man must refocus in order that he can see clearly. What I discovered was every setback that came my way took me out of focus of where I suppose to go and become. When the devil does this now I can't see straight because a blurry vision stole my identity. Now, the man takes the wrong path because of blindness and deception. This is a trick of the devil guys and we must overtake our sight. When I **Refocus** by knowing who I am and only looking up to God for the direction I reclaim my post. My post and my place are set in stone by God but takes a clear vision to find it and believe it.

The second Treatment Objective is **Rediscover.** Yes, sir, you must Rediscover the Purpose that was lost in the storm. See, I knew that coming out of a battle in Iraq the enemy wanted me to forget why I was here. I spent a lot of time with God and His word that I hold fast to my purpose for being born. When this takes place everything that may have been lost in your trauma is recovered. With everything that is in the man, he must meditate and spend much time with God that he **Rediscover Purpose.** When this happens no weapon formed against you shall prosper against your purpose. Now, the man began to come to himself that he was not here to be defeated.

The third Treatment Objective is **Restart.** Yes, what I mean here is you must hit your **Restart** button of life. Now that you know who you are and you have refocused, just do it. As a man, we do not want any idle time on our hands for what we are purposed to do. We must restart what we were first put on this earth to do and do it now. The sooner we hit the restart button of life the faster the recovery. God has a plan for every man that believes and the opportunity to see it done is now. I am confident that these were the preventive measures that kept me in the will of God. Sir, God has a plan for your life, and just because you may have stumbled does not mean it is over. All that may have happened is you may have hit a pothole or a setback. I believe it was a setback for a comeback. Hit your spiritual **Restart Button** and let's do it. Get your Fire Back!! God is ready to use you now. Child of God, don't let the devil have you to think that you have messed up to bad to restart. The devil is a liar. The restart button is available for all that believe and desire to start again. I believe the key in the man's restart is that he now be fruitful. The Bible says "And God blessed them, and God said unto them, Be fruitful, and multiply, and replenish the earth, and subdue it: and have dominion over the fish of the sea, and over the fowl of the air, and over every living thing that moveth upon the earth. (Gen:1.28).

When I hit my restart button in my life, I discovered if I can **be fruitful** and plant a seed which is the word of God (Luke8.11) I can come back. This would enable me to turn my entire world around as I function on the earth. What God would begin to do in my life with the seed was open me up to gifts inside of me to be fruitful. I believe God is about to show young men who trust in Him the blessing of **being fruitful.**

In November of 2021, I witnessed our city of Montgomery Alabama hold what was called a second chance job fair. This job fair was for ex-offenders hosted by our District Attorney that were looking to restart their lives. There were nearly 50 companies participating willingly to give many opportunities to hit the restart button of life. I was blessed by God to witness this knowing that I had ministered to great men in lockup. I knew some of these great men were soon to be free and I encouraged them to trust God on a restart. I believe these men shall hit their restart button and **be fruitful** as they make a difference. Precious one, God is in the business of restarting lives for His glory. I am a witness to this when it appeared all hope was gone for me from the valley of debt.

Tips For Troubleshooting

I am totally convinced that upon having a conversation with a man for five minutes I have 90% of who he is. Now, with this, I have obtained enough in most cases to determine his entire makeup and thoughts of a man. How do I do this one may ask? Well, for me in this time frame I am going to hear the resume of his mind. I have discovered over the years that words out of the man's mouth speak volume. What is critical for me in the conversation is to listen to what I call key persuasive dialogue. What is going on here is in his dialogue are some of his greatest thought processes about life. What I have learned is how those thoughts can be connected with everything in him including his heart.

The bible says " For out of the abundance of the heart the mouth speaks. (Matt:12.34). Beloved, one of the key methods I believe in troubleshooting for trouble is taking account of every word of the man. The reason why I believe this is important is that trouble starts from a word seed. As men, we were not made to speak on things that we did not expect to be so. While growing up in the projects I was hearing conversations in the park out of boys that grew wings. Some of the conversations that were troubling develop in less than five minutes that cost many ten years or greater. When I started working at the prison in 2012 there were men from my projects there for 20 years.

What I am saying is this is what I call **voice-activated trouble** that men must learn to capture immediately. What is also important is this is rooted in most men that soon participate or activate. I have talked with many inmates that are here because they stayed in the presence of the conversation. Beloved, this is a tip when you hear this in your environment it is time to leave. You do not want to allow the conversations to overpower common knowledge because it could lead to trouble. What voice-activated trouble does is it begins to sound so favorable that it must be attempted. What I learned was the more men discuss certain issues that can be troubling can come to pass.

The best thing for a man to do is to shift your direction of thought and move to a new and better situation. God desires you as a man to position yourself to His will but we must use God's wisdom. I know this tip for troubleshooting would have saved many of the young men I see here daily. What we must learn is that the enemy is very smart yet he will open himself up for company. This is the season for men especially young men to understand how voice-activated trouble is real. This voice can send a signal inside of a man and plant a seed of temptation without warning. Beloved, this is the hour where we as men must be able to discern troubling dialogue. This kind of communication in this season traps a good mind in a man and leads to a dark path. Let me encourage you as a man to take the five-minute challenge in a conversation with your next encounter. What I have learned in men is the message is really clear but our ears must be on. The bible says "He who has ears to hear, let him hear! (Matt:11.15). I must say to the young men that you cannot afford not to hear what the world is saying to men. It is critical that you learn the five-minute challenge to determine what is said to men from the world is true. Now, here's what I do know for sure. Everything that is spoken to the ears and minds of men is not true. Many words that are being voiced are pathways to trouble and into lockup.

Beloved, God has a future for you that is much bigger than what you may have encountered yet. I cannot overemphasize the importance of managing your distance away from the voices of trouble. In this time that we are living sometimes trouble speaks in codes and you must be conditioned. If there are things in your group or among your peers that are being said and you do not understand, leave. I have a wonderful young man in our prison that was a star quarterback for his high school. This young man said he never understood the words that were being said in the car. This young man was charged with robbery because he was in the car and charged with accessory.

Beloved, if you are not 100% sure of the conversation in five minutes it is your time to get away fast. Trouble has a way of maturing very quickly among men when there is no defensive mechanism in place. I say this because of the number of sex abuse charges among men who were caught sleeping. This is the time for men to be fully accountable for every voice and action within their reach. I am watching at a rate that is astounding of men who are allowing their future to fade under lack of knowledge. Take the five-minute challenge men that you might be free for the rest of your life.

Know Your Friends

We are living in a time now of so much violence that you and I have to be very careful. We are still living in a time where some are still unemployed and it has a bearing on many people's character. It is very critical that we as men must be certain and positively sure of who we call friends. Now, I am one to say that it is wonderful to have friends that you know are truly your friend. Working at the prison for six years now I also know that there are many men who did not know their friends. It is my prayer that from this point forward as I encourage our men that we know one another. This is a serious matter that has many great young men here in our lockup. What I have noticed is some of these men had good habits but fell victim to bad company.

The bible says "Do not be deceived; Evil company corrupts good habits. (1Corr: 15.33 nkj). My father used to make it very clear to me in the projects that if we went to jail because of bad company we will stay there. Now, he said this out of love because his teaching was firm on bad friendships. I can remember at 11 years old I asked my father could I go to the store with a friend. My father asked me who was he and he wanted to see who he was before he said I could. When I asked my friend to show himself to my father, my father said very convincible **No** and **Never.** Now, later as I grew older I found out that this same friend of mine was arrested as a teen and locked up.

Here's a tip for troubleshooting, most men that have a hidden agenda for trouble are visible when properly diagnosed. Men, we must ask God for the wisdom and knowledge that we carefully know our friends. You as a man must be wise enough to know when trouble has found your doorstep. I know what it feels like not to want to make your friend feel as though you don't trust him. The way to handle that properly is to let him know at the moment your spirit is not at rest with an act. Now, if the friend does not respect your feeling there may be trouble in the making.

Beloved, life, and your freedom are too precious to be walking on the edge of lockup that is in the invisible. Trust me when I say lockup can be in the invisible when you are not using wisdom under pressure. Men, we need to know who we have entrusted with our future when we step into the unknown. When you are not sure of a situation do not be afraid to ask questions now than later. I have great men here in the lockup that has said they wished they would have asked before they assumed. Now is the time to carefully take inventory of your friends that you may spend time with. I would rather for you do this now and be sure than do it later when the cell doors slam.

When the cell doors slam behind these men in lockup I believe it is a reminder that choice is now behind you. Beloved, I believe there is too much inside of you to be deceived by bad company. Let me suggest to you from some of my best men here at lockup to make a wise decision regarding the association. One important tip that is worthy to take notice of is the church attendance of your friend. Now, this doesn't make him a perfect man but it does I believe demonstrate a willingness to serve his creator. I believe if the man is willing to give God some time there can be a seed of hope. If your friend happens not to go to church try inviting him with you. Now if he refuses to go to church it is important that you pray for him but you must also watch.

The bible says "Watch and pray, that you enter not into temptation: the spirit indeed is willing, but the flesh is weak. (Matt:26.41). I am here to tell you beloved, you must watch your friends that you are trusting. Now, what is important to note is if he refuses to go to church with you he probably doesn't know God. The reason why you must watch is if he commits a crime and you are with him, again this is an accessory. Keep working with the friend about going to church so that he may get to know God. Beloved, it is critical for you to know that the line between lockup and freedom among men is very thin. In this hour that we are in you must know your friends and associates and know them well.

In my six years with these great men, I discovered that the best men can be taken out by bad associates. Let me submit to you that it is best to be alone and free than to have much company in lockup. You need to know that there are plenty in lockup that wish they can do it again. Now is not the time to be among someone that you are very suspicious of being in their presence. The moment this has shown up in your spirit God is trying to tell you something about that someone. Beloved, again your life is too precious to watch it go down due to an act of another. What I did even in the projects was I joked around with friends that I followed but I watched their every move.

What I am saying again to a great man out there with great potential is to be prayerful but please watch. I am not looking forward to meeting another great man in lockup because he was sleeping among the bad company. Keep your eyes open on your friends as you keep your eyes on your future. What many men have not realized is your environment can help you or hinder you in the blinking of an eye. You are in the driver's seat in which environment will you partake in your life. poison hope dysfunction can affect a man in a way that he thinks what he has can benefit those around him. You and I have the image of God that when we trust God we can trust his guidance.

What the enemy desires for us to do are to be led by his command that we fall into the trap of deception. When we call on God for His guidance the Holy Spirit will usher us in His presence so that we will be stable. This is why it is important to study the word of God and God himself will reveal to you the right path. Beloved, you do not need your path from God disturbed by bad company. You and I are being called by God to know our friends as well as love them that we may be complete. I believe God is pouring out his spirit in a mighty way for us to know that he is God. During these times it is important that we stay close to God through his word and in prayer for direction. I believe if we do this now we will have such an anointing on us that others will know of his power. We all have fake friends that we know really do not count us as worthy children of God. This is why we must stay in the word as we discover that he loves us so much and cares for us.

Many of our inmates at our facility understand now that there are many fake friends in and around us. I say this because before they knew it their friend had turned on them and they were in lockup. What I believe is the enemy has his army on assignment to gather God's saints and bound them. What we can do even now is stay on our knees that God moves by his spirit and lead us. I believe when the spirit of God leads us we cannot be connected with every breath from man. It will be best that we seek God and that all of our associates have a heart for God and his leading. I discovered that some that were so-called friends were hinders to the working of God in me.

What I mean here is that when I was in the presence of those that did not seek God they would change the subject of his goodness. We as men must be able to determine the right fruits for our spiritual development. What the enemy desires to do is lead us from God's goodness to his ways of destroying us. Beloved, if you are not in the habit of watching and praying you could be steps away from lockup. On the news one day there was a robbery in a neighboring city where 3 young men committed a robbery. What is so sad only one of the three pulled the trigger that killed a man and robbed him. The other two gentlemen with the shooter never knew that a robbery was taking place. They all will be facing twenty to thirty years in prison.

As I look at some of the faces in lockup I see so much pain of I did not know who I was really with. Beloved, these faces are real and they are real people and most of them come from good homes. The issue is they did not know how to contain the pressure of wanting to feel a part of something. This is a trap of the devil. Men, we are God's special people on this earth that represent his image. We have to stand on what we believe God is saying and know in our hearts when to say no. Growing up in the projects sometimes pushed me to the limits of all of God or most of the devil. This is the direction that the devil has set in stone in the minds of men that they make a choice.

Beloved, what you need to think about is God cares for you. He cares for you in a mighty way that you know it. Once you know that you have a God who cares in this manner, you make it right with God. One of the ways that you make it right with God is you be at the feet of Jesus day and night. In this manner what I discovered is the spirit of God is all over you and shields you from trouble and pain. This does not mean there will be no trials, but deliverance will come. The hand of God will keep you in right standing with God that shall keep you close to him. Many young men in our prison were overpowered with wrong relationships that appeared real. What I am trying to convey to men in this hour is to observe your relationships closely. When you keep your eyes on Jesus His presence invites you to His leading even with friends. Now is the time to be in prayer and meditation that you may be led by the spirit in your relationships. In this hour there is no room for uncertainty because the uncertainty has no benefits in lockup. Lockup if allowed can drain the true man out of you and bring forth the disturbed man.

God desires you to get to know Him so that He can live in you and that all the full potential in you is released on the earth. When you get to know God personally he will be your guide in your relationships now and forever. Each day as I began to know God in my worst hour the spirit led me to the right environments. This is the advantage we have when we get to know God personally that He takes control of us. Beloved, be encouraged that God loves you and he is a jealous God. God desires you to spend time with him who created you for a future than with those who desire you to have no future. Keep your eyes on God and you will become all that he has for you and your family.

Know Family History Tip

I believe it is important that when we decide to connect with a man it is important to know some history. Now, sometimes this is not easily obtained but it is accessible by association and communication. I believe the true essence of a man and what he is really about just comes out in his communication. Beloved, it does not matter if it is your friend, brother son, or neighbor what's in me will come out. I am just overwhelmed daily by the number of men in lockup due to not knowing their associates. We are living in a time that is much different than my time as a young man with relationships. What I suggest in the hour that we are in is to talk to your friend about his family. Find out in your own way if there are any others, brothers, or sisters, if so where are they.

What I have seen enough of in my six year study in the prison is the number of family members in lockup. I have talked with more fathers and sons as well as brothers and cousins of the same seed locked up. What am I saying? Parents make sure that you do all that you can do to know your boy's friends. I do not believe at this point that parents are doing all they can do to assist in their boy's development. I want to say to the boys and men trust me when I say this is a necessity now. When you have made up your mind that you will associate with this person again ask some questions. For the young man again it is critical that you know who you are riding with.

Find out if you can do your friend have relatives that are in prison and if so find out why are they there. What I am witnessing on a daily basis is how deep some seeds are rooted in family history. I believe in some way there are generational curses among some families that are tied to trouble and lockup. I have witnessed generational curses among families of sexual offenses that grew deep. In these families, they resulted in many divorces in the same family that grew wide. Beloved, I believe trouble can grow wide and deep and form generational curses until a believer of the family breaks the curse. I know for a fact right now of three families at our prison that suffer this terror.

What I am deeply hurt about these families is I grew up with all three families and know them very well. Beloved, one of these families comes from really great families that I witnessed grew up in the church. What the enemy does not mind is the man in the church just as long as he stays bound for lockup. Now, the way that the enemy keeps the man bound is to keep him in the company of like-minded men. If most of the people he associates with think the same the enemy grabs him. What the enemy does is make his mind sensitive to what he hears and sees among his peers. Once the mind of that man becomes receptive his mind embraces those thoughts good or bad.

What I have seen resulting from this way of living and lifestyle is the trouble that feeds the mind with lies that all is yours. Now, the problem with this thinking is the mind thinks that it can have it even if it is not his. I believe that it is critical for the man to be mindful of who he allows in his circle of influence.

Beloved, I know you need friends and associates we all do. What I am saying is for you to know who you are with. I made up my mind even when I was living in the projects that I am not going down on another man's bad judgment. Sir, you are much more important to God than to not know who is with you. Now is the time to begin to manage your friends and know their history or their story. God desires you to be his light and his representative here on the earth and you need to be watchful. I promise you that I really love people and love to fellowship with guys and have a great time. What we all must be mindful of is that the fellowship could come with grave consequences. Many are locked up here because of this.

The bible says " Wisdom is the principal thing, therefore get wisdom. and with all thy getting, get understanding. (Prov: 4.7). Beloved, it is the wisdom God desires you and me to have as we live upon this earth. When you apply sound wisdom in your life as a man wisdom will get to the source of the matter. What I discovered among most of these men in lockup is they never applied wisdom where needed. What I found was the wisdom from God kept me in a place of concern of travel. When applied the wisdom of God by faith I was able to search the heart of friends and their history. This wisdom comes from the word of God that I may use this in every situation.

Beloved, as you spend time with God and his word he will lead you and guide you that you apply his ways. What is important right now for you as a man is to trust God and ask him for his guidance. The guidance that you need from God will assist you in your selection of friends and acquaintances. Let me suggest to you to pray as well and when you pray regarding this matter God will fix it. What I have witnessed is when we walk in our opinions we have a tendency of getting it wrong. I am here to tell men after six years of study many men have got it wrong. What their wrong opinions and thoughts without wisdom and understanding resulted was lockup.

We are in a time sir as men that when we think we know someone we need to make absolutely sure we do. The best way I have found out is to know some history of his footsteps by communication. I promise you if the person you have decided to make permanent is clean he will not mind sharing history. I promise from the standpoint of listening to regrets from men in lockup it is worth it. What we must know is we as men can really display a life that is contrary to who we are. The issue with this is the law does not consider this when a crime is committed saying I did not know my friend. Beloved, what God has given you as a gift is worthy of keeping a shield of caution. When we do this with wisdom I believe the spirit of God will alarm you on who to trust. I just believe what God has given me in my assignment is worth being cautious of those I am not sure of. Let me encourage you sir that you have the image of God in you so why not protect it. Know who you are riding with and spending time with because it only takes one set of blue lights.

I am here as a witness to remind men that **blue lights** can truly bring you **dim lights** by way of lockup. This has come to many men due to them not knowing some history of the one they called friend. You as a man are much too precious to God on the earth to put your trust in the man. The bible says " Thus says the Lord: Cursed is the man who trusts in man and makes flesh his arm, whose heart departs from the Lord. (Jeremiah: 17.5) When the man puts all his trust in a man he opens himself to trouble. God never desires us as a man to depart from Him to submit to a man. I want to encourage you sir to seek God that no curse will be upon you that you bring him glory.

The devil desires for all of us to receive his council knowing that his council will bring the curse upon us. When you walk in the counsel of God you will have the favor of God that brings you insight of men. This comes as a blessing from God because he wants us to be successful in all we do for him. We are the apple of God's eye and in order for us to be effective, we must be alert in the earth. The enemy can really do a job on the man once he puts his trust in him for his direction. When the man does this the devil unloads a curse upon him that blinds him from seeing victory. The moment this happens you are led by false persuasion that blankets your true identity.

When this shows up in the life of the man it is critical that he quickly turns to God and pray for his intervention. There were times that if God's intervention did not show up for me I was headed for bad council. Beloved, the more God is a part of your everyday life the farther bad company pulls away. When you pray to him daily the power of God will shelter you that the curse can't touch you. You and I are here to bring the power of God to every place where God gets the glory. Let us as men know who it is that we are walking with as friends and associates that lockup has us not. We shall by faith get to the victorious place that God has for us that men find their place.

I believe you sir have been on the mind of God for some time now and it is time for you to be with God alone. When you do this now you will find that you cannot risk your place in history because of a lack of knowledge. This would be the lack of knowledge of the God you serve and the lack of knowledge of the bad company. The word of God is full of knowledge for you and I to get powerful instruction. By faith, the word of God can steer you into the right company that can bless you. What is important as a man is to know that God has a plan for you with him doing the leading. As a man, this is the season to be conscious of those around you that you will not be framed. The enemy again wants your entire life for him that he knows can lead you to lockup and locked down. Trust me once again sir when I say great men like you get misled and their future was taken away. Let me encourage you to love God now like you never have before so that you may love yourself. I promise when you do this you will be careful of the company you keep due to revealed knowledge. God will reveal to you his plan for you that will keep you free from lockup.

The Danger Of Losing Hope

What I have discovered about poison hope dysfunction is the root of it is a man who has lost hope. When the man has lost hope he loses much more than he thinks he has even when times are very tough. What he really loses is his trust in the God of hope (Rom:15.13) who is able to restore him. Each day as I walk to my office at the prison I see many men that have lost hope. I say this because as I hear their story lost hope is at the center of their situation that robbed their future. Beloved, what lost hope can do for you is set you up for failure when winning were at your fingertips. I witnessed this in Iraq as the enemy was trying his best to get me in the lost hope mindset.

The enemy knows that if he can get the man in the lost hope mindset he really can put himself and others in danger. I believe when hope is lost in the man part of his ability to overcome is minimized. When the man's hope is in God he now has an abundance of strength that brings overwhelming results. God gave me these overwhelming results in Iraq and I was able to come home unharmed. The danger of losing hope in the man is he now believes all things are against him and there is no way out. This way of thinking can lead the man to false ideas, make bad choices, and to lock up. God has given us hope that can bring us to all the things we need to win on the earth.

What I pray to do daily among men in the prison is to just walk upright before them so that they see hope. When I do that most of the time they will stop me and say something like "man I love those shoes". This will give me an opportunity to witness to them that you appear to be a man that has this style as well. Now, from that conversation, I build up their hope that they are more than this moment. This is what I said to a young man today when he stopped me about my shoes. When I finished the conversation with him I truly believe hope was restored because he said from that moment he believed. What he said from that conversation was he believed he can make a difference now.

Beloved, here is what is real; hope can make a difference wherever you are because hope gives you a different platform. My entire platform changed in Iraq when I never lost hope in what was before me. I watched God do things for me that no man could have done regardless of his position. The moment hope is lost you just accepted a lie from the devil that there is no hope for you. Precious one, the devil wants to make it personal with you and only you that you will not succeed. Let me encourage you that you have a hope in you that is much bigger than the one in the mirror. What the devil has done for many years now is to force a picture of lost hope in men.

The way that the devil has done that is to make hopeless men know each other. The real man and the real hope in me come when I discover in me that there is more in me than I can see. When I can believe that there is hope, I know that is the God in me. When I can embrace hope I regain what the world and its system may have stolen from me. As a man, I have much authority resting in me if I can only hold on to the hope that the devil tries to take from me. Beloved, the devil knows that a man becomes a dangerous vessel when hope is lost. The devil knows what makes the man dangerous is he is like him who believes he is fine without God. Sir, here's the problem, the world's system is too big for you and I to attempt to make it on our own. What I witness daily among many great men in lockup is most of them tried making it on their own.

Beloved, I have **BREAKING NEWS.** The system in this world which is led by the devil is a direct road to failure and lockup. The reason why many of these men are here in lockup is that they really thought they were right. The reason many thought they were right for what may have led them was poison hope dysfunction. Here's what I truly believe is so deadly to a man's future for this undiagnosed disorder. Sir, there are no symptoms of poison hope disorder and I believe it is on the rise in men. This is why I believe our prison is overcrowding because men are thinking they are right in their fault. The bible says" There is a way that seems right unto man but at the end thereof are the ways of death (Proverbs 14.12).

What is on the rise with poison hope disfunction is in many men is the end thereof of this mindset is lockup. I believe one of the strongest components of this disorder is a high dose of no hope that spreads fast. What I am witnessing at the prison is this sickness spreads to the core of the mind and rests. The only true treatment again for this disorder in men is their minds being renewed with the hope of God. When the mind is renewed with this hope every vessel where hope was lost is restored. The man now began to make a comeback on who he really is and why he is on the earth. I believe wherever he has lost his fire in becoming great in the earth gets recharged with high intensity.

God is a God that wants his man back and wants him back in the fire where his gift is a world changer. Beloved, trust me when I say that you were made to turn the hands of time back just with what you have. I discovered that when I began to pray and ask God to get me back to my creation. Now, I say that because I discovered that I was created to make a mark on history with my hope. The moment that I have no hope I just stepped into the realm of malfunction that leads to darkness. Sir, you too have been chosen to make a mark on your world than to make the state make a mark on you. I have seen now for six years working at lockup watching the state make its mark on men.

I am here to tell you this is a trick from the devil that is going day by day seeking whom he can devour. (1peter: 5.8) Beloved, you have a lot stored in you that shall come out of you through your hope in God. There are some men that I speak with daily in lockup who have much stored in them that are buried with no hope. What I speak over them is a word of encouragement that brings new birth for new life. Listen to me sir, don't get overtaken any longer by your dilemma, be overwhelmed with hope. What hope did for me in battle in Iraq was much more than any position, title, or fame could do. I have been literally given a new life because I did not lose hope under pressure. Another danger of losing hope is you never see the sun because no hope presented darkness for so long. In the nighttime of your storm, the birds of new life never could sing due to faded hope. I believe precious one you are on the verge of a new beginning with this moment with God. I believe God is calling you to this new hope that you and your gift will save many from lockup.

I truly believe having no hope for the man could cost him his highest possible achievement in life. What hope can do is put your mind above the impossibilities because hope never runs dry when it is active. When I was able to finish college and graduate as a chief warrant officer these were some of my greatest achievements. Now, because I grew up in a challenging environment in the projects the system made these look impossible. What the world kept flashing across the screen of my mind was insufficient. What happens in most of the minds of those that live through this is they give up. In the minds of these men, they have been beaten so badly by the system that hope is lost.

I believe there must be something bearing down on that man that says I am not here to be taken down by the system. I believe what the system of this world has done is set many of us up for lockup. I say that because there are not many agencies willing to help some families that are desperate. Unfortunately, there are some men out there that are willing to risk going to jail in order to feed their families. I have in our prison a great man who many love dearly shared with me his tough moment. While he was at home on probation he suffered job loss and had gone to several agencies for help. After watching his kids go hungry for so long he got desperate and lost hope.

When hope was lost he went to one of the local grocery stores and stole food for his kids and was arrested. I want to say right away that this was not the right thing to do. My prayer for us all in this situation is not to lose hope but stay in faith for the God of hope. When hope is lost it can paint a picture in your face of it will get worse. God desires us to trust in him regardless of how bad it looks. The bible says "And now Lord, what do I wait for and expect? My hope and expectations are in you. (Psalms 39.7

amp). When our hope is in God the power is in him as you wait for the blessing. God desires us not only to wait but we can wait expectantly knowing that God cares.

What the enemy has mastered in the men is pushing him over the fence that all expectations are gone. What men must know is when the wait is over in your eyes and in your heart, the head takes over. When this happens you are now operating on a full tank of bare flesh that is an easy lockup. I am sure that a lot of the young men I pass daily in the hallway of lockup were ruled by the flesh. What has happened in our world is because of this we have a world of men walking without any hope. What our nation is facing because of that is the shortage of men where men should be. When I look at the men daily in our prisons across our state and our country we are hurting. Three of the places I believe we truly hurt in our world with men are our school systems, our churches, and our home. My sister and friends who have been teaching for over thirty years have always shared with me this information. What they all have said is there is a terrible shortage of men teachers in the classroom. Now, I know there will be some say because of the pay or the challenges with kids.

What I will say based on what I witness daily is the lack of hope in men in one form or the other that takes away their true abilities. Here's what's true this is a problem in our world. I believe men were never made to be absent from something as big as education. I say this with the thinking of the bible that Adam was made in the image of God. As Adam was made to be the image of God man was made to represent God in key places. Our educational systems are key territories that must have God's image. Now, I am not saying that women are not the image of God because they are as well(Gen:1.27) and perform very well. What I am saying is the world brought enough pressure in the world to inflict no hope in the man.

What I am praying and believing God for in this hour is he is about to turn things around in this area. The way I can be a part of God's plan is to be a light of hope for men and encourage them that they are special to God. I was meditating on this issue and praying about this when an opportunity came. Just the other day at the prison I was introduced to a new male candidate for a correctional officer. This young man is a Christian and what was amazing was when he told me he was in graduate school. I was truly blessed when he told me that he was majoring in education. This young man went on to say that his ultimate goal was to be a principal after years of teaching.

Now, I know this was nobody but God that I will have an opportunity to help strengthen and encourage a young man. I will have an opportunity to let him know that he has all the abilities to be great in the classroom. I am believing God to start something great with him by reaching more men in the classroom through hope. Beloved, I don't know where you are in your journey but God has a plan for you. The world will always present signs for you to lose hope but God will always present hope that you win. With the hope that you and I can have with a loving God by faith, we can bring back hope in our communities. One other area I have witnessed I believe because of no hope in men is in the church.

I have been sitting in the pulpit now as a minister for nearly twenty years preaching the gospel. In that same number of years, I have witnessed a terrible decline of men in the pews.

Now, many must agree with me that again the schools and the church are vital to the world in which we live. What troubles me in these areas is the devil knows that if he can rule these two areas he can rule our world. One of the reasons I believe some men have left the church is they see few men themselves. With lost hope in men, we now have far more women in most churches than men. What the devil has done in most men is kept them before churchgoers who don't know God. It is the Christians who the devil tries to keep men from. What I have witnessed over the years is the loss of hope in men that have kept them bound. The danger of the lost hope in men has raised the level in men to acquire poison hope dysfunction.

When I look at the danger of lost hope in men I even see how it affects the church in being a role model. What troubles me about this is when I look at the divorce rate of the people in the church. Someone may say what does hope has to do with marriage? After thirty nine years marriage what I have learned is if hope is lost in marriage the marriage could be done. Beloved, God desires you as a man to change the direction of every broken highway of life. By faith, you and I have to believe that when we follow God's principles he will give us the strength to do it. Now, what the enemy desires is to keep our lives as men troubled that we fall and stumbled. When most men stumbled and the devil has led them all roads can lead to lockup.

Sir, trust me when I say there is much danger to losing hope than I can attempt to enlighten you in words. I speak daily with potentially great men in lockup who once were on top of their game while free. What most of these men tell me is their lives went from light to darkness in one breath of no hope. I pray that you as a man keep your eyes on the God of hope that your every breath is with him.

The Seed Of The Troubled Man

In my six years of study of the men in lockup, ,I have discovered that there is a seed that is planted in their minds. I believe the seed of the troubled man is he really doesn't know who he is. This is a man who has yet to discover his abilities or his faith. Now, what happens in the man is as long as he goes in life not knowing who he is the deeper the seed is planted. This is why the devil works hard on getting the man to quit school and keeping him out of the church. The reason for this is simple, the devil knows if the man is unlearned and doesn't know God his steps are always distorted. Beloved, as a man, when your steps are always distorted you are walking the steps for lockup and failure.

God called you and me with a mighty calling and what we as men must do is heed to our calling by faith. The way we do this first and foremost is to know that we are His children and we have a mission to accomplish. As I talk with these men in lockup daily some I can tell within minutes that they don't know who they are. Some think that they were born to be losers because they don't know their father. What I remind them is they may not know their earthly father, but they must know their heavenly father. My goal each and every day is to plant a seed of the word in their life. With the word seed planted in their life, I am confident they can be changed if it is fed properly.

The bible says "The seed is the word of God. (Luke 8.11). I believe the word seed planted in men's hearts can get their identity back. There are many men in our nation that have lost their identity through various hardships. As I have studied men in lockup for the past six years I have discovered valuable insight. One of the ways men can lose identity is what I simply call **CPC** or **Consistent Poverty Conditions**. This is a lifestyle where it doesn't matter where he changes his address poverty meets him there. If the man never discovers who he is and who he belongs to in the process he perishes under the condition. I witnessed this growing up when we moved from my first location as a child then to the projects.

In my growth in becoming an adult and watching the pattern of some of the guys, I saw identity being destroyed. Please understand here that it was not the location itself, it was the mindset that followed him. Unfortunately in some men their environment overpowers their strengths and causes them to fall. When your parents were not making much money such as mine and only enough to survive it is a challenge. When this is the situation and the family has to move they may have to settle for less temporarily. What is important for the man is by faith for him to know he doesn't have to settle permanently. When a man seeks the hand of God his life can change as well as his environment. This is because God is our source.

This is my teaching to the men at lockup that I use from a love perspective to assist them in getting their life back. God desires all of his people to know that he is a loving God and he will provide for us. My goal is to uproot the seed in man that the devil has planted underhanded to bind him. What I want to let all men know is that yes the seed is the word and it will break every stronghold. This is the stronghold that the enemy has maneuvered for many years to send men to lock up. What I have noticed in lockup is how when the word is planted in the man the new man is at peace. This is what I experienced at the prison as I spoke to the newcomers at the prison. I asked all the men how they were doing and one said "well the best I can at this place". Right away was an opportunity to plant a seed in one man to break the stronghold of his location.

I said to him "yeah but don't let the location affect the man in you that God has on his mind. I also said to him you are a little lower than the angels and crowned with honor and glory (Psalm 8.4). When I shared this with him I saw a new peace come over him and he knew now that God was with him. The Holy Spirit confirmed what I shared with him because the man sitting next to him responded. The man said "I just read that last night and we will study more of that tonight." When we pour out a seed of hope in man we can change his thought pattern for life. This is the hope that we have in God that we can put him in a position to override his circumstances. What the devil works hard on is keeping the man gazing at his troubles and condition.

Once the seed is planted in the man by faith I believe he can rise above the current circumstance and live. Beloved, I am here to tell you that now is the time to reclaim your place with God. The way that you do this is to declare now that no storm or place of my storm will rob my place in God. You are the victor even if you are challenged and not the victim with a seed of hope. Let me encourage you to only speak words that have been nurtured with the power of God. Now, your condition wants you to say what the condition has placed on the inside of you. This is what brings the trouble from the man that the devil knows can lead to lockup.

When the situation grows tall in the man it can grow above him and rob him of who he is in Christ. When this occurs the man is again wandering in the wilderness of who am I and falls in the hand of Satan. What the devil knows is that man must be fed the word in order for him to live in the earth. This is why the bible says "Man shall not live by bread alone, but by every word that proceeds out of the mouth of God. (Matt:4.4). I believe if the seed of the word is lost for the man it will be evident his identity is lost. The enemy will attack the man at this level and turn his world upside down. What normally happens when this is at its peak man began to encounter his greatest tests.

I believe we as men are at our highest points right now of being attacked on every side to see who we are. Beloved, I pray that you will not get lost in who you are while you are under fire by trials. What you are in need of when this occurs is to know that you are a greater man than your greatest fire. I believe every firestorm that comes against man is coming at his identity and his identity only. Now, a lot of things are connected to his identity such as his faith. When the attacks are strong upon your identity it will take strong faith to sustain. The moment you as a man do not apply strong faith the true man is weakened. This is where the man succumbs to the test and falls and many times falls hard. The enemy knows a hard fall for the man is the fall to lockup. The reason this is a hard fall is that no man was designed to be pinned down or bound. When the man is bound when he was created to rule a corrupt seed has been planted to destroy. What God desires for me is to know who I am under every trial that I may know who lives in me.

Here's what's very important under fire. If you are not sure who you are under fire you really will not know God. The reason this is true is if I can see myself and still don't know who I am, how could I know God who I can't see. When the devil plants that seed and taps my identity I am robbed of the best in me. Now, what happens is the man is tossing and turning in a world he can't survive on his own. What we witness on the news each night with the robberies and the murders is a lost man. This man is lost because his identity is lost because he is all over the place with a bad seed. My prayer is that he is brought to his knees in prayer and surrenders to the will of God.

I witness daily in lockup young men that allowed the bad seed to contaminate the good that they were born to do. Yes sir, I am here to tell every man that one bad seed planted in you has a mark for lockup. Now, what you may not know is every bad seed that is produced has a time zone in which to live. What am I saying?. If you are doing something that you and I know is wrong in due time welcome to lock up. I promise you that due time that you find yourself in lockup is the worst time. I say this because some of the greatest men with great gifts have found lockup to be at the worst time. They all mentioned that they knew there was a time clock ticking on the inside.

What I also discovered with men is that the bad seed in the man can cause him to sow bad seeds. The bad seeds can be seeds of robbery, driving under the influence, drugs, murder, etc… The bible says " For he who sows to the flesh will of the flesh reap corruption. (Gal:6.8). Your flesh as man has a tendency to give in to that bad seed. I want to let somebody know that hope can overpower that bad seed and change the course. The time clock I believe was a sign from God trying to plant a seed of hope over the seed of no hope that robs. What is robbed is the future and destiny that you were born to have under the guidance of a faithful God. Now is the time to make a decision to change course.

Beloved, you have the power to change the course of a bad seed that may have been planted for years. God has given you as a man the ability to take that seed and get it under your feet so that it dies a painful death. By faith, you are a man of destiny that is in route to a new life that will free you of corruption. Sir, I know that it may appear that all roads have kept you bound by circumstances. I am here to tell you that you have been chosen by God to be the seed of hope for man. I believe some of us as men have witnessed enough bad seeds in our lives that kept us from greatness. Today is the day for the true man to know that God is well able to get you back where you belong. I am here to tell you sir that your past has a tendency of planting a seed to hinder your future. I hear this in the conversation of men in lockup how their past would not allow them to go forward. What I want to encourage you is you have a future regardless of your past. God is a God who can set you far above what your past has presented you that his name gets the glory.

My past did not look bright coming from the projects and watching everyone else getting the breaks. I had a shift in my thinking and began to declare that I was not planting that seed in me. I knew if I stayed right there with that thinking it could turn into something that was less than God's view of me. Beloved, the enemy knows how to present the man with false accusations of the blessed life. Once I began to study the word and learn of God I stopped believing the lies the devil was speaking. What has happened to many of these guys here in lockup is they believed in the lies of the enemy. Once these lies began to take root they planted seeds and grew to become life. What man doesn't know without the wisdom of God is these lies are roads to lock up.

Men can no longer afford to walk in this world without the wisdom of God in their life. The reason for this is the devil knows the limit of man when he is powerless. The issue is man is powerless in this world without God because the devil has power. The bible says "The fear of the Lord is the beginning of wisdom(Psalm 111:10). Beloved, when you begin to fear or reverence God wisdom brings much insight. We as men can begin with wisdom to hear from God and find peace. God's wisdom directs us and leads us to his way of doing things that will make us whole. Now, things may not look any different right away, but our faith gets an increase.

We can walk in the wisdom of God knowing that what he has promised is true and be patient and free. When we hold on to the wisdom of God and walk in faith bad seeds get plucked up with confidence. I began to walk in the wisdom of God that uprooted bad seeds that were planted without knowledge. When I began to pray I saw a new me that now believed that I can do the impossible. What the devil is doing on a daily basis among great men is tossing him a seed of deception. What is robbing the best of men is this is a seed that has a pleasant outlook but dark results. The results are dark because they have a troubling end that in most cases will lead the man to lock up.

God has a plan for you sir while you be confident in what he is able to do for those who wait on him. I am here to tell all men that there is no greater seed that can be planted in us than the word of God. When the word of God is planted in us we can spring forth into the plan of God. The plan of God began to take root in me and I began to grow in the knowledge that gave me hope. This is the hope that allows the man to find his way to God's promise that keeps him in God's care. Beloved, this is your year to move whatever mountain is before you that keeps you from success. God is standing by to do great and marvelous things in your life when you trust him. The seed of that troubled man has kept him bound in order that he never sees the promised land of victory. There is victory for you sir and it is not found in being locked up but by being charged up for God.

Chapter 4

THE NEEDS OF THE TROUBLED MAN

When I walk into the prison daily I see many needs from men that can only be given by a vessel of compassion. When we as Christians embrace the humility of Jesus Christ and the love of Christ we make a difference. I believe when the man has been touched with poison hope dysfunction he is in need. One of the most important things that I think he needs is love which overshadows much. I have watched many men in this prison that I have watched for my entire six-year study. When I have talked with them and they share their pain as well as their case I can since their hurt. What chronic poison hope dysfunction had done to many of these men had robbed them of believing no one love them.

When we bring love to this troubled man we bring into him a touch that may have been lost some time. When the love factor was taken away, men tend to slump into a different vessel. I believe when we step into a troubled man's life and show him the love we can cover his wound. I say his wound because I believe the man has been wounded by something when he is troubled. The wound can come from something simple as a broken relationship that can spark anger. Now, this man can turn into another vessel that sends him on a different path not intended. When love is demonstrated it can bring him hope that can reach deep into his spirit and convert him.

The bible says " But God demonstrated his own love toward us, in that while we were yet sinners Christ died. (Romans 5.8). When I look at this scripture it shows me that Christ did not wait until I lived right. Saints, we cannot wait until a troubled man gets it right we must show him love in his worst. I am not saying we are to approve what his trouble maybe but to show him, love, despite his trouble. I truly believe in the men at our prison the love that I have shown them has changed them. I say this because of the difference I have seen in men who have been set free and become difference makers. Beloved, I am here to tell you that if you are troubled now God loves you.

I am here to tell somebody that if that child is continuing to make a mistake, don't make the mistake of showing any love. I promise you if this is your routine with your male child you are asking for trouble. Here in this prison where many great young men never felt loved are in a painful state of mind. Many are here alone with their trouble but are here also battered because no love was at home. What I have discovered is when a man is going through difficulties; his difficulties may love him more. This is why some of his difficulties never go away because love never fails. God demonstrates to us that we are still loveable even in our troubled ways.

I want to just encourage a man somewhere that feels as though you are a troublemaker that you are not. The only way that you may feel that way is you have looked to the wrong source for confirmation. Your situation cannot confirm because your situation did not create you or died for you. God has made it possible for every man to be touched by His love that he be made whole. When those of us that believe this activates this in men with troubled lives can affect the man. God has called us to be His light that shines love in the face of their trouble and brings deliverance. I believe if we desire to see men walking out their purpose in life, love must be in full force. I pour out my every breath of hope and love to these men in lockup daily that they feel love. I remember when I was shut out by peers on the job that knew they had it all and I had none.

The moment I began to feel loved by God and by those close to me, I began to receive revelation knowledge. What this has done for me is made me develop in my study that I can keep my eyes on Christ. Sir, you would not believe the stories I receive mostly from the project I work for called the eye clinic. This is a monthly eye exam clinic we perform. This is where I really get to pour out the Love of God because I talk about being blind, but now you can see. This opens up the door to show them that God loves them and they do not have to feel unwanted. I believe the fullness of love from one heart to another reinstates their true identity and purpose. The man was placed on the earth to do wonders and love clears his window shield of uncertainty.

Many men are giving in to trouble that enters their minds because of a lack of love that enters their hearts. When this happens the man falls for the mind that is not renewed which brings him on the path of lockup. I believe we are called by God to be his example that we show love in spite of criticism. Praying for the man's deliverance and loving him deeply is a road to recovery from poison hope dysfunction. Now is the time to love on those that might be troubled so that we can turn them around. The reason why I believe this is so is that when we were headed to hell, the love of God provides direction to heaven. Sir, even though your life may seem to be in hell, the love of God can provide abundant life.

In my six-year study with the troubled man in lockup, I discovered something of major significance. I discovered that trouble is not channeled by **Information** only, but must be channeled through **Transformation** that brings **Revelation.** Here's what I am saying. I've witnessed how the inmates are given information to help rehabilitate them. This method alone does not bring change to the total man. What transformation does is transform what information is given through faith and reveal his purpose. This is what Jesus did with a man named Saul who was a troubled man. (Acts 9:1-21). This man Saul had destroyed people in the church and had them sent to prison. When Saul was transformed, he became a new man and his purpose was revealed. I believe when the transformation takes place even with a troubled man, hope can be restored, as well as new life.

What Love Has To Do With It

In my six-year study working and talking to the men in lockup, I believe love has a lot to do with their troubles. I say this because many of them speak the same language when it comes to self-confidence. The Lack of being loved had robbed their self-confidence. What I believe is when we know that someone close to us appears troubled we must show an abundance of love. What we do not know for certain is what is the lack of love doing to them inside. I just believe that we as believers can help them and cover some painful moments that are invisible. Love can bring something unique into the man that can prevent his time in lockup. The bible says" And above all things have fervent love for one another, for love will cover a multitude of sins. (1 Peter 4.8).

I also believe that this same love can cover a multitude of pain and pressure in a man who is troubled. Now, what this will take is the faith in the love that we demonstrate among our brethren. When we show the love of God to a man who is troubled we release a love that can free him. We don't know is how long the man may have been troubled but the love of God can calm him. I believe when we demonstrate this love we open doors for his pain and pressure to be released. Here's what I do know when the pain that may reside in the troubled man is not released there could be consequences. What is, even more, is my concern is when this same man is touched with poison hope disfunction.

It is with much sadness and hurt in my heart that on October 1, 2017, 58 people were killed in Las Vegas Nevada. In this same tragedy over 400 people were wounded by a gunman while attending a concert. At this point, there is not much known about the gunman but we must agree he was troubled. I would also say that this man surely was a case of **chronic poison hope dysfunction** also eventually killed himself. This is recorded as the worst terrorist act and number of deaths in America's history. My prayer goes out to the families that lost loved ones in this tragedy. I truly believe that somewhere along the way for this one man all hope was gone for him in his mind.

What we do know about the killer from the news reports is he had a girlfriend who he had sent money. What I am concerned about is what if he was trying to gain her love back and he felt no one loved him anymore. All I am saying here is love can go deep into the heart of a man and change his entire world. Now, we will never know both sides of the story of this man's relationship with the lady. The point that I am making here is love truly has much to do with a man's life when troubled. I believe when a man is shown true love in his worst state of trouble much can be saved. God can turn him around from his troubled ways but he needs the love to start with us.

I do not believe that it is coincidental that I am in the middle of writing this book when such a tragedy has occurred. I truly believe that **chronic poison hope dysfunction** among men is on the rise and can be painful. I just believe that once all hope is appeared to be gone in the man trouble can be at the door. What must be carefully diagnosed is whether there are any signs of abnormal behavior of identity in the man. What I mean here is if it is someone close to you or you know well it is essential to know their identity. When you know the true essence of your identity the spirit of God can channel the love they need through you. The love that you can bring to them in their trouble can change their direction of travel. The only way that this can be done is when you stay connected to God in the process. Many of these men in lockup here at our prison never experienced unconditional love. I am confident that many could possibly be free if true love was introduced.

I believe when unconditional love is demonstrated in the life of a troubled man change is a breath away. When love is unconditional upon a man there is unlimited space in him to recover from wrong. This can come in him I believe because he has something to stand upon when he feels defeated. Many of these young men have shared with me that there was no reason for them to try to get right. Many have said because the home was so broken with no love and there was no room for improvement. I really hurt for these men because I know the proper love shown could steer them. Love has the power I believe to cover a multitude of hurt from past circumstances.

Beloved, here's what I want you to know. Jesus died for you and your sins as well as all your troubles. God has a plan for you sir that is much bigger than the pain that may be in you from your past. What the enemy wants you to think is because no one on the earth may have shown love no one loves you. I am here to tell you that the devil is a liar and he wants that lie to take you to lockup. God has his hand on you and he cares for you with a love that cannot be interrupted by the enemy. The only way that God's love can be interrupted is when the enemy speaks lies and you believe it. I love when I walk and shake the hands of these men in lockup because by faith I believe they feel God's love.

When I do this often with the men at our camp with many I develop a Godly relationship with ease. I say this because love is easy when it is of the heart of God unconditionally with no seed of judgment. I have witnessed some of the most troubled men in the last six years changed from a love connection. This I have seen when they have left prison and become great fathers and husbands. Parents, again please don't give up on that troubled child at home just show them more love. I am not saying cheer them on when they make a mistake but let them know that love is not lost. Many unfortunately showed no love when love was needed and they lost the child to lockup.

I am watching too many great men that had futures that were promising when trouble came by way of brokenness. The brokenness came when the chain of love was broken that they once knew went astray. Beloved, we serve a God that is ready to get you started again back on the highway of success. I want to encourage someone who may be at the edge of giving up that you do not have to quit. What I mean here also is you do not have to quit on life because there is much love for you. Once again, I don't know what it was that triggered the man that killed 58 people in Las Vegas. What I do believe is if there were someone he believed loved him unconditionally he may be alive and well. Right now across America, there are a lot of families in sorrow of the lives lost in the shootings. We as a nation will forever mourn the loss of so many precious lives by one man. What the Lord revealed to me about this situation is how one troubled man can affect so many.

This is why I want to again encourage someone that may have the opportunity to say I love you to someone to do so. Once again, if you know they may be a little troubled love is a key that unlocks curiosity in the mind. I say this as I think about a young man when I was in Iraq we knew was troubled and suicidal. Many were curious about his mindset to kill his own due to his conversations and acts. What the commander decided again was to take his weapon from him for his safety and others. What I decided to do with him was to meet with him often at the Chapel daily. What I wanted to do was to show him some brotherly unconditional love to help gain his confidence.

Upon doing this I was able to find the root of a lot of his problems which were financial and family problems. Once I began to speak to him daily about the love God has for him and our family of soldiers things changed. Now, I must say he needed this because he was really on the edge of ending everything. What he was feeling and what he shared was the world was caving in on him through his problems. Beloved, I want you to know that the world will not cave in on you or your problems with God. The love of God and because of who he is your problems by faith must cave in on God first. The love of God that he has for man has a lot to do with where he finds himself on the earth.

What the devil desire for the man is to listen to the world that has no knowledge of God's unconditional love. As children of God, we can step in on God's behalf show love to man, and bring him peace. The world continues to allow a man to walk in his trouble and troubled mind to lock up. I am saddened some days at work at our prison when some men's troubles were loved motivated. Our world is going through a tremendous amount of challenges with men, especially in identity. What the enemy is playing on right now is who he can keep in the dark world of **WHO AM I.** What I have learned even in my tests and trials is the enemy can push everything down your throat.

What I mean here is the enemy will push all of your debt, sickness, job problem etc.. on you until you don't love yourself. What has happened to the man is he is so far away from God that he only believes the devil loves him. This is why the man in his condition spends more time concentrating on who the devil calls him. God in his faithfulness has a calling on the man that must be received by faith. God has a love calling on every man who believes in him that will set him free. I believe with this unconditional love that same man can rise up and be accounted for again in his family. I am so grateful to God to be used by God to restore men on the earth with his love upon me. I am a witness that if it had not been for the love of God in my life I could possibly be locked up. Now, here's what's real about that. I know that I have made mistakes in my life and know how it feels to appear no one loves you but the devil. The moment I began to think of the love that I was overtaken with by God in my mess I was delivered. Deliverance is real and there is deliverance for men who have made mistakes.

The love of God is what makes the difference that can turn your life around and make you new again. With this kind of love within your heart as a man, you can wait for God until your change comes. I promise you the change will bring a new direction as it did for me when I waited patiently. The bible says " And the Lord direct your hearts into the love of God, and into the patient waiting for Christ. (2 Thess:3.5). What I spend a lot of time saying and teaching the men in lockup is waiting for God. I share with them that because God has great plans for them and loves them it will be worth the wait. What I discovered about the love of God is it brings strength from on high.

When men embrace this unconditional love from the heart of God's people it can make a major difference. When a man is being overwhelmed with life's setbacks he can feel less than a man. When this happens he can experience mental torture that tears into his manhood and his ability to function. When we bring him the love of Christ unconditionally we can rekindle new light. I believe within this light is his dreams and visions to be everything God called him to be at birth. What the enemy spends much time on with the man throughout his life is getting him into doubting his success. What I mean here is the enemy knows that God desires the man to be a success in every area.

This is why everyday of our lives as a man we have to stay before God hearing his voice through the word. What this does for us as a man is keeps us reminded that nothing on the earth can channel God's love. Now, for me I needed this very bad while getting attacked nightly in Iraq consistently. What also kept me focused on his love that I needed was reminding all the troops of his love. Beloved, God is working behind the scene for you as a man and his unconditional love is consistent. The love of God is constantly falling fresh upon you from heaven that all your needs are met. This does not mean that there will be no challenges but the challenges must obey God's command.

I believe that this is your season as a man to dig deeper into the love of God and see what he will do. I am here to tell you that love has a lot to do with your finish line and the destiny God has for you. Now is the time to learn of God and capture his love that the enemy will not capture us to lock up. Beloved, I am here to say again to you that you are much more needed in your home than here in lockup. What love has to do with every troubled man has to do with where he ends up. I believe the unconditional love of God has a shield itself that is bigger than the courtroom. My prayer is for the people of God is to show this unconditional love on every front and corner. When we do this I believe we can win more men who are free to be husbands and fathers. Trust me when I say I have looked into the eyes of many men in lockup with the potential to be presidents. The cells here in lockup care less about where you come from, but they do want to know where you are going. Saints, love has so much to do with the future of a troubled man. Let's show him love and pray the father will intercede and cleanse him from all his troubles.

A listening Ear For The Troubled Man

I believe there is much that we can do for those that may be troubled if we allow them to speak and we listen. What I have discovered is there are men that are bound inside because no one gives them a chance to be heard. What I have witnessed is that when I give an ear to hear I give hope an avenue of travel. One day at work at the at the prison I had one of our inmates tell me sir, I appreciate your spirit. This inmate works for us in our hospital as our runner and is a very quiet and intelligent man. This gentleman stated I don't speak to many people except you and one nurse. The inmate stated that we demonstrated having the heart to listen because no one else seems to care. Now, I know someone may say maybe no one listens to him because of what his crime may be.

The bible says "He who has ears to hear, let him hear. (Matt:11.15). I believe there are troubled men all around us that desire listening ears. When I listened to our inmate's story and allowed him to pour out his heart I saw something. What I began to see was a man who has a world of knowledge and heart for God. Now, he realizes his mistake but has a wealth of insight to change the world. What concerns me is all of this insight and his greatness and rebirth are bottled up due to a close world of listeners. I often wonder how much more peace would be in this world if there were more listeners than talkers. Parents, let me encourage you that if that child is troubled please give him your ear.

What I believe is when a man is troubled sometimes you can find where his pain is if your ears are open. I truly believe that if we want to hear from God we sometimes first must hear from people. What I mean here is in order to know what the man needs prayer for, I need to hear from him. When I pray to God on man's behalf I can hear from God and trust the Holy Spirit for direction. Now, I can believe God that what I just heard from God on mans' behalf will come to pass. A listening ear for the troubled man can turn his world around and bring hope.

I believe when we give a listening ear to a troubled man we allow nourishment into his confidence. What may have happened in his mind is that he is a nobody and all of his thoughts are none since. When we give ear to his thought process we can steer him to the truth as well as righteousness. The way I found that I can steer him to truth and righteousness is to allow all his conversations to be complete. When I respond to his conversation being led by the Holy Spirit the spirit will override natural thinking. When I apply what I was given by the Holy Spirit this has the power to set him free. This is the freedom that will deliver him from his trouble that can keep him from lockup.

Now, the enemy doesn't want this to take place therefore he will keep us from giving a man a listening ear. I believe God is calling us as believers to set our ears on Max so that we hear what man has to say. I really enjoy giving a listening ear daily to the inmates because I learn variable life resourceful information. This is information that will help me on bringing restoration to other troubled men. I really have been amazed at how much I have learned by giving a listening ear to troubled men. One of my goals in life is to reposition men's footsteps that have been positioned for failure by the devil. What I have discovered is the devil has planted many failures in man and hopes that he stays silent.

The reason the devil hopes the man stays silent is for the man to think that no one desires to hear him. What this began to do to the man over the years is build up pressure in the mind of a man of vengeance. I believe this vengeance takes place in man because his purpose is not being fulfilled to be heard. When a man can hear from God and obey him he can have much to say to change a nation. (Exodus :3). What I believe is every man who knows God has something significant to say that must be heard. I believe in this hour those men who trust God will change the lives of those who listen. Beloved, as a man, let me encourage you to get to know God so that you may have a voice for God.

I believe in the hour that we are in right now God is giving men words to say that is worthy of listening ears. What is significant is for the people to wait before criticizing what is in the words of the man. I believe even when the man is troubled he can release expressions that define his trouble. I have had the opportunity to speak with men who were having trouble in their marriages. What I discovered was within a short period without asking part of his trouble was his wife's ears. Anytime in a marriage when one set of ears is not listening can bring failure in the marriage. When trouble shows up in the marriage and someone is not listening there is no room for recovery.

I believe this is the same with a troubled man when there is no listening ear how can he recover from his dilemma. Now, we truly believe that God will listen to this man when he calls in faith. What we need to know as believers are God desires us to be his ears and eyes here on the earth to be his disciples. Beloved, you need to know that God will hear you when you pray that you may walk in him. This only requires you to know that you can always recover and be free from lockup. The devil desires all of us as men to never be heard that all of our dreams and desires die a tragic death. When we can stay strong as men who know God our voice will be heard for God.

Again I want to encourage someone who may be going through with a man to give his voice a chance. I believe if you listen to him with a favorable ear you may detect something that you didn't know was there. What I have learned working here in lockup is men can hold their pain when they feel unworthy. What made them feel unworthy were dead ears when they needed attention. What those death ears did unknowingly was open doors for the worst to come out in the man. I submit to you sir that you are worth being heard as a man with the image of God living in you. My prayer is for you to know that God is always willing to give you a listening ear when you call. As I listen to some of the men in lockup many times I can hear their cry for a listening ear in a fight. I hear this when they bring the man next door to my office to the emergency room. This is when they have been involved in a fight and must come to the E.R. for a body chart. As I listen to his rage about what started it I often hear "I'm tired of people thinking I am nobody". What this tells me is nobody has heard him enough to prove that he is somebody.

Precious one, you will be surprised how much freedom you can place in a man when he is given an ear for proper identification. Now, even though he may be a troubled person **opportunity** presents **discovery.** This can be the place where the man and the listener unveil under pressure his true purpose. I believe new discovery is made about the man once someone listens with an attentive ear. This is what happened in the life of Joseph while in prison when Pharaoh needed someone to interpret his dream. (Gen:41). When Joseph was given an ear to hear what he had to say things changed. Now, we realize Joseph was not a troubled man but he was bound and needed an ear to set him free.

What I believe is regardless of the man's challenges when listening ears are available freedom is possible. What I have discovered about man's trouble is sometimes for so long they have had only their own ears. Now, the problem with that is in my six-year study here in lockup I have discovered repercussions. What I discovered is that when many of these men only had their own ears to hear them some developed mental problems. I am so amazed at the young men that are locked up with mental problems. Now, the few that I have been able to speak with in-dept always had low self-esteem. Once I found out one of the key components of his problem I went to him when I could and gave him my ear. What I discovered I was able to pull more out of him when I just showed up.

I did this when I issued eyeglasses to these young men and was amazed at what I could discover in a short period. Just like Joseph in the bible, I truly believe that men have much inside of them even when bound. Some may be bound with issues of different types but I believe they can voice to us their pain. I just believe that we are in a crucial time on planet earth for special voices to be heard. Now, since we really don't know who these special voices are let's give that man near you a chance. This may be his only chance to be heard which has an impact on him getting delivered from bondage. I believe we who have by faith a heart for God will make our ear available for all men.

What I have discovered about men also when given a listening ear is they can reveal what you may already expect. I believe when you allow the man to be heard long enough he will release every setback he has. What I believe we can do in some cases with trouble men is save him a trip from lockup. While we give men a listening ear to him, he unloads sometimes unknowingly hidden darkness. What we can do as a source of medicine for his pain is widen our abilities to hear him. I have spoken to some of these men, and I can tell that if they had a listening ear, trouble would not have taken them. I know some of this may seem like an opinion of a man but the numbers don't lie. I have the numbers of far too many sons, husbands, and friends that wish this was just a fairy tale. Here's what's real, in lock-up it does not matter what the outside world believes as long as they are locked up.

What I desire to do is to keep great men at home, in school, working in the church and working behind the fences. My prayer is to reach men from all corners of the earth and lend them an ear of hope. I believe when lending them my ear they can be heard by someone that comes from their world. Now, I say this because I have walked in some very seemingly disappointing shoes of hard times. Yes, times were hard in the projects and on the west side where drug deals were made before your eyes. Many times it appeared that this was a norm and not doing wrong made you feel uncomfortable. When I witnessed one neighbor get locked up I began to believe it could have been me.

I made a choice that my life could make a difference if I believe and be willing to help another man believe. When I made a decision to be a **difference-maker** than a **lawbreaker** I saw something new. What I saw was if I could get a listening ear for my somewhat mellow voice I might be able to help someone. What I didn't know was at the time that God had a plan for me all the time. What I believe is God has a plan even for those men that may be troubled by their environment like I was. What will make the difference in bringing them out of their environment is an ear of hope. This will be the ear to tell them my brother you are a fingernail from a turnaround.

Once again this requires first allowing him to get out all of his pain that he might fall upon sensitive ears. Beloved, God is calling all of us as believers to be his ears by faith that we may lead the lost to him. My prayer is to help with all that is in me to help build up men from where they have been torn. Working in the prison I am witnessing how the enemy is tearing down the best of men. The enemy is playing a very serious game in putting great men in a position where their voice has no power. The way the devil is doing this is shutting out the path for man to know he is redeemed. When the man is in the uncertainty of being heard by the people, he can easily believe he is not heard by God.

Precious one, if you don't give the man an ear to hear who he can see, what makes you believe he thinks God hears who he can't see. I believe giving the troubled man an ear to listen to his story can reset his outlook. You and I can be the change agent that brings him by faith to a place for true repentance. We can do this while we listen to him and demonstrate the love of God and his righteousness. What is real is when these cells at lockup slam upon the man he hears those loud and clear. My job is to listen to the man that I can slam the doors of misconception. I believe when I slam those doors I can give him hope from God that shall be loud and clear. This hope shall be a God-sent hope in his heart that shall set him free that lockup is under his feet. Beloved, open your ears as well as your heart to that troubled man and discover newness in him. I believe when you hear him even as he weeps you may hear that his pain was deep. We will never know how much love we can show when we give a listening ear to one troubled man. When we do this in love we might see how significant we were as a part of God's plan.

A Heart That Cares For The Troubled Man

I believe in order to reach the heart of a troubled man it will take a heart that cares and the man knows it. What this shall require in every situation is having the heart to go against troubling odds to help someone. What I discovered while working in lockup is the man cares less about how much you know. What the troubled man is truly interested in is how much anyone cares. Here's what I also learned about troubled men, they know a true heart when they see and hear one. Poison hope dysfunction takes away men's ability to have real hope, but not their ability to discern. When we love God and desire the heart of God we can soothe some of the most troubled men.

When the troubled man knows someone cares I believe he now has his eyes on what change can mean. Most of the men here at the prison always are seeking hard and wide for a caring heart. What I have noticed is they really desire change but outside pressure has overwhelmed their effort. I believe this is what we have in troubled men all over the world where violence has emerged greatly. When a heart that cares shows up on a troubled man I believe his gages of anger calms. What I believe brings this calm is the heart like God that shows him love from head to toe. What I mean here is there is a heart that cares about you for who you are regardless of what you have done.

I think what a lot of people fail to realize is most troubled men have hit rock bottom on winning a popularity contest. They know that most of their family and friends have given up on them being that model man. I believe by faith that there are men at this level that are one heart that cares away from a miracle. Beloved, if you are one that feels that no one cares anymore let me be a voice from God. God cares for you and you are much loved by God and he is willing to bring you peace. Precious one, regardless of where that man may be right now God is calling for us to show him we care. Now, that's all is required of you and God will do the rest because he is God.

Many parents, friends, and the family I believe have missed the mark on being a change agent for God in the lives of men. The reason why I believe this is the case is they think that they are the ones that have to do it. You need to know that all God desires for you and me is to demonstrate his love now. I am watching men coming into our prison daily with nobody caring about my attitude and mindset daily. When I get to know them and talk with them very few have something nice to say about home. Now, for me, this is a sign that we as a church must work harder to reach that broken home. I believe with a heart that cares about the man we can bring change to the man through love.

The bible says "A new commandment I give unto you, that ye love one another; as I have loved you, that ye also love one another. By this shall all men know that ye are my disciples, if ye have love one to another. (John 13: 34-35). I believe that troubled men can be the men that shall see that we are God's disciples. They can see it when they see and feel the heart that cares when we trust in God. I really have been blessed by the men that have left the prison and are making a difference at home. What I am even grateful to God about is him allowing me to be used by him to bring change. I believe beloved that you too have that ability if you just ask God to give you a heart like his. With a heart like God you can reach if not that troubled person in your life maybe someone in your community. In this violent time among troubled men, there is a lot of room for a caring heart.

I also believe that there are many men that are near trouble and really need that caring heart to show up. When that caring heart shows up it can be an element of hope that keeps a man free from lockup. As I am watching men with this poison hope disorder continue to be made known I am concerned. I am hurt when I watch the news and see the enemy unload this sickness upon the earth. This again for me is great men with no hope that robs their freedom to bind them in lockup. I was speaking to an inmate today who happens to be a preacher who was robbed by this enemy of deception. Beloved, again at this point the enemy doesn't care who he affects with this poison. Trust me when I say he has robbed and affected many church leaders that are here in lockup.

What is significant to the devil is as long as he can get this infection in a man's hope he can take him down. This is why the heart that cares must be effective in his ability to reach one man so that he may keep hope alive. This preacher that I spoke to today was being released after several years locked up with hope. What he mentioned to me as he was headed home was his hope was poisoned with dope. This great man of God also mentioned that he lost his family but believe hope will get them back. I encouraged him that the power that God gave him is still much alive if he believes. Now, here's what I want to convey to Christians. No one is so strong in the word that the enemy will not try you with this poison hope.

While we are sleeping the enemy is wide awake coming at the best of us to still our joy and deposit destruction. Let us be that heart that cares and encourage a man that he is capable of winning over trouble. What the enemy would love to do is bring poison hope disorder to an entire seed. Once this disorder spreads in one seed I believe it can destroy cities, States, and eventually nations. When we look at all the terrorist acts on the news we must wonder how far this will go. The answer to this question I believe depends on our faith in God and the power of our words. I believe the faith we have in God and the power of our words will reflect the care we have for his people.

I thank God that he has given me hope through knowing him that I can spread his love in these dark times. Yes, we are living in some trying times but we have the ability by faith to win this race through Christ. I am called by God for this very moment to stand right in the midst of hard times to show his love. When we lean on God to demonstrate his love the heart that cares will come alive. When the love of Jesus comes alive daily in us the darkness fades away at his presence in us. What I am finding out daily at the prison also is a caring heart can find the source of torment. What I mean is sometimes the true pain in a man only comes out when kindness goes in. When you really desire to find the pulse of the pain the heartbeat of the kindness must be right. I was shocked today at work in the prison when I saw a young man in leg irons. This was a young man that I had been talking with for months about turning his life around. This is a mild-mannered person who speaks very softly and calmly and appears to be well in mending his past.

When I asked him what happened for him to be in leg irons going to restricted housing I really was shocked. This very mannered calm young man mentioned to me that he was caught selling drugs. What was most surprising was when he opened up to me about the torment in him. Now, he would not reveal this to anyone else but he always mentioned how he felt comfortable of my care. Saints, we have to get this down on the importance of our hearts of care to reach these men. There are so many men that are walking in this world battered and torn by this torment. What I have discovered is this torment is only giving away to poison hope disorder.

This same torment is on the doorstep of many homes and is robbing futures and sending great men to prison. I believe God is giving and has already given many of us hearts that care to save many alive. What will be necessary for those that are in faith of having hearts that care is standing firm in believing. We will have to believe that we are called by God to make a difference. Daily I was looking forward at the prison to pour out this care upon men. I attempt this upon those that are in prison always and especially those that are going home. I really try even harder upon those that are headed home soon because I don't want them to return.

What I have learned in this journey is this is a trend that has plagued many troubled men and kept them hostage. Beloved, by faith you and I can set many young men free with just a touch of God's care. I am truly amazed by the effort that it takes on reaching the heart of troubled men by faith. Many times it is really a matter of knowing that I am on the earth to bring light to a dark pathway. When we rely on God to help another man I believe we have taken off the leg irons of his life. There is an avenue of approach that is required to make this happen with grace and get sure results. The first way of approaching for me has been to pray and ask God to give me the word for this man's trouble.

Secondly, I ask God to search my heart that it is just like his that I might speedily show him that God cares. Now, when I do this I allow the Holy Spirit to take over and I find myself fully emerging. My ultimate goal is to touch a troubled man where he might be hurting to bring him God's care. Now, the moment flesh gets involved when we are trying to show a heart that cares this man goes silent. I began to get concerned when a troubled man becomes silent knowing that he is troubled inside. I believe when a troubled man is silent without a caring heart many things can be built. A heart that cares I believe can spring forth a conversation that stamps out what is building. The conversation can be a conversation of hope that saves him and possibly others. What I have discovered about poison hope disorder is it is not sensitive to trouble it may cause. Our nation once again has been traumatized by what I believe poison hope disorder can bring. Once again I am concerned about what if a heart that cares would have been available.

On November 5, 2017, a mentally ill young man walked into a Church in Sutherland Springs Texas and killed 26 people. This shooting is the most victims killed in American history in a mass shooting attack at church. My heart and my prayers go out to the people and families that lost loved ones in the attack. One of my many concerns about the tragedy is was there a heart that cares available to reach the shooter. What is clear for me is that the shooter truly had lost hope that he must end his life and others. What I am getting a clear picture of what God revealed to me is poison hope is real. My prayer is that God will give me and all that believe a heart like his to reach the hopeless.

I just truly believe that if there were hearts that care for a troubled man lives may have been saved in Texas. Reports speak of all the sources that knew of this troubled man but no concern was for others. I believe if there was one heart that cares for the life of a troubled man a whole community could have been saved. Precious one, your heart that cares could make a difference in reaching one man. My prayer to you is to speak to God that he gives you the words to encourage that one in your heart. God is looking for those of us who love him to trust him to be a light of hope. We can bring hope just by demonstrating the love of God to a troubled person that God is able.

When we do this we can touch the most troubled spot in the heart of a man whose hope is poisoned within. Sometimes what I have found with some of these men in lockup is they knew not of the possibility. Most men with no hope due to poison hope disorder think that they are at a dead in. Unfortunately for troubled men, they have no regard when their actions leave others dead from their disorder. The shooter in Texas at the church had no regard that children and teenagers were killed. Precious one, by faith we have the ability through God to bring a heart that cares and saves others. I believe that God is pouring out an abundance of power in the hearts of caring people.

My prayer is that the true believers continue to seek God that we act now in reaching lost people on earth. I believe the time has come for those that have hearts that care to come to the front of the line. What I mean here is we must come to the front of the line where many men are in the lineup. What is so important is we don't have time to be at the back of the line of uncertainty. Every single day I believe the devil is reaching into the minds of men and bringing hopelessness. Now, what the devil is doing is choosing his own path on how he will bring it. What I am witnessing in the prison is even the greatest of Christian men don't understand this disorder. The reason they do not know is only the spirit of God has revealed it to me. Child of God in this season of troubled men you and I need to pray that we embrace a heart that cares. I believe when we do this we can through God's power save great men from the hand of the enemy. What I have witnessed in the six years working in the prison is the devil has a mighty hand upon men.

What is a real concern for me at this point is how I am seeing this disorder playing out in the life of influential men. What I see is the day is coming for more of these great men moving in the direction of lockup. This is where the enemy wants great men that the world can continue to follow his lead. God is fully aware and is empowering believers with a much better plan that wins every time. What this will take is believers praying daily and worshipping God that we have a heart like his. I believe with a heart like God's we can touch this earth and restore the hearts of men.

A Vision For The Troubled Man

I truly believe that one of the things that can keep a man on the course is a vision that can be reachable. In order for this man to have a vision, he must be encouraged that he can succeed. One of the elements that I have discovered that have bound most inmates is their inability to dream. Now, what I believe has assisted them in not having a vision is their surroundings and their influence. The bible says "Where there is no vision, the people perish: but he that keepeth the law, happy is he. (Prov:29.18). When we can assist a troubled man with a vision we can possibly save him from lockup. I knew coming out of high school and living in the projects there were not many options.

What was certain was there were many boys in my neighborhood getting in much trouble and getting locked up. Now, I did not get in much trouble but the trouble was building up around me to capture me. What truly blessed me was my older brother who was in the military and my father planted in me a vision. A vision was planted in me with encouragement that I could possibly be great as a soldier. Now, I had to hear this often while I did not know which direction I would go if I didn't choose the military. This changed my entire world when I embraced the vision with great encouragement. In this hour we are in we need to encourage our young men with a vision or lock-up is waiting.

What I have learned to do each day that I talk with these young men I encourage them that they all have gifts. When I find out where their gift may be I have them to understand that God can use them. It is extremely important that every man knows that they can be used by God when they trust him. When a troubled man is being terrorized by their trouble I believe he has lost identity with himself. Now, when he has lost identity with himself it takes minimum pressure to take hope away. When the man has re-established himself with his gift he can now feel his way to destiny. When a vision is placed before him through confidence and encouragement hope is regained.

I believe we as believers must always have on our helmet of encouragement for the man of trouble. When we can get him focused on a vision that is in his reach we can possibly save a generation. When God made the man he made him with a vision to have dominion in all the earth. By faith, I believe when we speak a word of God filled with hope we can turn man's trouble into triumph. What the enemy desires for us to do are to continue to kick a man when he has fallen. God has called us to lift the man up even when he has fallen as he did for us when we fell in sin. I know without a doubt that when I kept the vision in sight for the military my crooked places became straight.

The enemy knows that if we continue to kick the man while he is down his road only leads to lockup. Now, his vision may not be to be a doctor or a lawyer but whatever he has a passion for that can feed a family. God can make it happen. I have talked to many young men in lockup that have great gifts but were never encouraged. Here's what's real, men that may be troubled will not encourage themselves due to doubt. Beloved, most of these men here in lockup I discovered their trouble was influenced by doubt. The doubt made a pathway into their heart and took away their hope to excel. When a believer can step in and plant a seed of hope for a vision a light can be turned on. This can be a light that changes a man thinking from I can't to I can do all things through Christ. (Phill:4.13). I believe when a troubled man embraces his vision with faith a new man is created.

God desires I believe all of mankind to have a vision with possibilities that he may see the goodness of God. The reason the devil hopes man never has a vision is he stays average with no goals and ambitions. When the man in this state hits a rough spot anger sets in because he feels he has no help. When the man feels he has no help or no one on his side he begins to go after his provisions with force. What the devil knows that he has done at this point is put the man in a point of confusion. I see the point of confusion on these young men as they process through our prison. Sir, let me encourage you that as a man you need a vision of your life that you may always pursue greatness.

I am here to tell you with faith and hope your vision can keep you out of trouble because it becomes the real you. This is the man that you know best because it reminds you of why you were born. The moment you know and learn why you were born and a vision is incorporated the journey begins. I believe with the vision the troubled man sees through a different set of eyes. God through faith will pour His love and His power into this man that he makes a change for God's glory. When this man can stay focused on the will of God with the vision trouble no longer can bind him. God in His own way grants him a new determination that he works overtime to turn his life around.

Our job as believers desiring a troubled man's life to turn around is to stay in prayer for him day and night. I believe the level of his confidence shifts toward his vision as those who care for him encourage him. I am so grateful to God that I hear from men that were in lockup that are free and focused on their vision. Now, some of these men were troubled but not trampled from a vision from God. See, precious one there are men that may be in your path with trouble but not trampled from destiny. God has called you and me to speak to a man in our path and return to sender his trouble. When the vision is rested upon his heart for God's glory and to bless others trouble is swallowed up.

I believe the troubled man is swallowed up in the beauty of holiness as a vision takes him to a victorious place. What we who care for him and love him must do is to trust God in his glorious work in the man. Each day as I went to work in the prison my heart was on speaking hope in a man for a vision. Now, I am not even concerned about what he is there for but I am about what he was born for. Every man that walks the planet earth was given breath by God to impact his environment for God. When this man has been tapped with the hand of the devil his ability to impact has tarnished. I believe when man's ability has been tarnished trouble slips in through an open door of despair. A man in despair with no vision to realign his way of life can soon become a troubled life. The trouble in this man can intensify because without the vision he can become idle. What I believe the idle mind of the troubled man is doing is working overtime in his failures.

What I mean here is the devil has the mind of a troubled man focused clearly on how tough his struggle is. When the troubled man is a high school dropout without a job the enemy works in his low place. When the man is in this place and rejection is on every hand he is vulnerable to stay in his low place. What the believer has to do in faith is to build him up in the word that he still is a child of God. We can find ways as well as help him through prayer and fasting and watch a vision come alive. When we trust in God as believers we shall always be a doorway of hope for the lost. What I believe God has given me as well as all believers is that we can be a blessing to men.

I believe this is why we are the salt of the earth (Matt:5.13) because we can give flavor to broken men. When we come to him with a willing heart to bless him God will give us His power to change him. The way that I shall always seek after a troubled man is to look past his outer man. Precious one, the vision that the troubled man needs is paramount to his recovery to his true identity. What we must do if possible is to get the man to make some notes of the things that he has a passion for. The bible says "write the vision and make it plain upon tables, that he may run that read it. (Habakkuk 2:2). I discovered that if a man can move upon what he writes, he can move upon the written word.

What we have to work on with a troubled man again is his confidence in himself and what gift is he favored with. Believers have the ability to enhance I believe a man's potential when we speak with authority. God has given believers the authority needed to bless a man by faith when we trust him. When a man can write the vision that is on his heart for God there are amazing dividends. What I discovered is required is to look at that vision daily with eyes of faith and confidence. When we can do this as men of faith God moves ahead of us with his plan and make the path clear. A troubled man is haunted by his failure and needs to design his path for victory.

I have been blessed with this mindset and have watched God bring the vision to pass due to consistent praying. What we must encourage the troubled man is his vision is possible if he would learn to pray. God desires even the troubled man to have a vision that he finds his way back to him. What has happened to the troubled man is the enemy has darkened his path to write his ticket to greatness. Now, the devil did this by punishing the man with the world's way of being recognized. God desires us to look to him and his way that he may get the glory for what he has done. Jesus said I am the way, the truth, and the life. No man comes to the Father except through me. (John 14.6). When the troubled man can trust God for his vision his trouble gets new light. This is the light that can bring him to know that he was born to be the light of the world for God. What most men think is when failure or hardship shows up I have lost the meaning of being great. I discovered that my vision has a hidden ingredient in it that matches the gift that I was born with.

Now, this came through overlooking how the world saw me and where the world placed me based on my economics. The vision that God gave me didn't require me to be a scholar or make the dean's list. What my vision did require is knowing that Jesus is the way that I find my way from trouble. Precious one, that man in your life that may be troubled needs to know Jesus is the way. When you can encourage him that Jesus is the way with his vision, the provision will overtake his troubles. I was not the smartest in school as a matter of fact I barely made it through college. What opened my eyes to my future was a vision to show others how much I care for others.

Once again, I had no idea my vision would take me across the country to Iraq to do something amazing for God. What really also was amazing was doing something amazing for God that I saw in a vision. I saw myself preaching the gospel at home to soldiers and civilians in Iraq if I would only believe. I believe once the troubled man can get the vision in every vessel the vision shall come. What the devil hope is the troubled man only sees himself defeated that lockup rule his world. I have seen enough men in my six years working at the prison that has allowed lockup to rule their world. When I say this I mean the number of men I have seen get out of prison and come back.

I am confident that the reason any man returns to prison is there is no vision or no belief in a vision. I promise you if the man has the vision and believes in it God has the last say so on it coming to pass. I am confident that no one in Iraq could have held back the vision that God had placed in me. Preaching the gospel in Iraq to the men and women there tore down walls in me that were impossible. Child of God, you get a vision in that man that is troubled failure doesn't have a chance with the blood. Your job is to believe in God and believe the vision will stand strong when received. God is a good God and the moment the vision is sowed in the heart of the man it can spring up bountifully.

I believe now is the time for the troubled man to take the extra step of faith and take hold of a vision. What the man needs to know again is that he is not here to just be here but here to be a blessing. As believers, we must be bold enough to tell the man even if he has a troubled past that it is not over. God still has a plan of greatness for his life that has major implications for his surroundings. You and I precious one can be a voice for God and stir up a vision in someone who lost hope. God is calling us to be strong in him in faith that our faith causes something to leap in a man. What I am believing God to do in a troubled man is to cause the vision to leap and the enemy to weep. I desire the enemy in his life to weep that he has just lost a man he thought was his. By faith, I shall trust God that his life and his vision shall keep him clear from the enemy and lock up. Beloved, this is the season for you and me to pray unto God that we are vision-minded. When we are vision minded we can transform a bad seed of hopelessness into greatness.

I witnessed daily in our prison men that appeared that a vision for their lives is next to impossible. What troubles me is the thinking of these men appears to be the same way of thinking in many. I see this even as I walk in major department chains and grocery stores among young men's lives. Beloved, if you and I do nothing to bring hope to this generation of men we too have no vision. Let's not think that troubled men cannot be delivered from their troubles because they may be the ones. The Bible says "For behold, I create new heavens and a new earth: and the former shall not be remembered, nor come into mind. (Isaiah 65.17). Beloved, God can set the troubled man free with a vision and his troubles will not be remembered. I believe much of the gun violence across our nation is because of men without a vision. It is my goal, prayer, and desire to bring men from **Guns** and **Violence** to **Sons** of **Visions.**

Chapter 5

A MESSAGE FOR ALL BOYS AND ATHLETES

One thing is certain that I have found about men is the devil has a problem with their gifts and talents. Now, I first want to say that the devil will never win over young men who trust in their God. The issue at hand in this hour is when our boys and athletes call the next play in their life. What the devil is after in a male athlete is a turnover. Now, what the devil knows is that turnovers are killers in any sport. I must say here these turnovers are killers of dreams that lead to lockup. I have witnessed it at the prison more than I desire. When this young man commits a turnover, the devil sees it as he is turned over to him. What the spirit of the Lord is showing me is that the devil is causing men to make bad plays. I have discovered in my six-year study at the prison that our boys and athletes are vulnerable. What is really even depressing is how easy our young men are falling into many traps. Now, what the enemy is doing is allowing boys and athletes to be overtaken by their gifts. Now, let me explain what I mean here, because I know that gifts always have a positive viewpoint.

When our boys, as well as young men, are overtaken by their athletic gifts they have a tendency of escaping wisdom. I truly love and enjoy seeing our young men using their gifts to play sports and playing well. What I have witnessed in six years working in the prison is great athletes are not excluded from lockup. What most of these great athletes fail to realize is they are not above the law. Many of these young men come from great homes but broken home discipline. The reason why I know this was the case is many of them admitted it and most displayed it. When I would talk to them as a father to his son they mentioned that they fail to listen.

I want to encourage every young man with talents on the field or the courts that there is an evil one at hand. What I also want to let you know is that the evil one (the devil) desires to lockup you and your gift. I have talked to in lockup some of the most talented athletes I believe ever created. Now, some of these are not from just their words but from reading about them and watching them. Beloved, as a young man this is the time to revisit who you are and where you are going. I am here to tell you that if you are blessed with great parents you need to obey them now. Most of these great athletes missed their opportunity for greatness because they did not obey.

Growing up in the projects I watched great potential athletes miss their calling because of one bad choice. The worst of their choice was the decision to not obey their parents and follow the crowd. This was all done by the devil that led them to bad company knowing that they had talent. What is even troubling for me now forty years later is I still see some of those athletes locked up. What I want to convey to our boys and young men with these gifts is that enemy is still alive. The same devil that was stealing boys from their gifts and talents has raised the bar. Now, what the enemy wants to do is as quick as possible get boys to pull away from their great home.

The reason why the devil wants to do this early is he doesn't want them to grow in the knowledge of God. What the enemy desires are for the athlete to grow in the knowledge where trouble abides. In November of 2017 3 UCLA basketball players were arrested in China for stealing expensive sunglasses. Now, wait just a minute, players from a high-profile university such as UCLA stealing? It was reported that if these young gifted basketball players were convicted they could have received 3-10 years in prison. It was reported the sunglasses were returned and the charges were dropped. Beloved, trust me when I say this is what the enemy is doing behind the curtain. The enemy is allowing some of our boys to be great athletes as long as stay under his command.

Now, again this is not all of our young men but it is more than enough of them that are falling victim. The reason many of them are falling is that they are following the wrong crowds and voices. Parents, I want to encourage with all that is in me, to talk to your boys with a passion to save them. While you are talking to them it is vital that you teach them identity with great choices. When young men become their own identity they can make their own decision and not follow the decision of others. I am not sure which one of these three basketball players made the decision to steal. The issue is whoever made the decision all of them will go down together if charged for stealing. I want to speak to all boys and say to you don't allow the decision of another boy to bring you to lockup.

The bible says "And if the blind leads the blind, both will fall into the ditch. In the case of these UCLA basketball players if charged they all will fall into lockup. I am watching this over and over daily among too many great young men with great talent. Now is the time for our boys to develop self-discipline. This self-discipline must come with listening and following the leadership of parents. Now, as young boys, it is easy to think that you have gathered all the facts of life. Unfortunately, I am talking with many here in lockup that thought they had it as well but trouble interfered.

When you follow God and the leadership of your parents you can go a long way and have a long life.

In my six years employed at the prison, I have been watching young men go and come and some never get it right. Here's what I believe for young men. God desires you to be great and to have great lives as young people. What I am committed to do is to keep talking to our young men about winning. In our prison system in Alabama, we have a program that is called The Dunk Program. This program allows parole violators to come back to prison for 45 days or less for their violation depending on each situation. I am not sure what Dunk stands for in our prison system but the Spirit of the Lord gave me his insight. God spoke to me at about 4.am in the morning and gave me words for his young men today. First of all the D stands for **Deliverance.**

I believe God desires every man to be delivered from every setback or sin that causes him to stumble. The bible says "The righteous cry out, and the Lord delivers them out of all their troubles. (Psalm 34.17). What I believe is each one must cry out to God for deliverance in order to be totally free. Sir, if you cry out to God as this scripture says you can be delivered from all your troubles. You can be delivered from all your troubles and watch God bless you that your gifts flourish. Now, I must say the enemy does not want you delivered that you stay bound and lockup ready. Next, the U stands for **Used.** Regardless of your troubles or past God still desires to **use** you for his glory. The reason why God desires to use you is he wants to show you that he still loves you. You do not have to fall at the hand of the devil that could lead you to lock up as a young man. You have been chosen by God to be set apart from the enemy's trap and receive God's best for your life.

The N stands for **Needs.** The bible says " And my God shall supply all of your **needs** according to his riches and glory. (Phill:4.19). I believe when boys and men decide to follow God there is no **Need** to worry. I am a witness that God will provide you with every need because you chose to be obedient. You choose to be obedient to God and your parents as boys and God begins to open doors just to bless you. I witnessed God bring the blessing from the projects all the way to becoming a first in my State.

The K stands for **Knowledge.** The bible says "My people are destroyed for the lack of **knowledge.** Beloved, you can gain much knowledge through the word as a young man that makes a difference. What the word of God knowledge does for you as a young man keeps your future bright. The word knowledge keeps your future bright and you make good choices that keep you from lockup. The future of the UCLA basketball players could be destroyed if they get charged. What eventually would cause their trouble would be their lack of knowledge which destroys destinies. The State's **Dunk** program for what I see is an opportunity to take inventory of yourself to get it right.

I pray that the UCLA basketball players get a chance to take inventory of their bad choice that could lead to lockup. I want to share with our boys and young men that one bad choice can set you back. The bad choice can go very deep inside of you and cause your entire way of thinking to shift. Now, the reason your way of thinking shifts is because your thinking takes over your judgment. Unfortunately, I am looking at many young men daily in lockup whose judgment fell short of the law. When your judgment falls short of the law you lose every time and the judge and jury win. My suggestion to our boys and young men is that you stay in school and get much knowledge as you can.

What I have noticed happens when our boys make one bad choice it speaks softly to their ability to succeed. What I mean here is if you are still in school that soft voice began to affect your education. The reason why it begins to do that is this is the devil's way of making you think you need no education. What happens next is the devil begins to allow you to get away with a few more bad choices. Next, your way of thinking becomes comfortable with your achievements. In most cases, the next really bad choice for this young man in school is his choice to drop out. The reason why I know this is true is what the enemy was doing while living in the projects. The enemy was doing it back then and he is still doing it right now with more dynamics. The devil knows that he can destroy a young man because of a lack of knowledge. The devil may have caused a young man to quit school, now he knows he can control his future. Without word knowledge and no knowledge of who he is most young men are in route to lockup.

God revealed something to me that is so amazing that speaks volumes to what is going on with young men. When I lived in the projects I lived by three important places in our neighborhood. Now, walking to school daily from the projects I had to first walk past the first two. The first place I walked past was the church which was across the street. The next place was the police department and the city jail. The final stop was my elementary school which was zoned for us in the projects. Now, what the Spirit revealed to me was in life I could choose the church, school, or the middle which was jail. The city jail was in between the church and the school. What we are witnessing is what I witnessed while working at the prison. Today many young men are not in church or in school. What has happened these young men have chosen the middle of the three which is jail. This is a revelation from heaven of what we are experiencing now on the streets of America with gun violence.

I want to speak to many parents and many young men. When you decide not to be in church and quit school you lose. Now, you lose because you have made the choice that will eventually lead to lockup. I want to say that the spirit revealed this to me from heaven that I must bring to the earth. As an anointed man of God by faith, I am able to hear from God what the spirit is saying with clarity. I have more to say about this than I can say in this book. I spoke to many men at the prison in their 20s and 30s that has sixth-grade education. Now, again I saw this daily at the prison while the devil is having his way in the lives of young men. The bible says "I call heaven and earth to record this day against you, that I have set before you life and death, blessing and cursing: therefore choose life. (Deut:30.19). What I witnessed for six years working at the prison many men are making the wrong choice. I am here to encourage a young man to choose life as this scripture does. What the devil desires are for you to choose life as well. The only thing wrong with his life he desires for you is life in prison

The Basketball Courts vs The Probate Courts

Living in the projects in my teen years was challenging times but the basketball courts were better than probate courts. I discovered that on the basketball courts you can **shoot it out** and lose and go home. In the probate courts when you **shoot it out** and lose you don't go home for a long time. What is significant for our boys and young men is to know that one of these courts is not for play. When the UCLA basketball players went to China they had the opportunity to **Dunk** the ball. Once again, if these basketball players are found guilty the probate courts could decide to **Dunk** them. I witness many young men daily at the prison playing basketball on the courts provided. My heart hurts for them because I know they desire to be at the gym. My prayer and concern are to teach our boys and young men before the prison cells reach them.

What boys can learn on the basketball courts is you have a lot of gifts and talents in you and for you. Now, everyone may not make it to the NBA neither did I but I discovered there was some endurance in me. Beloved, I promise you there is much endurance in you that is designed to be used for the good. What I am witnessing on the news and at work in the prison many of our boys and men are lost. Where young men are lost is in their ability to discover the endurance that can change their life. What I am seeing is many of our young men are using their abilities for bad than good. Watching the shootings and killings on the news among our young men concerns me. What I say now that I speak to many of these young men daily at work is they are not all bad young men.

What is needed I believe is more men with compassion to see young men become great men from their own endurance. I believe when our boys and young men see and hear from true examples lives are changed. Once again, coming out of the projects and staying on the basketball courts kept me from the probate courts. I was intense about being on the basketball court so much I would stay several hours. Many times I would go to the basketball courts after breakfast and stayed until lunch during the summer. Now, you must know that there was a lot of heat and pressure that I had to endure. What God can do in the life of a young man is channel his endurance for His glory.

What I believe the basketball court and the pressure in the heat did for me has deposited endurance for success. What I had to do was to channel the heat and pressure to endure the tough times of life. I knew that life was full of heat and pressure that I would have to endure and trust God. I was able to channel the pressure of heat and pressure to become a great soldier, father, and husband. What I am saying is this, many of our young men that are getting in much trouble need endurance training. Many of them are dealing with much heat and pressure of their troubled surroundings. What is overpowering many of these young men is the inability to endure their pressure.

God has a better plan for our young men and it is my prayer to channel their endurance to win over their pressures. My goal first is to let young men know that they are much loved by God and he desires them to win. By faith, I believe every young man who believes has a seed of endurance in them. The bible says "Thou therefore endure hardness as a good soldier of Jesus Christ. (2Tim:2.3). Beloved, as a young man there is a seed of endurance that is waiting to be called on by you. Regardless of your financial situation, God can do something amazing with your endurance. Don't allow the pressure that may be around you cause you to give in to its call on you.

This is what I believe happens with many of our boys and young men leads to trouble and eventually lock up. The heat and pressure of the world cloud young men's hope causing them to quit school. I submit to you sir that I am looking at young men of your same status and thoughts in lockup. I say that to let you know that do not think you are smarter than the enemy of deception. This is a trick of the devil to sway boys and young men to fight a losing battle with little or no endurance. As a young man, I made up my mind that even though I was not the smartest in school I would endure. The reason I would endure was the projects I lived in were just across the street from lockup. I realized that as a young man growing up lockup was just a breath away from a bad choice. Lockup was closer to me than I wanted it to be.

Young man, I want to let you know from what I am seeing every day lockup is closer to you than you think. The enemy is right now baiting every young man who thinks that he is good enough to beat his system. I really believe these UCLA basketball players believed because they were good they could beat the devil's system. I believe where you go to school or where you come from will not make you. As a young man what will make you are your decisions and choices you make under pressure. Now, coming out of the projects I know what it is to endure hardness due to our tough economics. My father had seven children to raise after the death of my mother while living in the projects. My mother died when I was 12 years and God provided for us.

I learned through tough times how to endure my environment and make good choices and trust God. When I did this I began to see new light and new hope of being what God called me to be for his glory. This did not mean that I was not going to be tempted by the devil because I was day and night. What made the difference in me as a young man was I didn't want to throw away an opportunity to make a difference. I knew coming out of the projects I was under the radar of society to fail and end up in lockup. This was because many assumed I would either quit school or turn to drugs or other trouble. Beloved, as boys and young men we can change the entire thinking of the world about us.

In order to do this, we must be willing to walk upright as young men and make good choices and decisions. Today is the day that you decide that you will no longer give in to what the world has labeled you. While I was spending time on the basketball courts enduring defeats, I stayed out of probate courts and the hot seats. What was so amazing about living so close to the police department was what I could see. I could see so many young lives being destroyed at an early age that was not nice. The reason I didn't want it was I did not want to be a victim of my circumstances. Once again, I was not giving in to what society wanted but to what I believed I could endure. I believe as boys and young men God places gifts in us that must go through a pressure test. All that our young boys and young men are faced with daily are pressure tests that they are failing. Now, on the basketball court, we learn how to endure under pressure to stay ahead.

When I was trying out for my high school basketball team we worked hard on pressure points from all points. We were learning how to overcome the pressure from the opposition trying to take us down. Now, we spent a lot of time on this because we knew this will be where winning will be determined. What the devil is doing to our boys right now is applying much pressure in every area. The pressure is being applied in the classroom, the home, and on the streets, with the intent to take young men down. What I am seeing daily that is showing up at Kilby correctional for men is shocking.

Beloved, I am here to tell you that what I am seeing among our boys and men is not for you.

I am seeing young men coming daily because of the lack of discipline to handle the pressure of life as teens. You were never made to live as a young man from the world's pressure without self-discipline. I am here to tell you that the self-discipline that you need starts at home obeying your parents. I thank God that my father was as hard as he was on me in the projects that I develop discipline. If I would have made the decision to not follow his guidance I knew lockup was waiting. What you need to know that is major to your future is your parents or parent cares for you. I am here to tell you that regardless of the pressure against you there is room for you.

I am here to encourage our young men that there is hope and you can endure if you hold on long enough. One of the things that the basketball court did was provided me with the discipline required for pressure. Now, I must admit I was learning this discipline on the basketball court not knowing it was for life. I have been abundantly blessed through the discipline I learned from home and the basketball courts. Child of God, you have everything in you and every right to be the best of the best. The only reason why you don't make it to the top is you give in to the lies of the devil. The lies that he sold to most of these young men here in lockup is their environment disqualified them from victory.

You need to know that the devil is a liar and he is a liar because I made it out of the projects through his army. The devil had an army coming against me with the same tricks he has coming today. I am here to tell you that there is a highway of grace God has for you to stay in faith for your future. When the pressure of the world came at me in great numbers I stayed the course that I might be a witness. What I wanted to be a witness to was for boys and men that came from my world. What my world looked like was you do not meet the standards required to be called successful. The enemy knew if I bought into that mindset I could be trapped and bound by the system's perception. I did not buy into that mindset but endured my hardships and setbacks in faith. What I love about working at the prison is a lot of these young men come from my world. I can feel their pulse of maybe not their trouble but certainly their pain while in the trouble. Their pain is similar to the pain I felt as a young man going to school but can't compete with my peers. The reason I couldn't compete with most of my peers was they lived a life that pleased the world.

My ability to endure under these outside pressures kept me strong enough to believe one day I would rise. Beloved, you must know as a young man that you will **rise up** once you can endure the **set-up.** I thank God that I stayed on the basketball courts pursuing discipline to rise up from my inadequacies. Beloved, this is what shall make you great that you bring home the trophy of overcoming. I believe every one of these young men I see coming in here in lockup can rise up from their inadequacies. The way that they can rise up and become great leaders is to say that I AM Somebody. See, here's the key, the moment you say that you are somebody your mind began to take shape.

What I discovered happening to me in the worst circumstances was that my mind began to take on the view of the heavens. This all came by faith to believe that God can really trust in me and that I know he will see me through. Precious one, God is not fading away from his promises for you because you can't see him. You need to know that God is well able and is well capable of bringing you out of bondage. What I see the enemy doing in our young men is just keeping them bound with the killings. The enemy knows that if he can keep our boys and men with the killings he keeps them in the probate courts. The **probate** court is the devil's hunted house for our boys that should be on the **basketball courts.**

Beloved, now is the time for boys who desire to have a future to keep their minds and hearts on doing right. I believe if our young men can focus on doing the right thing with the right motives they can succeed. I had as a boy growing up in the projects all the right ingredients to end up at lockup. What I truly believe kept me focused was I wanted to do the right thing and that propelled me above wrong. I knew very little about the probate courts as a teenager but knew a lot about the basketball court. I do remember that I did not want to be a PRO in the probate court, but did want to be a PRO on the basketball court. I did not want to get the two confused or misunderstood. I knew one could save me from lockup and the other one send me to lockup.

Today on the way home from work at the prison, I saw a remarkable reminder of what the basketball court really means. As I was headed home I passed a wonderful and beautiful local church that has a basketball court outside. I saw boys playing basketball on the church property enjoying themselves and at peace. What the spirit of the Lord revealed to me confirmed this message of hope. The church is responsible for introducing our boys and young men to the right court of interest. Allowing these young men to play basketball on their **court** and property keeps them from the **judicial court**. What I also notice is the church basketball court is open to the general public, not just members. When I see this as I am driving home from the prison I praise God for what I see. Now, this might seem small to some, but I promise over a period of time this becomes large. The reason I believe this can become large is what I see daily in boys and men at the prison.

The bible says "Enter into his gates with thanksgiving, And into his courts with praise. Be thankful to Him, and bless his name. (Psalm 100:4). I truly believe as this church allows boys and men to enter their gates and their courts we can give thanks. We can give thanks to God because these are a few that are kept from probate courts. Again, the basketball courts for me did wonders in my life that I cannot forget. The church must do greater work in providing hope to youth in whatever way possible that will please God. I am not saying that every church must get a basketball court. I am saying many of our boys need role models and a source that can occupy their idle time.

The basketball court worked my muscle of hope in me because I wanted to win every game I played. What I later understood was there was a connection there for me with God as I see it with this church. Now, I desire to win in every aspect of life that I can bless others that they may know I care. 40 years later today since graduating from high school I keep a basketball in my car. I keep the basketball in my car as a reminder of how it kept me on the ball court and not the probate court. Young people, there is an enemy that is working overtime to take you from your game. You need to know that there is a God who has already worked it out that you can win if you obey. What I also discovered on the basketball courts was it was about making goals. Yes, we all know the team that makes the most goals or points wins the game. Listen to me parents of young men. Life for a young man is making goals for his young life. The more goals he set for his life, the harder he will work to make the goals. Like on the basketball court, the players work hard to make a goal. Now, if they never make any goals, he has no chance of winning. Here is what I discovered about life from a basketball point of view that helped me greatly. **"LIFE IS LIKE A FREE THROW SHOT, YOU MUST STAY FOCUSED, OR YOU MAY END UP AN AIR BALL."** Child of God, as a young man it is critical that you set goals and **focus** because becoming an **Air Ball** means you **hit nothing but Air.** You were not made to be an **Air Ball,** but a **Fire Ball** for greatness. If you set goals for yourself that are attainable with hope, you can win every time. Now, the way you win as a young man is by having a relationship with Christ. What this will do for you is set the stage for you as not only an athlete but as a young man. Once you spend time with Christ and in His word as a young man and athlete, you have the potential to make history. Now, you can make history in whatever sport you chose as a young man as long as you seek Christ. We all witnessed this in not only the great State of Alabama but across the nation. On December 11, 2021, we witnessed history being made by an exceptionally great **young** athlete.

This was the night the 2021 Heisman Trophy Award was given to Bryce Young, quarterback for The University Of Alabama. Bryce Young made history as the first quarterback to receive this award from the university. Not only did we all witness his amazing talent on the field, but we witnessed his heart for Christ. We also witnessed the heart of Christ on his mother and father that is imitated in their son. What I pray as well as truly believe is that God has used this **young** man to set the stage. What I mean here is Bryce is setting the stage for other **young** athletes on the priority of life. I also believe he is a role model for all young men. What the Lord revealed to me in my spirit about Bryce is his last name is **Young** for a reason. I believe his last name speaks to many **young** men who have good eyesight on the field, but no sight of Christ. Today is the day for the young male athlete to seek Christ like never before. I believe when the young athlete seeks Christ first, he too shall walk away with an award that shall make history.

High School Dropout Trouble

One of the most devastating statistics that I have noticed in this six-year study of lockup is the dropout rate. The devil I believe over the last twenty years has used this tool to send boys and men to prison. What really is a tragedy is among the young men coming to prison now most can barely spell their names. When I call men down to my office to receive and sign for their eyeglasses sometimes it is depressing. Many not only have spelling problems but some even have problems counting. When I look at this huge nightmare upon our young men I see a problem that is becoming uncontrollable. I want to make it very clear to especially boys that are in school today. If you drop out of school trouble has a success rate that will outsmart you on the streets. **NEWSFLASH** to our **boys**, if you **DROP OUT** of school statistics proves you will **DROP-INTO Prison.**

The reason why I know this is the number of young men that I speak to daily bowed to trouble due to lack of knowledge. The young men that I speak to daily that are under 22 three out of four are dropouts. Now, I must say some of them are great guys but made bad decisions to quit school. Here's what's real about quitting school. As men, we were made to be the head of our households and our wives. The bible says "For the husband is head of the wife, as Christ is head of the church; and he is savior of the body. (Ephes:5.23). Now, we know this does not mean that you must be highly educated to be a husband. What I do know is the devil doesn't want you to have anything in your head. If the enemy can get you to quit school and never return he knows that you belong to him.

The devil knows that if you quit school you have a slim chance of being the best you can be on earth. Now, I know there are great stories of those who excelled and succeeded after quitting school. What I want the young men to know today is that these are rare and most quitters are coming to lock up. I want you as a young man to know that you are better than the voice you hear to quit school. The potential that is within you is hidden behind your troubled world that deceives. What I have found about these young men in lockup today is they really want to be someone. The truth is they really are. What they are suffering now is the guilt behind their decision of quitting school.

What I try daily to encourage them all is they are not out of the race if they can turn around their ways. What their ways have been from quitting schools is I can make it on the street on my own. I want to say something to a son that is contemplating quitting school. You are one bad choice from your worst nightmare. I promise you that I have some young men in lockup that if they could talk to you they would. I promise they would tell you don't quit school. I know that because these are great young men that desire to see others not damaged. I believe they would tell you that quitting school was their first base to a home run. The home run was a direct run from home that their parents warned them that was straight to lockup.

Now, the enemy has the one that quit school feeling freedom initially but really it is freedom for the devil. The reason why it is freedom for the devil is the quitter has no knowledge of what freedom really is. The devil has just been given freedom from the one that quit school to play with his future at will. When most boys quit school their future grows dim that they can't see right from wrong. Many of the young men that are here in lockup that quit school had no clue they were going wrong. Trouble just showed up at their doorstep and due to no knowledge, they accepted. I believe staying in school for me while living in the projects brought wisdom from my educators.

I had a great teacher by the name of Mr. Edward Patterson who went to be with the Lord desired all boys to win. As my bricklayer instructor his wisdom in his teaching was for a greater life for young men. I truly thank God for his training along with my father for the tough times we endured. Mr. Patterson knew that living in the projects we faced tough obstacles that could temp us. My ability to stay focus during the tough times and tough decision came easily with his love for us. In the same building, there was also a bricklayer instructor name Mr. Davis who called every student Love. Mr. Davis who also is deceased taught and provided wisdom and love that kept us in school.

Having these two great men along with my father while in school provided hope that I could finish school. Beloved, as a young man you need an example and a model of hope that you can hear their voice. My prayer for you is to get to know God and he will lead you and guide you to that example. What the devil wants from you is to hang around those who have no future and no hope. This type of company will keep you from wisdom and knowledge and keep you in darkness. When the enemy can keep our youth in the darkness he knows he can easily lead them to lockup. I see this on a daily basis as I see young men that I would have loved to have mentored as a father.

Now, I am not saying that I am the perfect father but I do believe I could have kept one of these souls from lockup. When you allow quitting school to come to your mind it is a setup for you to mess up. The bible says "He stores up sound wisdom for the upright; He is a shield to those who walk uprightly. (Proverbs 2:7). Beloved as a young man in this season you need sound wisdom to stay in school. I say this because the world's pressure is stronger against you than it is for you right now. Today is the day that you make up your mind that the strong wind of the world will not persuade you. I speak to many young men daily who say they never imagined being locked up and uneducated.

One of the major discoveries I noticed about the dropouts in lockup was nearly all of them were in public schools. What I would do when encouraging them was I would ask them what school they attended. Nearly 100% of these young men were dropouts from public schools across the state. Here's my point. In my six-year study and working with these men in lockup no dropouts came from private schools. Never in my entire time did I have a young man to say he dropped out of Lamp. Lamp is one of our top magnet schools in the state and ranks high across the nation. I also have never had any of these young men say they attended Booker T. Washington magnet school in Montgomery. This school is another one of our top magnet schools. All I am saying is our public school system in our state needs major attention. I say that because when we look at the news at the many troubles with the administration there are some concerns. I have witnessed the revolving doors of leadership in public schools that should concern many parents. What I am concerned about is with all the drama in the last ten years the effect is devastating to learning.

Now, I must say that I came through the public school system and was glad that I did and received a great education. I realize that our public school system cannot compete with funding with private schools. What I do believe is we can compete if the effort is made to produce quality learning. Quality learning comes from quality minds that are focused on educating our children without compromise. What I see happening is all the drama with the school board is manifesting in the classrooms. The results are many of our boys especially are quitting with ease I believe due to a broken system. The public school system concerns me in the building of men in the education process. In the process, great young minds are being destroyed.

Here's what's real sir, the enemy is quick and fast at getting you to take on his mind and his world. Some of these guys were decent students in school but without a mentor to tell them that they can win. I am here to tell you that the enemy is recruiting great minds to stock his storehouse. What is happening after that what I am told by young men in lockup is the devil then drops the bomb. The bomb I understand is always an unexpected bombshell with no way out but to prison. Here is a word from God that I have for all boys in school and parents to drop in your spirit. The devil was **Cast out** (Rev:12.9) and hope you get **Put out** (of school) that he may torture you while you **Sit out** that you lose hope that you **Drop Out.** When I look at the number of young **dropouts** in lockup the enemy strategy is working. The devil has been mad for a long time that he was cast out of heaven. Now he wants to get back at God by torturing His first creation which was the man.

What we must know is that it is only in the mind of a young man that he cannot stay and finish school. Now, what I want parents and children to know is the devil will do this to the mind if you let him. Remember, the bible says "In whom the god of this world has blinded the minds of them which believe not.(2Corr:4.4). Notice once again, he blinded our children's minds that they can drop out, not their eyes. The reason the devil didn't blind their eyes is that he want them to see and be deceived. Yes, the devil wants them to see all the things of the world that he offers as a dropout. See, with their eyes they can see all the great luxuries the world offers all day long. The luxuries of this world for a dropout always lead to lockup.

For our boys, they see ways they can make money without having the education necessary to do it. The problem with this mindset is due to no education your ability to reason with smart choices is absent. What the enemy has done in your thinking as a dropout is think you will always win. I promise you that I speak to more young men in lockup daily that was taken by that thinking. I am here to tell all of my young men you have a destiny from God that requires your decision. The decision is for you to make the decision that you will be man enough to stay in school. God does not want you to be lost in the darkness of unlearned for the work he has for you.

I say unlearned because as a man you need to know how to handle decisions when the enemy comes after you. When a man is unlearned and has no knowledge due to no education the devil can use him. How the devil uses him is he attacks his knowledge by mixing up his decision-making process. I have heard many of these young men that quit school and are fathers of little children. My heart hurts for them when they say how much they miss their kids and how much their kids need them. When I talk and have deep conversations with the man I find out that the enemy mixed him up. Sir, as a young man you must know there is no easy fix for staying focused and complete.

What I mean is you need to stay focused on what you are required to do to succeed and complete your assignment. Now,

Perfecting Man From Lockup

there are ways that you can get help when you cannot help yourself finish school. I know that it looks like you cannot make it through all that the school place on you to do. Trust me when I say that if I was able to do it coming from difficult and dark times you can too. You just cannot be blindsided by the strong currents of the issues you may have at your home. I am here to tell you that there is more man and more mind hidden in you than you can see. What you as a young man must do as I did while in school and that was to match my will with my desire.

Now, my desire was to finish school so that I might join the Army. The problem was I was struggling in school and was not doing well. My father said I was not quitting school and you are not going to the army until you finish. I found a way to dig my heels in so that I get my motivation up. I needed my motivation and my will elevated that I could graduate to meet my desire. Now, how did I do that, it was simple. I saw the results of other boys around me that quit school.

I began to study much harder in school and rather than thinking of graduating I was thinking of my ticket to the army. I had a strong desire to go to the army that might have been greater than my will to finish school. Sir, I believe that you do have a desire to be something, but I am not sure of your will. What I will say to you is to take a look at your life and decide whether you are comfortable where you are headed. I believe every man has a desire to win in something that requires will and strong desire. What I do know through experience is as a man my desire can outlast my struggle. When my desire rests deeply on the inside of me through prayer I will not quit what I desire.

The bible says "Delight thyself in the Lord, and he shall give you the desires of your heart.(Psalm 37.4). I want to say to all of our young men in school that if you can breathe, you can breathe the desire to win. What will be important for you like it was for me is to develop a relationship with the Lord. When I did this quitting anything that I desired to do did not match the forces that were with me. Upon joining the army, I later decided that I wanted to attempt going to college to get a degree. Now, I knew that I barely made it through high school, but the desire came upon me. Knowing that I wasn't as smart and not quite committed as I needed to be it took years to accomplish my desire. I must say it took me nearly 20 years in school and out of school, but I completed what I started. I received my bachelor's degree from Troy University.

What happened, I did what I believe every young man regardless of where he comes from can accomplish. Sir, I want to say this to you before you quit school. You have the ability to reach higher than the label placed upon you. I know what it is to have a label placed on you coming from public housing. What you can do without having any pressure applied is say to yourself I am not a quitter. I believe the more that you say that the stronger your armor gets on the inside of you to succeed. Quitting school is not for the best of the best and I believe you have been chosen as the best. I know that it might not look like you are the best but you are and the enemy is working hard. The enemy is working hard that you decide to quit school and miss your calling in the earth.

Here is what I have witnessed in my six-year study that the enemy has done with men who drop out of school.

Grade At Drop Out Offense Average Years In Prison

Grade At Drop Out	Offense	Average Years In Prison
7th	Drug Distribution	5-15
8th	Robbery 1/Sex Offense	5-60
9th	Robbery II/Car Thief	5-20

10th	Murder/Manslaughter Sex offense	10-99
11th	Murder/Sodomy	20-50
12th	Drug Distribution	20-30

What I believe the devil has done is stamped a label of offense for each grade level that is consistent. I have watched this for six consecutive years and I see that the devil has masterminded these statistics. Notice in the above statistics that a seventh-grader dropout comes to jail for drug distribution. What the spirit revealed to me is the reason a child so young can sell drugs is from selling his cookies for the school project. Yes, I know I became really good in the sixth grade at selling my vanilla cookies for my school **project** in the **projects.** Now, I am not saying all school selling projects are bad because there are many great ones. Young man, let me tell you that you do not have to fall to the latest schemes of the devil.

The devil is still using the same tactics today of reeling in our boys at an early age to become bad salesmen. My wife and I received a knock on the door by two young boys about 10 or 11 years old. These young boys told us they were selling cookies for their school and showed us the pamphlets. We paid them $5.00 which they said they needed in advance and the cookies would be here in a week. The boys never came back and I don't believe my neighbors never received theirs either. Young men, this is a true pathway for lockup at an early age for quick money. This again is how many of our young men are quitting school early from an early addition.

What I believe your calling is certainly is to stay in school that you might demonstrate that you are bigger than any label. I have witnessed enough of our young men in lockup hold on to their devil-given label. What the enemy desire is for our boys in school to hold on to the label as it paints their future. I am here to tell you as a young man your future is in your hand and you can hold on. I believe you can hold on because you know that you may be the only one left in your family with hope. I believe all you have to do from here is to stay in school and watch God bless you in all you do. When you get through this hurdle of finishing school I can see greatness coming through you. The reason this will take place is that you are a mighty man from God to be a light. Many will learn from you and from what you shall become by staying in school and doing great things.

What In The Jail Do You Want

After six years of working with the prison system, I discovered most men had no idea of prison life. When I walked the halls and I saw the faces I wanted to ask them what in the jail do you want? Now, I want to be very clear to my young men that there is no choice on your bunkmate. What it is important for you to know is your place of rest at home is much better than in prison. One of the choices that you do not get in prison is do you want a single or double. What I promise you can expect is double trouble like you have never experienced. When I watch the operation in the prison I say to myself Lord thank you for allowing me to obey my parents and keeping me.

I say this because I know that I couldn't keep myself with the terrible life that can be upon a young man. Now, young man, I am here to tell you that I don't know what you know about prison. One thing for sure I can tell you it doesn't matter what you may have been told by a friend or relative. What I am here to tell you is after six years of watching this life it will be your worst nightmare. You have a life far better ahead of you that has destiny upon it than life in lockup. You need to know that there is a nationwide problem of overcrowded prisons. What I want to know from you is do you enjoy a peaceful night of sleep at home.

Well, I am here to tell you here in lockup is not a place to desire your peaceful night of sleep if you can sleep. I have had too many young men tell me more than enough that they have not slept in a month. Many are concerned about their life while sleeping afraid of the next bunkmate. Precious one, listen to me, you were not made to be bound but if trouble lies deep in you lockup awaits you. When I hear the young men, especially the repeats who keep coming back of their misery I have a question. I ask them what in the jail do you want and what are you expecting behind bars? When you commit an act that can bring you to lockup you can't expect Renaissance hotel treatments. Now, it doesn't matter what the act was if found guilty you are coming to jail. Let me say you and I are not exempt from coming to jail for an act of crime regardless of our title or position. None of us are exempt from a crime this includes law enforcement officers as well. Even if you are a law enforcement officer who would put his knees on a man's neck and kill him and be found guilty, jail awaits you too. Now, I really have a question for you because you know better, What In The Jail Do You Want?

Our local newspaper did an article on our prison system entitled **"Crying Out For Help"**. The inside sub-title was called **"American Horror Story"** in 2019. I knew of the troubling living conditions and nightmares inmates endure from working there for six years. After reading this article and hearing from the inmates of their horror stories I wanted to cry. I read of inmates saying they were afraid to go to sleep because so many had knives in their possessions. Many were afraid they would not wake up. There were many stories in this article of inmates in wheelchairs that get physical harm and nothing done about it. What was even worse was when some inmates mentioned how others get beaten and raped. When many were beaten and raped the report says the inmates are left in the same dorm when reported.

Sir, I ask you again, what in the jail do you want after hearing of these types of conditions in prison. Now, I must say, this is not even close to half of the horror stories that are in this news article. One inmate mentioned if he had only been there one week and had seen an inmate stabbed in the face. Now, keep in mind no inmates are allowed no weapons, but the story mentions of many weapons among the inmates. Precious one, what I am attempting to do is to keep our men from lockup. My prayer is especially for young men is to stay in school and know that you are somebody. You were not made to spend your life in prison, but to find purpose and hope.

What I have witnessed in many young men that arrive here in lockup is hope goes to a lower level than before. I witness this in most young men who have dropped out of school because of no confidence. When the devil sees that your hope goes now he goes after whatever is keeping you breathing. When these bars slam shut around you some of these guys' minds slam shut as well. What I believe the enemy is doing with this is taking advantage of no confidence and no hope. Once again, to my young boys and young men, your mind can get tortured in a short time in lockup. My concern is the number of young men under twenty years of age that become mental health patience.

I experienced how this can affect a man one day when I was accidentally locked up with the inmates. This happened because I was issuing an inmate a pair of crutches in our hospital ward and the officer didn't see me. The officer locked the cells and walked away. What I noticed was how the enemy can trap your mind by the slamming of the bars. Sir, when you are locked up and bound by cells it has a tendency of robbing your future. I noticed that in a short time that a mental block can form in the man in a short time. I was locked up for five minutes. I believe because the man was never designed to be bound a mental seed can form. When this mental seed is formed immediately a seed of hope must be born to set him free. I believe if a seed of hope is not born, a seed of depression dominates his mind. Here is where mental health can begin to take shape. This is a major problem across our state prisons. Now, I was set free because my seed of hope while locked up accidentally gave me joy that this was for a minute. Now, let me say I watched this happen more than I wanted to great young men.

Now, this is what is troublesome in a major way to me because I know that these young men are much brighter. We have a major problem currently going on in the mental health world for the prison system. The problem is so big that our state is having a huge problem of not enough staffing for the inmates. Now, for me as a believer by faith, I know where the problem begins and where it could end. Once again, we are faced with the god of the world who blinded the minds. (2Corr:4.4). Every time I think and hear about our mental health problem in prison I think about what the devil is doing. First of all the god of this world is the devil and he is affecting minds.

Today in our local newspaper the state's mental health commissioner stated that "we know the prisons are the largest mental hospitals in our country". Young men, **What In The Jail Do You Want?.** Did you hear what was just said? Do you want to come to jail for the crime that you commit just to be in a position to develop mental illness? Now, let me be clear I am not saying this happens to every young man that comes to prison. I must say that more than enough has become affected that the state mental health department is shaken. What the devil is doing with this is sitting back laughing at how he has affected young minds. Young man let me say to you to keep your right mind out of trouble and out of lockup.

The bible says the mind is being blinded which means causing minds not to function properly to their ability. I have seen the line of these young men waiting in lockup to see the mental health personnel. Young man, you need to know that there is an abundance of problems in prison that are affecting great minds. I suggest you to stay out of trouble and away from the prison so that you may accomplish your dream. I believe the moment you began to believe in yourself and in God, you can dream again. I am hurt when I see all these young men so young in prison with mental problems. What I see daily is the devil is trying to do all that he can to steal the great minds of great men.

When you commit a crime and are coming to lock up much can be expected that will not be with comfort. Sir, I suggest you to be all that you can while at home otherwise, I must ask you an important question. **WHAT IN THE JAIL DO YOU WANT?** I am wondering with the 40 or more new young men admitted a day are they seeking gold. In the six years, I have worked in the prison the closest word I have seen to gold is **mold.** This is because some of the young men get sick from the mold in the older prisons. I know personally, that this is in our prison because it is around the faucets in my supply room. These added problems in our prisons do not make your stay a pleasant one.

When I also see so many young men visiting the mental health office I am just concerned with the future for many. There are many of the young men that come through lockup that are not here for life. What concerns me is when some of them are released in their short stay they go home with mental illness. This is not a great way to go home greeting your family having acquired a mental problem. What I believe affects so many of these young men is the initial shock to a locked-up world. Young man, your world is hit drastically with an overwhelming shock of reality that can stun the mind. My question to you as a young man is why would you want to come to an environment of disruption.

The disruption that is a part of the life of lockup can send your way of thinking to a place that is far off course. You were made as a man to come to this earth and have dominion over the earth including its issues. (Gen:1.26). I want to say to every young man that this earth needs your mind sound. The reason your mind needs to be sound is that you can dream dreams and believe they will come. In some cases, the enemy will try to block your mind that you can never recover. Now, I am not saying that there is no recovery from mental illness because there is which takes hope. God wants your mind as a man strong and pure that he can use you and I as his vessel.

What I see the devil is doing here in lockup in young men is putting a mental mark that goes deep. I say it goes deep because when the mind is affected mentally in lockup it can lock up your hope. I had one man tell me something that he experienced while in prison that would affect most minds. This gentleman told me that he had spent thirty years in prison and had seen 25 deaths while locked up. What he said was most devastating was when he witnessed one inmate head amputated. Now, sir, this type of violence goes on in prison and could cause major mental problems. Again, I must ask **What in the jail do you want?** Do you want to possibly witness your bunk mate's head cut off if not yours?

I promise you as a young man it is much better to sacrifice time in the classroom than time in the lockup room. I have seen young men come out of being locked up in our segregation totally disoriented. I truly understand why they could be disoriented because in segregation it is you, a toilet, and a bed. When I look at the amount of space I think about my closet for my shoes which will mess with my mind. Precious one, you do not belong in that lifestyle, maybe your buddy but not you. Now is the time for you to understand that there is no fun in prison and certainly not no comfort. I promise you even though you may not be in true luxury at home all chances die in lockup.

What is troubling to me is when I see so many young men that come to prison daily with high expectations. When I say high expectations I mean they think that it is just doing my time and getting out. I have **BREAKING NEWS** for those young men. You will do your time and your time can do you if you underestimate the system. When you commit a crime please understand if found guilty you must pay the cost. Now, the easiest thing for you as a young man is to stay out of lockup and be wise. Sir, again, **What In The Jail Do You Want,** do you want to come here and set a new standard. I am here to tell you that in jail there are no rewards or medals given to the most intelligent law breaker.

I can tell you that there are many young men that are doing great things when they stay in school. Staying in school creates an avenue of hope that gives rise to faith that can do the impossible. When I entered Robert E. Lee high school in Montgomery, Alabama in 1975 I knew I was in need of hope. I knew that I needed hope because once again I was not on the dean's list coming out of junior high. I heard a voice in me saying stay the course or stay in school and greatness can develop. Living in the projects the only way greatness would come appeared to be through sports. I played sports but was not big enough to excel in sports therefore I needed an avenue to pursue.

Since I knew no scholarships were not coming my way from sports I needed to maximize my staying power. When I began to maximize staying power by staying in school another door of excellence opened. What I am saying to young men is that when you maximize your staying power God can move. God can move on your behalf and create an open door simply because of your labor. Young man, God loves you and wants to do great things in your life but you must want the same thing. The bible says "If thou can believe all things are possible for them that believe (Mark 9.23). I believe greatness will begin in every young man the moment he rises from his fall. Now, as a man you may have fallen but the longer you stay there the longer the enemy works. While you are not moving as a young man the devil is moving constantly to steal your freedom. What I have witnessed in six years working at a prison is how the freedom stealer has robbed great young men.

Precious one, now is the time to be a man in your thinking and change everything.

What most of these young men I am witnessing to needed was someone who feels the wound they feel. I can feel their wound through my journey of life and I can share words by faith to bring them hope. I want to bring hope now to the young men that have a chance to be someone who didn't quit. I am not only talking about quitting school but also quitting on seeking greatness. I knew once again that I was not going to be in the top five in academics coming out of high school. I also had seen and heard of enough of the guys in the projects that were going to prison real fast. Now, I must say as well most of them quit school at a young age and were overtaken by temptation.

Sir, this new form of temptation that the devil has today, especially through social media will wear you out. What is even more damaging to your freedom as a young man is the number of ways to stay connected. Now is the time for you as a man to decide who you will stay connected with. I must say to you that you have an opportunity to stay connected with God and be free. When you decide or the devil decide for you to stay connected with him you give up your right to be free. What I am seeing daily in lockup are many young men that have lost their race to freedom. What I am saying to you as a young man is yes staying connected with God brings greater.

What I am seeing on the news daily for young men is the same I saw when I was a teenager for those who chose to quit. These young men just quit believing that they could rise above their storms and succeed. The jail cells have the same ring to them that they had 40 years ago when I finished high school. Now, they may build new prisons but the ring to those cells will not change when they slam. Why is that someone may say? I believe those are the sounds of if you don't change we will not either. I believe it is saying we will always bring the pressure to make you miserable. These sounds from those slammed cells to me are also saying we are going to crush your thinking.

Sir, **WHAT IN THE JAIL DO YOU WANT.** Lockup is not going to be getting you ready to make your next movie. I am here to tell you that it is not also going to make you ready for your next number one song. What could happen for you if you are not strong in your faith is leaving here really confused. That is what I witnessed in the guys that return back to lockup so quickly after they leave. What I would have witnessed in talking to them for five minutes is that the slamming of those cells took effect. What I believe is the mental application that goes inside young men is devastating. This is why it is critical for you as a young man to focus on what you want to become.

The moment trouble takes on your life I am here as a witness that these cells will take on your life. I had a young man that was released after his third time in lockup and promised me that I would see him in church. Well, I never saw him in church but I did see him back here for his fourth trip. Now, what I am convinced of in him is that these cells have taken hold of his future without him knowing it. Until this young man is able to endure under the world's pressure lockup will be his resting place. Sir, you do not have to allow pressure to rule you when you stand tall as a man. God is waiting on all men to come to know him so that he can guide them and lead them.

Now, I want to say this to mothers and fathers. **WHAT IN THE JAIL DO YOU WANT FOR YOUR SON.** Here's what I want to say to parents. I know that it is a challenging time right now raising boys. The moment they began to walk on their own in the public the moment Satan began his attack. I want to say to you as parents that it is critical that you be the best you can be to your son or sons. In lockup for a young man, it is brutal and crushing to his insides and to his mind. Lockup has its own way of putting a mark on him if he is not in faith that will limit his potential. Let me encourage you with all that is in you for your son to allow him to find his way to Jesus Christ.

When your son finds Jesus Christ he has found himself a way that he can be free from giving in to temptation. This does not mean that he or none of us will not make mistakes but we are covered by the blood. The bible says "If the Son therefore shall make you free, ye shall be free indeed. (John 8.36). While your son is in the covering he can keep his eyes on his future while God keeps his eyes on him and his future. Remember, the enemy wants to put your son in his army that he is never free. My heart hurts for the mothers who gave birth to some of these great young men I have counseled. It is my prayer that mothers and fathers continue to pray for their boys. Here in prison, it can be a chamber of disillusion where all hope is gone and so can a young man's future.

Identity And Lockup

What I can be sure about now more than ever is that lockup is truly a place that can rob a man of his identity. Now, the way the devil does it in lockup is he will attempt to use leadership if it is possible. This is why I was grateful to God that I knew what my assignment was while I was an employee at the prison. While doing my daily duties as a supply clerk I often had young men at the prison working with me. These were young men helping me unload my orders or as workers on the hospital ward. Many times at the prison men would come to me to service their wheelchair, crutches, or eyeglasses. One day I had two young men come one helping the other one who was on crutches.

When I issued one new crutches for his broken ones they always must sign an equipment sheet. When I ask him what his name was he said yes we both have the same first name. The young man said our first name is Emmanuel and I said really, and do you know what your names mean. Now, they both shouted out yes sir, our names mean **GOD WITH US.** (Matthew 1.23). I said to them praise the Lord guys ,but do you know that the two of you are special. I also told them that they could be two powerful forces of change in their dorm and in the lives of men. Now, they were amazed at what I said to them because of what the enemy has allowed in their lives.

This is what the enemy is about and what he is doing in the lives of young men who have no identity. What the enemy desires to do in these two young men's lives is to bind their identity with lockup. In order that true men rise up and be the man God has them to be their identity must be recognized. When I say that I mean as a man he must learn how to allow who he is as a man to rise high above circumstances. The enemy knows that if he can take away his identity he can replace it with lies. What I have learned is there are two most important days in the life of a man. Those two days are the day that he was born and secondly the day that he discovers why he was born. I believe within these two days lies an identity that affects every breath a man breathes with purpose.

As a believer, my job at this prison is to build up young men lives with truth and identity that the enemy has stolen. I told these two Emmanuel's that they must grow closer to God while they are in prison. I said to them that what the enemy desires to do to you both is rob you of your true identity. One of the young men said "you know sir I am here for robbery" but no one was hurt neither was I. I then said to him you see son the enemy was trying to connect robbery with who you are. I wanted him to know that the devil can't take what God has already given him. (2Peter1.3) I continued with him that God has a master plan for your life and you must pray to God for the answer. This is all that the enemy is doing all over the world so that he can get men to lockup.

What the devil knows is if he can get the man to think that he has no place he will go on the attack. I shared with both of the young men to make sure that they get to the chapel to attend worship service. They both mentioned that they would and one of them said what is the name of your church. Now, watch how God works. The young men at our prison come from all over our state. I asked them both what city are they from as I ask all of them while I am witnessing to them. The younger of the two said I am from Montgomery and I said praise the Lord son I am as well. I then gave Emmanuel the name of my church and told him that upon his release how to reach me.

As believers, this is what God expects of us that we plant seeds in the heart of young men that can bless them. When we reach out to save the one I believe God will do the rest to restore his identity. The bible says "I have planted, Apollos watered; but God gave the increase. (1Corr:3.6). Now, I am not sure whether I will ever see these young men again, but I do know that I planted a seed. I believe by faith that God will give the increase that they get to know him in a greater way. This is what I have been called by God to do after seeing what I have seen what the devil is doing. The devil is reaching as far as he can reach into the souls of young men and defeating them. One of the ways that the enemy is doing this is by taking them out of their identity.

Child of God, when the enemy can take you out of your identity he can redirect your world to his world. When this is done no matter what defense you may have your defense will not match the power of the devil. The devil will use his experience of robbing identity and lead boys and men to trouble. Once the enemy leads you down the road to trouble the table is spread from your identity to lockup. Sir, you do not have to stay on the road to trouble because that is not your identity. By faith, you have all the abilities to locate the hope in you that you rise above every fault. Regardless of what shortfall that you may have there is much hope in you that can rebound from your fall.

Let me encourage you and every young man on the planet that there is a way out of a troubled past. When God made you He created you with a purpose that is far greater than any trouble or setback. Let me encourage you to learn to pray to God that you may know him and know your identity. What the devil hopes you never knew is to know your identity that your identity knows lockup. The way that the enemy works on your identity with lockup first is to personally find your greatest need. Yes, if the devil knows your greatest need is money he will do everything to keep you broke. Now, if you are still living with your parents the enemy will do all he can to keep your parents broke. I know this is true because he tried it with me while living in the projects. What the devil was trying to get me to do was rob that he can rob me of my identity to lockup. I also know that the devil is still doing this today as I talk to the young men that are coming to prison daily. Child of God, the best way to walk in your identity is to allow God to walk with you.

The way this is done is simply to study the word of God and believe in who God has called you and wait. Now, I know sometimes it may seem that you have been waiting long enough and nothing has happened. I am here to tell you that your real and true identity demands waiting and patience in order to develop. Sir, trust me most of my life which includes 28years of military and 21 years of federal service was tough. I truly was blessed overall but was always looked upon as incompetent and not worthy of promotion. What really was even worst was the people that I trusted as friends laugh at me. It really seem as though nothing was happening after I had been waiting for years.

I heard the voice of God speak to me in a still small voice and said your identity is far greater than your pressure. What I knew was it was time for me to find out can I function and succeed when I know who I am. What I am saying here is when I believe in God of my identity I can overcome every setback. When I made up my mind to go to warrant officer school and graduated I stepped into my identity. The reason why I knew I stepped into my identity is that I raised the bar in identity in the Alabama Army National Guard. Precious one, even though it may not seem like anything might be happening for you I believe you have **raised the bar of potential.** What the devil wants from you is **below the bar potential.**

The reason why he wants you to underestimate your identity is he can waive trouble at you for you to bite. I am here to tell you that you are not without the power in you to override the devil's temptation. I believe the more you work on your identity that you are here with purpose you will see an increase. You will see an increase in opportunities that God has for you free than you can get in lockup. Sir, as a young man I just believe you are the one that God is about to use for real change. Now, don't be afraid of change because trust me change is great when it is in your DNA as a man. By faith you have the ability to change all the negative images that may have been appearing all your life.

This is what the enemy was doing to me for years because for most of my life I had only seen images of barely making it. Now, this was not of God and what the enemy was trying to plant was a seed of hopelessness. What the enemy knew was this would be a seed that grows **wild weeds** in my identity. Now, if I never rise above these **wild weeds** I could begin to **smoke and sell weeds** and end up in lockup. I know this may sound corny but young man I am telling you what the enemy is doing daily right now. I even command you to rise up from thinking that you are nobody and I speak blessing over you. You no longer by faith have the right to surrender your future to the devil.

God is standing by waiting on you as a man to reclaim your identity so that you can take back your place in the earth. Now, you can do that and you have the ability to do it when you can believe in yourself. It is time for man to know that we were not made to settle for what's left but for what we declare. Sir, I have a question for you? Have you made any declarations this year for your life? I believe that it is critical that every man make declarations for their life that they come to pass. The bible says You will also declare a thing and it will be established. Thou shalt also decree a thing, and it shall be established unto thee. (Job:22.28) When you walk in your true identity you can declare some things in your life by faith and tear down walls.

I believe this is your year to claim your identity back as you make declarations and watch the blessings unfold. Many of us have watched the enemy have his way because our situations had us silenced. **NO MORE.** We will keep our eyes focused on the prize that we may be free and not bound. I also believe that every man that has even been troubled is about to call on Jesus that lockup has no place in him. The reason why he cannot be bound is there is much work for him to do in the earth.

Chapter 6

SATANS WEAPONS OF MASS TO LOCKUP

I truly believe what the devil has done over the years is release weapons of **mass** destruction to lockup. I say they are of **mass** destruction because I have witnessed a **mass** of men come daily to lockup. What has been even more devastating for me is how the devil has marked his territory on who he chooses. The bible says "For the weapons of our warfare are not carnal, but mighty through God to the pulling down of strongholds. (2 Corr:10.4.). What I have witnessed during my time working in prison takes your breath away. I say this because what amazes me is there is no natural strategy for winning this battle. I am watching some of the greatest men get tapped by the devil's deception.

When I look back six years ago when God started me on this assignment, I watched each year how the devil reloads. When the devil reloads his weapon, he makes each round stronger than the one before. What I mean here is when I talk with young men and they share their trouble, the enemy came with power. Now, regardless of what the offense was, it was so strong upon the man that he had no defense. Every time I heard the story I said to the man that his only hope was calling on God. Sir, what I am saying to you is the devil is coming at your best man in you with power. Now is the time for men to bow before God for him and his family or the enemy will destroy his family.

One of the weapons that I have noticed that the devil is using on men with families is greed and sex crimes. The devil knows that if he can get the man to become an addict to greed he can flash financial deception. You and I as a man have the image of God on us that has the capacity to defeat this foe. What it will take is for men to stand strong in their faith that there is no question about who their God is. I believe when we begin to seek God with all that is in us chains can't hold us. When I say this I mean the devil can no longer lead a man to the path that is a sure way to lockup. The reason this deception would no longer work on the man is that he is now aware of his purpose.

In my walk with God, I have noticed that the devil is constantly coming up with ways to deceive the man. Now, in his deception, it is always designed to penetrate that a stronghold is released if possible unknowingly. When I look at some of the devil's weapons that he has used they have caused mass destruction. Two of the most significant areas the devil is after to destroy are the family and the church. When I look at a large portion of the men in our prison when I arrive at work this is what I see. I know that when we see all the violence on the news we might see one man arrested. This was my thinking as well until I started this six-year assignment from God to expose the devil's work.

What the devil is doing is releasing strongholds (a lie to deceive) to do mass construction as well as a mass lockup. In January 2018, a man and his wife in California chained 13 family members in their home for years, I see the mass destruction of lives. I am here to share with all of God's people that the enemy has released weapons of mass destruction on people. Now, what he has done is target men that he destroys God's design for the family. What I do know is we are in a critical time for boys and men to decide with conviction who they will serve. If the choice is uncertain the devil knows just what to bring to help your decision. We as men now must be strong in our faith.

What the enemy is doing is working I believe on getting the man to bow down to his lowest state of being. Now, the devil knows if he can push this man to his limit he will act before the man even thinks. This is why I am confident that the only hope for man to find his strength and purpose is the word of God. Working with the eye doctor at the prison I have looked through the eyes of many educated men. Some of these men were at the top of their game in their respective professions. What I am here to say to men is the devil has not slept since he was cast out from heaven. I believe he has spent many hours day and night breaking through men strongest mechanism.

Over the years the devil has worked hard and is continuing to work hard to defeat the man and do it in mass. What I am seeing daily in lockup is how his efforts are coming through as a mass of men come daily. Sir and mam let me encourage you that the enemy is after the best son as well as the best husband. What the enemy has done is loaded and reloaded his weapons that he takes out the best. This is the season that all men must seek God that they know we have the greatest weapon. Our greatest weapon as men is the sword of the spirit, which is the word of God. (Epes:6.17). Brethren, without this sword upon us the devil's weapons of mass is overpowering the greatest. When the devil overpowers the man, he can send him to hopelessness and to lockup.

What I am about to reveal is what I have witnessed among some of the greatest men in lockup that is taking names. Now, yes many have fallen by the devil's sword and his weapon of mass to lockup. I am fully persuaded that we have an advocate in Christ who is our lawyer who never lost a case. What it will take from men in this hour is to get to know Christ that we do not bow to every trick. God has a plan for every man who trust Him that he finds his place of dominion in the earth. What the devil wants to do is to take out every man with true identity and to take them out in mass.

How Great Men Get Locked Up

One thing that I am certain about in my six years working in the prison is all the men were not bad people. What I saw was a potentially great man who made a bad choice. What I am also sure about is all the men in prison again are not men who do not know God. What I have witnessed for sure is the devil has plunged his way to get great hearts to crumble in shame. This concerns me because I use to think that no way, great men who knew God would do better. Sir, what I have discovered and I am sure many others have is the devil also desires great men. What I believe is that great men sometimes lend themselves out to the wiles of the devil. (Epes:6.11). This is the hour that great men demonstrate wisdom that lockup remains far from him.

The bible says "Happy is the man that finds wisdom, and the man that get understanding. (Prov:3.13). What the devil truly desires to do is to bring down shame from the top so that he may show his power. We here in Alabama have had a clear view of that when our Governor went down in shame. Now, this Governor did not get locked up, but was investigated for possibilities. You and I know that to be considered for the Governor's office many in your state consider you great. What the devil presses hard to do is to get you to lend yourself to one wrong or sinful act.

This was not the first time that the enemy took down our Governor who once was a great man in lockup. In 2006 our once Governor was sentenced to 78 months in prison for excepting a bribe. What all this tells us is that regardless of how high the natural man can rise being great, lockup can find him. Now, in order for lockup to find the great man, he must surrender the true image of God inside of him. The only way this happens is the natural man who was a great succumbs to his flesh. This is why you and I as a man must always stay before the feet of Jesus so that we stay righteous. What the enemy works extremely hard on is finding the weak spot in the heart of man.

God has called us as men to be great for Him and to be great by Him because we live in a world of darkness. Sir, this is a season for you and I as men to know that the enemy is after the man that makes you great. By faith, that man is your spirit man or that man that walks in the spirit and imitates God. I truly believe that every man who lives by faith has a strong desire to imitate God and find his purpose. What the devil is doing right now is coming after great men so hard that he is seeking us all. What I mean here is the devil is ripping at the heart of every man until he gets him in defeat. What I am seeing at the prison that I work at is he cares less about what side of the track you come from.

What we as men must do is to become very familiar with the areas that we may be weak in and become very strong. The reason for this is I am watching great men all over the world fall victim to violence and sin. Now, as I see it daily at lockup where I work it is an inside view of what the devil has expanded. The devil has expanded his boundaries and territory on where and how to reach great men. Sir, now is the time for you and I to be in our best image of God like we have never been before. One of the ways I see great men getting locked up is that he thinks **his position makes the difference.** This thinking is wrong and shall always be wrong when you use it to take advantage of another. In 2017 we saw a mass of great men across the country in many areas fall prey to this mindset. This I truly believe is the setup of the devil's weapon of mass that can destroy great men.

When I look at the opioid abuse across the country by doctors and many going to prison I see something. Now, what I see is what the natural eye can't see or the general public can see looking from the outside. The devil is coming now from what I call a secret platform to destroy great men. Let me put it another way, he is destroying great men in their skill set that they fall from grace. You and I know that for as many doctors that are falling to this opioid takes a powerful foe. It is time for the man to know that the devil has the power to destroy the greatest educated mind. What it will take in this hour by even the greatest of men is to keep our eyes on Christ.

One of the reasons great men are getting locked up is they have taken their eyes off Christ, and put their eyes on themselves. What I am saying is great men are walking in their flesh which is dangerous. I say dangerous because the flesh is sending many men down dangerous roads to lockup. Sir, if the enemy is strong enough to send the Governor who is also a doctor to act on his flesh what about you. The number one factor then that is sending great men to lockup is his flesh is ruling him. When I look at all of these great men that have been called out on their flesh it is astounding. Sir, it's like this, if it is in your mind to go and rob the store, that is a flesh moment waiting for a response.

When a man responds to a signal from his flesh it doesn't matter what it is it must process through the spirit. Now, in order for the man to know how to do this, he must be walking in the spirit. (Gal:5.16). What the devil is doing in this season is releasing temptation upon men to see who he serves. What we are witnessing all over the country is unfortunately many great men are not serving God. Now, they may go to church, but that is fine with the devil as long as you are overpowered in the flesh. The bible says "For I know that in me (that is, in my flesh) dwells no good thing. (Rom:7.18). I am here to tell you that in the last six years great men have given in to no good things. What I saw was many were giving in to bad things based on what I saw in new cases daily.

What is significant for our understanding is great men taken by their flesh is no excuse in the courtroom. What I am really seeing in lockup is the judge's desire to make examples out of great men. Sir, I believe you are a great man who desires to do great things. Let me challenge you to revisit your purpose. All the enemy is doing is slowly taking great men out of his place as king. What the devil desires is to take your position away and bring you to shame as he has done many in 2017. When God made you a man He had a plan for you to be gentle, kind, loving, and respectful. When God made you he put all of this in you from the beginning leaving you with a choice.

What I am seeing daily on the news and what is coming to prison is great men who made one bad choice too many. Child of God, you do not have to mind the flesh when he sends you signals of a bad choice. What is happening across the country is many great men are listening closely to the flesh. When this occurs, the flesh is lying to great men telling them to go on and do it and you will be alright. Now, I want you to know that that is a lie from the devil's pit and he knows it. Another reason I am finding great men getting locked up is simply they are not using the right judgment. When I say that I mean great men are putting themselves in a position to be under the radar.

When I say this come on guys some things are too easy to bring to the conclusion of what if. If I am a married man as I am I will not go alone over to a single lady's house because she asked for prayer. Now, if I went there to pray with her I am certainly bringing my wife or I will not go. We as men must be diligent when placing ourselves in an awkward position that has a seed of destruction. Sometimes great men lose their sense of great awareness due to being proud of their name and position.

The bible says "Pride goes before destruction and a haughty spirit before a fall. (Proverbs 16.18). I have never seen as many great men fall all in one time in my life as I have seen in 2017 in America. I believe what we have seen in these men is only a foretaste of how many are falling in lockup. Men, we as men must begin to use great judgment in all things if we are going to remain free. What the enemy wants to do is to confuse your judgments and thoughts life that you make a bad decision. One bad decision is causing great men that have been great for a long time in shackles overnight. What is important is a bad decision can easily be greater than your bank account.

We all watched a billionaire resigns who was once a great man but fell to sexual harassment as many others did. The enemy is not intimidated by your financial status as long as you fall and fall hard. What is important for men to know is the enemy hopes that we stay full of pride and our eyes closed. With our eyes closed, they are closed to the enemy's scheme to set us back from God's plan. In order that we stay with the plan God has for our lives as great men our eyes must be open. Now, our eyes cannot be open to all that God has for us with pride being at the forefront of life. What I have witnessed in lockup in men is that pride creates a cloud over great judgment in great men.

This is a stronghold as well that is keeping our boys from seeing their fathers being the example they should be. When the devil maximizes his efforts in keeping great men bound sons are left for the devil's den. I say this once again as I continue to watch young men come to prison as a partner to his father. One day I saw a young man who looked very intelligent and asked him where was he from. When the young man said he was from Montgomery I said what part and what about family. The young man said now, my older brother and father are in jail and I am the youngest of boys. I then said to myself Lord, I pray that the eyes of our men are open and that their sons are saved.

What I believe that will be required by men again is a greater judgment on their decisions for a greater life. Sir, I am here to say to you that if your judgment is flawed in this hour I suggest to you get in the word. The word of God is the only answer for men that they might find the ways of God for good judgment. The bible says "The meek will he guide in judgment: and the meek will he teach his way. (Psalm 25.9) What the devil is doing on a major scale right now is allowing great men to guide themselves. Now, what the devil know is when some men become successful he takes the credit. What God desires in men is to allow him to teach them his way for great judgment. I am a witness that when great men trust in our Great God a shield of direction is granted. With this shield, we are able to stay in the hand of God that our pathway is full of grace. When God is doing the leading our minds and hearts are clear for great judgment and great testimonies.

The devil is not in favor for **great** men to have **great** testimonies. What the devil desires is great trouble that leads to lockup. Sir, now is the time that we keep our eyes on Christ that we may follow his way. What I have discovered is that yes I want to do great things for Christ that may lead men to follow him. I know that the devil is always after me that I may fall to his plan that I may be in his number. The problem with the devil's number is it can easily become a state number for men in lockup. What I do know is the number the devil desires in great men is growing quickly in lockup. What I want to say again to all men is we were made by God to do great things for him.

Another reason that I believe great men get locked up is found in their association with the wrong environment. The bible says "Blessed is the man that walketh not in the council of the ungodly, nor standeth in the way of sinners, nor sit in the seat of the scornful. (Psalm 1.1). I discovered early as a young man that bad company connects to bad decisions and eventually bad results. You and I as men must be wise on our choices for who we decide on making our circle of influence. The enemy is really smart on how he makes his connection through men that has great potential. This is why it is crucial that all young men be at their best while the devil is at his worst.

What I want to say to young men is that if the environment or conversation makes you feel uncomfortable leave. I say this because many men here in lockup are here because they didn't follow their spirit. What I mean here is they were in a situation that didn't feel right but they act right away. Sir, one bad person in your company of friends can spoil your future for many years if you allow it. Now is the time to learn how to manage your company as you manage your future. I am here to say to you that sometimes you might have to be to yourself that you may grow in knowledge. God can lead you to the right environment where you can make good decisions.

What is important for you to know is that your future as a man is much greater than the wrong company. Most men that are coming daily are coming from the bad environment that surrounded them. I believe it only takes days of communication from bad sources to lead to years of frustration. God has called men to be great leaders, husbands, and fathers that his name will get glory. The bible says " Verily, verily, I say unto you, He that believe on me, the works that I do shall he do also; and **greater** works than these shall he do: because I go to the father.(John 14.12). Sir, please don't miss this. God desires you to do greater works than he did therefore greatness is in you. What the devil is after now is taking the **greater** out of you to lead you to lockup. I truly believe the devil is on a witch hunt to get the greater men in lockup that no wonders are performed. These wonders are the things that are impossible by men on their own and only by God. My prayer is that men come to know God much greater than they have before that they may be free.

When I look at the world today many homes are absent of some of these great men because they are in lockup. Now, yes I know some caused it on themselves by bad decisions but others were framed. What I have seen and heard in lockup is many were framed by bad company in sheep's clothing. Child of God, let me suggest to you as a man again to keep your eyes on Christ that you can win. Jesus has said that greater things shall you do and the greater could be hidden in doubt. Now is the time for men to walk in faith that the greater will come out and stand strong. When the greater man stands strong his faith will be strong as he becomes wise in every decision.

An Achilles Heel To Great Men-Sex Crimes

One of the things that I have really been shocked greatly by the prison is the number of sex crimes. What even has been truly shocking is the caliber of men that are falling prey to the devil's trap. What is important for men to know is the enemy knows how to bait the man who lacks confidence. I believe the enemy has a set time in which to attack the man where he knows he is weak. I am confident that what can bring the man to his knees in the natural is when sex has overtaken his identity. This is all that I see as I have watched great men fall in 2017 with all the sexual harassment charges. The devil knows that sex crimes are an Achilles heel that will sideline the man.

What I understand about an achilles heel is that it is really painful and can take a player out of his normal behavior. This is all that I am seeing with many great men being taken out of their norm as a man. Sir, I am here to tell you that your only defense against the devil's stronghold in this is the word of God. Once again this stronghold that the enemy has released is ripping through many homes. What I am confident in about this entire sexual harassment outcry is the flesh is ruling. When the flesh is ruling the man he has nothing in him strong enough to feed his sexual motives. What even is a fact is his money or his power cannot help him because his desires are stronger.

What I am seeing with this in the prison where I work is the man's sexual desires overtake all of him. The reason why I say this is because I have had the deepest conversation with the greatest men. When I say the greatest men I mean these are men with great families including wives and children. What I am trying to convey to the man in this hour is you are not too good to be taken. Now, I must admit in talking with some of these men that are locked up some just were not thinking. These were men who trusted people who they knew would not set them up. Most of these men again were just overpowered by a force that was much stronger than them.

I want to make it clear to all men that the enemy is after you and me to bow down to his sexual temptations. What is amazing to me again is when I witness these 40 new men per day coming to prison. I am continuing to be taken in my heart by the number of men that are taken from their family and their church. Yes, I say church because you would not believe the number of great men taken from the church. Sir, listen to me once again, the devil cares less about you talking like you know God. What he does care about is that he keeps your mind on Pornography that you fall into the devil's pit.

Yes, pornography is taking the mind of men by storm and causing major havoc in their lives and future. This I discovered is a silent storm in the mind of men that has no physical or outer symptoms. The symptoms are on the inside of the man that takes his desires to a deep pit. I discovered talking to men in lockup that the pit invades the mind with pleasure and deceit. God desires you to keep your mind on him so that he guides and protects you from the pit.

I have been hurt day after day as I continue to see young church leaders as men coming to lockup. What I have witnessed over the last year is how strong that demonic sex abuse stronghold has gripped the church. Many of these are from the seed of pornography. My heart really was hurt when I witnessed a great young youth pastor in lockup. What was even shocking is when he conveyed to me that the enemy used sex to trap him. Sir, as a man and especially as a man of God the enemy is after contaminating your mind with sex. Now, I am here to say to men that this is an attack from the devil that is truly taking prisoners. One of the things that the devil is using mightily is social media to dominate in this area. What concerns me as well is how this stronghold from the devil is able to reach the young to rob their future. Child of God, I am here to tell you from experience that the enemy desires to reach you early.

When I was only fifteen years old the enemy came after me to rob my future by introducing me to Pornography magazines. Now, the enemy came after me real hard and gained my attention for a short period. I believe the only way that I was able to break free was I cried out loud to Jesus for his deliverance. I must admit that it did not come overnight and the hand of God kept me grounded in Him. Sir, there was a calling on my life as a child of God, but the devil tried hard to make me reject it. I am here to tell every man that the enemy is after the greatest call on your life through sexual desires. The only hope for you to break free from this power that is stronger than you is the God of hope.

I must say the attack on my life as a young man by the devil is not the end of my story. More will come in the sequel of this book. You don't want to miss it. I am blessed by God to have been delivered and set free for well over 40 years I am now preparing to celebrate 40 years of marriage with the devil and Pornography under my feet. I said all that to say to men that the devil desires to tear us up through sexual desires. I have seen enough of great men go down in lockup behind sex and am willing to share my story. I am also doing this because I want to help a man save himself and perhaps his family. When I look again at all of these men called out in 2017 on sexual harassment, we have a problem. I am speaking of all those national men figures that really lost their identity.

Once again, the devil does not care that you are a sports athlete, commentator, or news anchor you can fall. The reason why you can fall is that you have succumbed to the desires that the enemy brings. What the enemy brings before men is excitement to his eyes that may be appealing to his flesh. Now, the fact of the matter is the devil cares less about whether you are married or single. The bible says "For all that is in the world, the lust of the flesh, the lust of the eyes, and the pride of life is not of the Father but is of the world. (1John 2.16). All the temptation the devil has brought to the flesh for sexual harassment is of the world. What we are seeing around this world, as a result, are great men losing the battle.

I want to say to all men right now is because what this scripture above is saying it is now time to get real. When I say this I mean it is time to get real with you and real about the God that made and created you. What I am witnessing coming to lockup for sexual crimes are men that were not true to God. When the man is not true to knowing God and obeying God his sexual desires gets the best of him. The devil knows that one of the setbacks of a good man is when he is overtaken by the lust of the eyes. When I look at all of these guys that have been called out with sexual harassment this is significant. If I could encourage a man who desires to follow God fully let me make a suggestion. I would like to ask all men to make a **covenant** with your **eyes** that they obey God's command. Now, I know a lot may be said there but I promise you your eyes can be a vehicle of light or darkness. I can assure you based on conversations I have had with men here in lockup it is true.

As a married man I have a covenant with my eyes because I believe without a covenant my flesh can deceive. Making a covenant with my eyes binds me by faith as well as disciplines me to stay true to my wife. Sir, married or single you need to know that the lust of the eyes is more powerful than you. Lust of the eyes is more powerful even than a billionaire who resigned from his duties because of sexual harassment. What am I saying here, it is time for men to turn to God and not to your flesh. I have watched for too long how the lust of the eyes and the flesh has ruined great men. When I think of my nearly 40 years in the workplace I can see how great men get locked up.

I witnessed so much infidelity and adultery among married men through the lust of the eyes that was horrible. One of the greatest things the devil desires is to keep his army strong among strong men. I am here to tell all men that sex crimes may be good for you at the moment but bad in the end. I am witnessing great men having some very bad days in lockup that did not have to be. Most of these powerful men across the country that have been fired their accusers were at the workplace. Again what the devil desires is to get the strong man so that he can show their weakness. Sir, I am here to tell you that your **workplace** can become your **worst place** if your eyes are in the **wrong place.**

The bible says " Give no place to the devil (Ephes:4.27). Now, if I was the writer of that verse I would have said "give no place to the devil (especially the workplace). I say that because I know that is a place where the devil know how to use time. The devil knows daily that we spend more time on the job than we do at home. What the devil has done is used one of our most precious body parts (eyes) to focus on what's seen the most. In addition to that the enemy dresses up sin or adultery with good work ethics. The man will spend as long as it takes on the job to get the job done.

Beloved, these are weapons of the devil that is taking great men in great numbers to their greatest pitfall. What these underhanded routes to sin that the devil has used is leading men to lockup. Sex crimes or sexual harassment are truly on an all-time high and is taking great men hostage more than ever. What I believe the devil has done in many men is blinded their minds that they no longer understands no. Sir, it doesn't matter whether she consented are not Rape binds integrity. Even if you are a man of good morals and integrity your words has little authority in a sex crime. Sir, here's what's important for you to know is your future is greater than a sex act. Now, I'm telling you that you must take control of your feelings before your feelings take you. I have some brilliant men in here in lockup that almost overcame their sexual desires. What is so painful about these men is many of them were leaders in prominent places and positions. Again sir, our governor of our State was overtaken by this same demon that is stripping titles.

I believe this Achilles heel of sexual desires in great men is planting a false mentality in destinies and visions. What the false mentality is saying to men is no one will ever find out that I did this and she will not tell. Sir, let me tell you, you are as wrong as anything because your sex desire that was wrong will find you. What is painful as what I am seeing right now in lockup is they find you in lockup. I want to say to my single young man that may be dating right now, that when she says **No** that means **No**. I have spoken with enough of great young men here in lockup that in a second something came over them. According to them after their date encourage them about sex they could not refrain.

Now, again this is a trick of the devil that he is in control of every thought and action of every man. You and I as a man by faith were created in the image of God and have the power to take every thought captive. (2Corr:10.5). Sir, you no longer have to be overtaken by your sex drive, rather you can drive out the devil. When you really know that you are a child of the most high God you can walk away. Sir, now is the time to walk away from that uncertain female that you know might ruin you. I would even say to some of God's best men that now is the time for you to turn from those thoughts. I know a young man right now that is a leader in the church that is addicted to Pornography.

I am praying for this young man because he will not be honest with me but men this again is a master stronghold. I cannot overemphasize enough that this is an Achilles heel that is putting men on the injury reserve. The problem with this injury for many men here at lockup it is a permanent injury. The injury is permanent because some of these great men have life in prison for their sex crimes. Sir, I want to say to you that life is too short for you to be walking a sexual road that can be too long. I pray that you will call on Jesus Christ to deliver you from destroying the blessings he has for you. I believe sir that you are much too sharp to be tied down by a sexual desire that is unclean.

What is important for men to know about sex if you are not married as I said already is your sin will find you. The bible says " But if you do not do so, then take note, you have sinned and be sure your sin will find you out. (Numbers 32.23). Notice how many of these men that were called out for their sexual sins in 2017 happened many years ago. Sir, it will not go away and you can find yourself locked up. My brother, the easiest thing for you to do is to do the right thing and be free. I believe that the enemy has set up man with sexual sins that he holds him captive. I am hurt daily as I talk to these great men in lockup that have been held captive from family and friends. The reason why it really almost brings tears to me of these men is I always think it could have been me. I say that because I know when the devil attacked me as I mentioned I could have fallen. Thanks be to God that he is willing to deliver those that desire deliverance. While the devil is on an all-time high in attacking the man with sex crimes now is the time to know him.

Brethren, if you do not know God in this hour the devil is going to tug at your flesh until he get your attention. I am here to tell all men that the enemy has got true men attention and that he is not joking. I never knew that the enemy could use something that God blessed and turn it into bad and bring bad results. Precious one, your sexual desires can bring you such bad results and cause many pain. Sir, I believe you are so close to your dream of seeing God do great things for you. Please do not allow the devil to push you to the limit with one bad sexual move and change your entire world. Sexual crimes will change your entire world and trust me when I say great men especially.

Sir, I am here to tell you that there is a very thin line between consent to sex and getting charged with rape. Let me encourage you as a man that the best move is to walk away and be free. The moment you have to face a judge in many cases your story will not hold up to make you free. In most cases with many men once again the flesh on its own made a decision against your will. This is the danger when the man is led by his flesh that will always succumb to what looks and feel good. This is a call to all men that the enemy again is turning the heat up on your flesh. What I have witnessed in lockup for six years in a row is that great men are falling hard on sex crimes.

In April 2018 we watched the man who was once **America's Dad** found guilty of sex crimes. On Sept. 25, 2018 he was sentenced to 3-10 years in prison. Now, let's think about this, we are talking about a man who was strong in his gift and what he knew. We must also acknowledge that we are talking about a man who is well educated and wealthy. We also must consider a man that touched the hearts of many parents on raising children. Brethren, we are talking about a man that many men admired greatly for his exceptional style. I am one of them. Sir, I am here to tell you once again that the enemy cares less about our gifts, talents, or name. The enemy's job is to tear the man down to a piece of bread (Prov:6.26) that he may fail.

I believe this is what the enemy is attempting to do for this man by sending him to lockup at the age of 80. Working at the prison for men for six years I am here to tell you lockup is rough on any 80 year old. What I am trying to convey to all men again is that you are not bigger than the stronghold of sexual addition. I am also trying to inspire men to walk upright as men so that the sexual demon doesn't affect you. Yes, this sexual demon that is extremely powerful is tearing down walls. Sir, I am confident of this very thing, that now is the time for you and I to seek God like never before. When we look back over 2017 and 2018 of great men who went down in sex crimes it is painful. The reason I say painful is because many of the national figures we all admired with a passion. I truly believe what the enemy has done is sent a message to all men that he is after us all. I also believe what the devil wants us to know is in the sexual offenses world he is in control of the natural. What I am saying here is if you are walking in the natural world your sex desires is controlled by the devil.

What I believe as well is the enemy allows men to go for a long period in his sinful nature and then attacks. I believe what the enemy attacks is the man's name and his accomplishments that he falls quick and fast. I am hurt for some men because of some of their accomplishments that helped others. The fact of the matter is when you are convicted of a sex crime and found guilty lockup awaits you. Sir, now is the time for you to come closer to God and cry out to him if you are on the edge. Yes, if you are on the edge and being led by the enemy of sexual crime you can defeat that enemy. Now, a lot of these big-name men may not have been preached to about this sexual demon.

Sir, I want to speak to you right now that it is time for you to stop your way of thinking about that sexual offense. I want to also warn men that if it has been any time to know your female associates it is right now. I speak to many men daily in lockup that was one day innocent and the next day guilty. Yes, one day the sex was consensual but after bad blood the next day it was rape. Men, let's be men that walk upright so that we can be a light in our world as well as in our community. We are experiencing some shameful moments in the life of great men across America and abroad. All of this is because the devil is mad that God is raising great men to become heads of household. What the devil is trying to do right now is to destroy the man and his image through sexual offenses.

The Man And A Gun

I truly believe that we are living in challenging times when we look at our world when man misuses a gun. The problem is not the man having a **gun permit;** the problem is when he **permits the gun.** Our prisons all over the country are overcrowded with these violent crimes. What is at an all time high right now is when our young people are losing their lives over nothing. What even more is a huge tragedy is how often school shootings are occurring in America. On February 14, 2018 a 19 year old man entered a Florida school and killed seventeen people. This was one of the worst school shootings in America that shocked our entire nation.

What we are witnessing in many of our neighborhoods and now our schools are many great lives lost in gunfire. What is also a tragedy is our not so concerned leaders and politicians who can make a difference. I believe as our nations continue to undergo much violence the destiny of men will undergo darkness. This darkness will have a lasting effect on lives that shall reach far into family roots. I am seeing this unfold right now in lockup as mentioned as I see fathers and sons in lockup. Sir, you have the mind if you only believe to channel your way of thinking about pulling a trigger. What you must know as a man now is when you pull the trigger on someone you are pulling on destiny.

I am seeing again 40 new inmates coming into lockup and many have pulled the trigger instead of pulling away. What the gun in the hand of most of these men said to them was you have the power. Now, I say that because I have talked to enough of these men in lockup that decided to shoot someone. Sir, listen to me well, you do not need a gun to tell you that you have the power. What you need to know is that God created you with power that is already in you by faith. What the enemy is doing in every man that misuses a firearm is robbing his future with lies and fairytale. Great young men are being locked up for life simply because they didn't use their power to walk away.

I truly believe that the devil is making it easier on a daily basis to get guns in the hand of the man. Now, he is doing this on purpose because we must know that the enemy is after removing the man. Yes, I will always believe that the devil desire to have all homes with fathers missing due to lockup. Now, we all know that there are many great mothers doing great jobs at home by themselves. What the devil wants to do is to break up God's design of the family and is doing it through troubled men. When we see the violence on the news somewhere a gun will be a major player. What we witness when the case is settled in most cases is a man is **dead** and the other man **dead wrong.**

What the devil has done in this case is removed two men from their purpose while he celebrates his work. What God desires in our lives as his people is that we live in peace so that we might be a light for peace. The bible says "Blessed are the peacemakers, for they shall be called sons of God. (Matthew 5.9). I believe the devil desires to keep gun violence in the man that he never becomes a son of God. The devil knows with peace upon the man he has great potential to change his world. When the man fulfills his role as a son he can change his world and the environment around him. I made up my mind with faith that I would not allow a gun to change me as a peacemaker. The devil knows that he is doing a job on men for lockup when the gun breaks him as a peacemaker.

When the man walks out of his identity as a true man for God he can still function in his calling.

    This is what I had to do even at war knowing that at war a gun is a part of my mission as a soldier in combat. While deployed in Baghdad Iraq from 2004-2005 having my gun with me would not interrupt my identity. When we were convoying into West Baghdad the people of Iraq were waving their AK47 rifles at us. Now, we are at war and we know that if we were fired upon that could have caused trouble. What I knew was that I had prayed before we departed and that my destiny was at state. I want to say to all men that have a gun if used improperly your destiny is at state. God kept his hand on me while in Iraq and he was my shield without me being trigger happy.

    I must say that in Iraq I know that we were in a battle for our lives every single day and we needed God. What I want to share with men is that we are in a battle right now and we need God. What I know that we do not need is the gun violence that is dominating our world in the lives of men. I am talking to some great men here in lockup that just allowed their guns to get the best of them. The gun is taking the best of their years such as a young man I talked with who is serving 20 years. Sir, I am saying to you that the gun is not the best answer for every battle. When you know your purpose on the earth as a man no battle can overtake you when you believe.

    I believed that when I was in Iraq and the battle really began to get bloody my gun was not my supreme source. I trusted God that he was my only source and my protection under every weight of violence. This was because I decided not to put my trust in what my gun can do over what my God can do. I fully trusted God that even in all the violence and corruption around me in war I could live. My faith was in God that my purpose was much bigger than even the most violent moment in my life. Now, my purpose while in Iraq was to bring a message of hope through the gospel. Now, yes I did perform my military duty as a property book officer. God kept his hand on me and allowed not a scratch that I might tell a man to believe.

Sir, I understand that you feel that you must have your gun and I have no problem with that at all with a permit. What I am concerned with men is that they no longer allow a gun to have them in their first encounter. My purpose on the earth has been enlarged by God through my experience at war. Again, I want to say to men that we are in a war with the devil that he is trying to interrupt our purpose. When I see these young men entering here in lockup daily for gun violence I truly hurt. I hurt because I know their purpose is hurt by the **pulling of a trigger** instead of **pulling away.** I believe as a man of God my job is to reach men and bring them to hope even in horror. Sir, I am here to tell you that there were many moments of horror while in Baghdad Iraq. What I had to do was stretch out on this hope without overreacting with my gun in my hand. Unfortunately, sometimes men are given poor examples even by those that suppose to be leaders at church. I truly was disappointed in the words that I heard from a pastor on national television.

The pastor said that he was going to visit young men in a bad neighborhood to reach them that they know God. What really troubled me was when he said he told his wife not to worry because he has Smith and Wesson with him. I was baffled because he as a pastor relied on his gun than his God. What I am trying to convey to young men is that we serve a God that is bigger than Mr. Smith and Mr. Wesson. In fact while I was in Iraq serving my county I was serving a God who created Smith and Wesson. Here is what's real, when you have been before a real test like war you can be confident. You can be confident that your faith in God will outlast your faith in a Smith and Wesson.

In America today we are battling gun laws as to what is right and what is wrong in order to set guidelines. What I am concerned about is will and can these laws stand up to what is in the heart of man. The bible says "The law of his God is in his heart; none of his steps shall slide. (Psalm 37.31). My goal is to get the laws of God in man's heart that he has no need to depend on Smith or Wesson. Here's what's key, I believe what is rooted in the heart of the man is what he shall stand on. What we are witnessing in our nation are many men whose heart is rooted in violence. I believe the only way that the man's heart is cleaned is this man gets to know God. In this hour when the man has these laws in his heart our streets, neighborhood, and schools are safe.

The reason why our world can be safe is that man's heart is restored so that he can now make a difference. When our schools are not safe for our kids due to gun violence and shootings major changes are needed. What the devil is doing right now is celebrating that we cannot move toward the true laws. Since the law of God is not being taught or seen laws are being broken by our young people. The result of this is I am seeing young men with no hope of being locked up for gun violence. It is my prayer that the true man rises up and declare in his heart that I am willing to turn around. Sir, I believe that if you are willing to turn around and align your heart with the laws of God change will come.

I know within the last six months I have witnessed great men get locked up that should have locked up their guns. What is much more damaging to our world is many of these young men just needed a word. What they needed yes was a word of God but also needed someone to point out their purpose. I say that because again I can see in their teary eyes as I speak with them a cry for help. I also see and hear of their world that was missing a heart of God from an example of God. What I see also is with no example many of these young men have no future in sight with no way out. What the enemy has done is by allowing them to use guns on each other while they are without goals. Each day what I am witnessing coming to lockup are men who had guns but never had goals. I say that because once again when I get their history the majority quit school with no goals in view. Sir, for most young men a gun is a setup for your failure that blinds many of their goals.

I believe the enemy set it up that as long as the man has no goals he can stumble in the darkness of the unknown. As the country is spending many hours trying to come up with gun laws men are still shooting. What is happening in the process is men are getting the guns and the unknown is overtaking them. When I say unknown the darkness is causing them to drift to the unknown to commit hideous crimes. Unfortunately many with no goals with these guns are drifting to again mental illness. When I look at the 19 year old that killed the seventeen people at the school in Florida it is clear. Young man now is the time to take your hand off the gun and your head in the book.

On August 3, 2019 our nation was devastated as a shooter went inside a Wal-Mart in EL-Paso, Texas killing 20 people. Two died days later to make a total of 22. 13 hours later a shooter in Dayton, Ohio killed nine people inside a bar including his sister. We all have heard this before, a bullet has no name on it, unfortunately, even if a family member is in its path. What are we seeing here in America one may ask? Truly what I see is we need prayer for our nation that we love one another. What I am also seeing is how the devil has invaded the mind of man. What the devil has done is fixed the mind of the lost that with a gun you have power. The problem with this power is it is of the devil and unwanted in our world. My prayer is with the families of these precious people whose lives were lost in these great cities and States. Let me suggest to every young man to the book with hope which is the word of God that you see a future. I am here to tell you that there is no future for you with that gun only a bed for you in lockup. Most of these men that are in lockup for gun violence have what I call gun hidden talent. I say that because after being here with them for six years I see how the gun robbed their talent. Many talents were robbed because the guns overshadowed what was truly in their hearts. One day I was walking down the hall as I did daily at the prison with my cart and a young inmate asked me sir you need some help. I said well yes young man I appreciate it and he unloaded the supplies off my cart.

As I do always I asked him where was he from and I noticed he just looked to me like a great football player. I said to him man you look like Mr. Football of Alabama, and he said man you are exactly right. The young man then said I wasn't quiet Mr. Football of the state but was a great running back. I said to him then you played high school or college, he then said I quit high school and trouble arrived. I was looking at someone with a good skill set but a wrong mindset. The young man then said I really loved running the football and I loved what I did. What happened was his offense robbed him of really what was in his heart to lockup. I believe what we are witnessing is how the enemy has reached the ears and hearts of men through gun violence. What I also see happening is those ears and hearts of men that are weak are being influenced.

Just one week after the school shooting in Florida I witnessed on the news other attempts across the country. Many of these attempts were coming through social media and schools were put on lockdown. What I began to see in all of this is how we are in a gun society of lockdown and lockup. I am writing this when we are only two weeks from the Florida school shooting. Here in my city of Montgomery Alabama, a man was arrested for bringing a gun to a local nursing college. The school was put on lockdown with no one injured and the man was placed in lockup. Here's what I am saying to men, in this hour your ears are tuned in to the devil or to God. It doesn't matter where you are this is a call to either you will respond to the word of God or the devil. Many men are coming to prison for gun violence simply because they are responding to the devil. As a man of God whose first name (Jeff) means **God's**

peace and last name (Mathews) means **gift of God** I declare **peace** over you.

As a child of God, I can by faith declare **peace** over all men as I witness men falling in **pieces**. I am witnessing men falling into pieces day after day as I see great men going to lockup. What this is to me is I see men falling to pieces in areas that we suppose to have power over. Yes, we as men with the image of God are supposed to have power over violence like I was given in Iraq. This same man is falling to pieces in his home, on his job, community, and nearly on every side. I declare the peace of God upon every man from this day forward that the curse is broken. I believe by faith that every man that reads this feels the peace of God in his heart and lay down his gun. Yes sir, notice again now that the meaning of my first and last name has the name **God** in it's meaning.

Now, you don't have to take my word but look it up and what I declare is there is by faith a mighty God in me. There is power in God's name and I speak in that name. I also realize that I am not the only one with my name but I do believe I am the only one with my purpose. Yes sir, my fingerprints and yours by faith have purpose on them to do a mighty work for God. Notice how everybody else has come out of the closet in the world about themselves. I believe it is time for the people of God to do the same for the glory of God. What I am doing is being as bold as a lion with my name (Proverbs 28.1) All I am doing is reminding the enemy what the bible says about those of us who believe. Again, the bible says "because as he is so are we in this world. (1John4.17). I declare that you sir is a mighty man who is bigger than gun violence.

The Gun vs The Keeper

I believe that many that carry a gun believe that their gun is their keeper and their protector of life. I am not calling everyone that carries a gun a **bad person.** What I am saying is in most men their gun causes them to make a bad decision. Trust me when I say after six years of working in the prison it just happens. When the flesh begins to act on the flesh it acts upon what is happening in the natural. The two of these connect and when they do in most cases trouble arises. Men are pouring into lockup in record numbers today due to rising trouble from gun violence. I am confident that no matter what gun control laws are established they will not speak volume.

They will not speak volume until man speaks to God who established laws for man in the time of trouble. For me, in Iraq, I had to speak to God and know He would keep me alive under tough pressure. The bible says "The Lord will deliver him in the time and trouble. The Lord will preserve him and keep him alive. (Psalm 41.1-2). Again, even in war, I had to put my trust in My Lord that He keeps me alive for His purpose. I believe when the man knows who their God really is they will truly know He is our keeper. What I am seeing in lockup among men is the gun itself is keeping the man in lockup. God never intended the man to put his trust in a gun as his keeper but God as his keeper.

The moment God gave me his word that he was my keeper I began to see him keeping me in every area. God will keep the man from all hurt, harm, or danger once he gets himself out of the way. What I have seen in men across the country is them putting themself in the way with a gun as their keeper. Sir, I am here to tell you that what the gun is doing is binding great men and keeping them hopeless. What I learned from my hope in God is that my faith and hope have more power than any gun. When I rely on the gun I only see what the gun can do once I pull the trigger for its power. What I discovered in Iraq is when I trust in God I see what God could do without me pulling a thing.

My God has kept me through many storms because I trusted in him that he cares for my total being. God is my keeper not only for my protection but also for my well-being that I might be a powerful witness. Sir, you can be a powerful witness for God with your life than the power from any loaded gun. When you put your trust in God you have discovered the keeper that keeps you in his care. When I speak to the men in lockup my ultimate goal is to get them to know that he is our keeper. I often share with them of the deepest wounds that life brought me that I thought it was over. In my witness experience, I ask God to use me that I find every vein of weakness in their body of no hope.

What I believe is most men are at their lowest point when they believe nothing can keep them from self-destruction. Talking with many of the men here some see themselves worthless due to little success. The world I believe is watching many young men go down easily not knowing the keeper of all. God has given us hope when we know of his power that is far beyond any method created. When I returned home from Iraq which was my greatest challenge in faith I had a new direction. With my new direction, God put a fence around all of my hope as well as my dreams. Sir, when your trust shifts to new heights God brings to us a greater window of hope that keeps us. We as men no longer have to think that it is us alone that bring us the life that we desire. When we choose God as our keeper over a gun God can now show himself strong on our behalf.

God began to show himself strong for me as I have never seen before when I kept him in my heart. What I discovered was keeping God in my heart I now can breathe fresh air of dependency. I have made God Lord in my life and I depend on him that he will not ever leave me. Now, the enemy wants me to lose this hope that I develop fear that I might have need of a gun. What the love of God does for the believer is draws them closer to God's heart and wipes away all fears. I knew in combat when the enemy would be after my life daily I needed to draw near to God. When men draw near to God, their heart and mind get conditioned for the peace of God to flow.

I believe with the flow of God's presence around us through faith we are confident that he is our keeper. When the man relies on the gun as his keeper the flow of God's presence diminishes. I believe his presence diminishes because God is a jealous God (Joshua 24.19). While I put all of my trust in God while undergoing countless attacks in Iraq I just trusted God. Sir, here's what's important for you to know. God is a keeper, and you must get to know Him. When you get to know God like I do you will have written on the breastplate of your heart **I TRUST GOD.** Now, after I settled this in my heart there was no question about who was my keeper.

Since making God my keeper and I trust in Him heaven has poured out more blessings than I can receive. God has kept his hand on my life in a way that all I have to do is walk in faith and the promise is kept. Yes, God is a promise keeper, and he is the greatest promise keeper I know on the earth. What the man needs to know is when you trust in the promises there is no need for fear. Most of the men that I witness in lockup for gun violence really lived in fear without their guns. When I hear the stories the first thing that jumps out to me was the man was in fear that he was defeated without a gun.

Sir, the moment you can put your gun down you can pick your identity up that you are the image of God. When you do that you have just reintroduced yourself to the one that God called king. Yes, you are in God's eyes king (Rev:1.5) and you are a king without a gun but with identity and mercy. What the devil desires is that you never know that you may fight a fight that is not yours. The fight that I am speaking of is the fight that is bringing great young men to lockup on a daily basis. What is also painful to me as a veteran of war is when I see what a gun is doing among our war heroes. On March 9, 2018 a veteran of the Afghanistan war shot and killed 3 people including himself. This shooting occurred in California shocking the residents and great lives were lost. It was determined that the veteran suffered PTSD and was once a resident of the center. As a veteran, it is my belief that some PTSD can lead to the common denominator in troubled men I discovered in lockup. This common denominator is called again Poison Hope Dysfunction.

What I have witnessed in talking to other veterans that have PTSD is it has a tendency to cause them to lose hope. This is why it is my prayer precious one that if you are a PTSD patient I pray that you are being treated. I say this because I do not want you to ever feel hopeless with a tendency to quit. Most importantly I am concerned for those veterans that have a gun and is not being properly treated. What a gun will do is again take over the thinking of any man that the gun is a keeper. I am consistently praying that I hear of no more of our war heroes taking lives with these guns including their own. Once again, I just believe this veteran in California along with illness lost hope.

Sir, you do not have to lose hope because I am here to tell you that from this day forward God the keeper is with you. Regardless of what giant walls are before you, there is a great force of power working with you. Now, again we as men must take a look at why we are here and whose side are we on. When we realize that we are on God's side we have no reason to think that we cannot recover. I say recover because most of us as men have been trampled by some form of a storm. I say that we are in the right moment for God to take away every hardship that was sent to take us out. Now, again we must remove what the world may have brought our way to discourage us.

Here's what the devil is doing. The devil is on a daily basis discovering new ways to discourage the best of men. Why is this one may ask? I believe he is doing this to get you to believe what you have been believing is not so. All of this is to get you to discover a new keeper in your life the devil. When the devil gets men to believe this lie the first thing he does is to get them armed and loaded. The reason the devil starts the man off this way is he wants to get him to feel dominant. Yes, the devil wants the man to feel dominant that he can rule over every matter or source. This is how I am watching the devil march young men here in lockup one by one.

When I have a sit down with these guys I began to see how the enemy is baiting our young men foul by foul. When I say foul I mean they are being faked into a foul like the player on the basketball court. When they are faked by the devil with a bad choice they foul by using a gun and take the penalty. I try day after day to speak to these guys to let them know that they are being used. They are being used again by the devil who means them or their life no good but only bad. The same God that I trusted in Iraq who kept me from destruction wants to use men that he shall keep them. Sir, I am here again to tell you that in war I came into a place with God that kept me sheltered. What I discovered was he can shelter all men who trust him and make him their Lord. I pray that all men will make a plea before God as we are in a place in a world of imitation. Sir, I believe as men either we will imitate the devil or we will imitate God and there is no middle. This is why I believe again the bible says "No one can serve two masters: either he will love one and hate the other. (Matt:5.24).

Guns Down And Hands Up

I believe in this hour that we are in it is truly time for the man to put the guns down and get his hands up. Now, I know this sounds familiar from the world but this one is not of the world but of God. When I look at the gun violence in our world what I really see that men hands are in the wrong place. We are living in a time that I believe when the man hands are up blessings shall come down upon him. The blessings shall come down upon him because uplifted hands are a sign of holy submission. What I believe God desires from men in this hour is submission to him that he will provide. When my hands are up to God I truly can experience a place with God where there is victory.

When Moses was with Joshua fighting with the enemy he went on a hill and Aaron and Hur went with him. Moses begin to get tired and when is hands were down the enemy would win the battle. The bible says " Aaron and Hur went on both sides of Moses and each of them lifted up his hands and victory was won. (Exodus 17.8-13). When men place their hands down on the gun in violence the enemy win and the man is defeated. When the man hands are lifted up to God victory is forthcoming. I believe when our hands are up with **hope** on one side and **faith** on the other side we succeed. God can do amazing things for us when we have our hands lifted up to him in praise.

When young men hands are down and down on the gun it could be a signal his hands are down in the classroom. The enemy has mastered keeping his hands down also in the classroom that he asks no questions. When the young man asks no questions in school the devil allows him to lose interest due to no knowledge. When this occurs in most young men in the classroom he eventually drops out of school. This is a trick of the devil that has planted in young men that he develops no knowledge. The bible says "My people are destroyed for the lack of knowledge. (Hosea 4.6). I am watching young men coming to lockup daily at the rate of 40 per day due to lack of knowledge. This lack of knowledge has kept men hands down on the guns and not lifted up to God.

When men hands are lifted up in hope and faith they are up in worship to an almighty God our redeemer and protector. This is how it was for me while in Iraq and we needed a savior and protector. When we came to worship at the chapel in Baghdad Iraq as soldiers, all of our guns were down on the floor. Our hands were off our guns while our hands were up in worship while the power of God shielded us. While our hands were up in praise and worship we experienced God's mighty works. I witnessed the mighty hands of God protecting his children regardless of outside attacks. I believe what God desires for all men are to trust Him while we praise Him.

When young men get to know God and to lift their hands up in worship to him he can cover them with ease. I know that God can cover them as he covered us in the darkest hour of war in a desert. Guns down and hands up is a sign of surrender, not to the devil but to an almighty God. I believe when men put their guns down and their hands up the scales can fall from their eyes. As long as men hands are down on the gun they cannot see what their future holds that is far above. What I discovered even in combat is when your hands are up you still believed there is more life. When I see these young men marching down the hallway of lockup daily I see no hope for true life. What I do see is many that because their hands were down on their gun they were given life. That is life in prison.

Sir, you still have an opportunity to know that there is more life for you when you surrender your life to Christ. Keeping your hands down on a gun only keeps you from the power in you as a man. See here's the secret. The more the man's hand is down on the gun for the violence he never can rise to dominance. What the enemy has set up with men with all the gun violence is a stripping party of power. The devil knows that you have power as a man when you truly know who you are. I believe the central portion of the heart of the man is knowing his power and where his power comes from. The more the man's hands are lifted up in worship the less he has concerns. I knew that my life was in danger while in the war in Iraq, but as long as my hands were lifted concerns vanished.

The bible says " The Lord will perfect that which concerns me.(Psalms 138.8). When my gun was down in war and my hands were lifted up heaven was perfecting my needs. I want to speak to those men who are not in law enforcement with their guns at their side. Yes, I understand it is your right by law if you have the license for your gun. What I am saying is this, I have witnessed working at the prison is the license was not the judge. Many great men have made bad decisions to rely on their guns than rely on God. What lifted hands up to God I believe does is keep your mind at ease. What I believe the enemy is doing is allowing all the violence to be seen to stir up concerns.

The devil knows that if he can stir up concerns and worry among the people he can get gun sales up. Now, this is what the devil desires, that is gun **sales up** that he can keep men **hands down.** When the devil has this system working as he does, he knows that he is going against the desires of God. The desires of God in this hour is for guns down and hands up that we all can have abundant life. What the devil has done is caused a disruption in the earth with violence to keep hands down. I want to encourage that man that is so close to the edge is having his hands up has dividends. One of the most dividends that you can have with your hands up is your freedom. There is a freedom that comes with uplifted hands that I truly cannot explain in words.

Notice when David was facing Goliath, he was on the attack against him without a gun in his hand. What we witnessed was David defeated Goliath with a slingshot and one stone and power, not a gun. (1Sam:17.50). Why someone may say? I believe this because a gun **demonstrates the power of a gun. The slingshot demonstrates the power of man without a gun with God.** What this also demonstrates I believe is man has the power to defeat every giant in his life through faith in God. We must also notice that David needed only one stone out of the five that he had available to defeat Goliath. I also believe this demonstrated the oneness of power established with God and man. Sir, again all you and I need is to be one with God and we can watch God do mighty work. My goal is to change young men from **Guns of Violence** to **Sons Of Visions** in Jesus' name. My goal also is to see this done in Christ through the Book Of Mathews Ministries which I am the founder. Sir, please don't miss what I am trying to explain. I truly understand and respect your right by law to carry a weapon. I am only trying to reach young men from falling into the hands of lockup.

Since I discovered the power of having my hands up in worship to God I have watched my every Goliath fall. We must also remember the bible says "Behold I have given unto you power to tread on serpents and scorpions, and over all the power over the enemy: and nothing shall by any means hurt you. (Luke:10.19). I believe Goliath witnessed this power as a giant serpent from a man. Child of God, your giant can witness this same power in you by faith. I have witnessed from job problem, to money problem, etc... fall to lifted hands. I know that if all of my problems fell whatever your problems and concerns are they can fall too. What I do know is this, looking at all the problems of gun violence on the news is not the answer. What I am even really praying about now is when I hear about arming teachers in the classroom. The children I believe will be in danger of a teacher who may be going through personal problems. What a tragedy if we live in a world where lifted hands are up to man who could bring you and your hands down.

In California, in March 2018 a teacher accidentally fired his gun in the classroom injuring three students. I just believe with the exception of law enforcement having a gun in a place where hands are lifted up in school does not match. Guns down hands up is a decision that does not mix and yields different results. When the man decides that he will lay down his weapon creativity by faith can increase. I believe in this decision that man can allow room for God's hand to go to work on his behalf. I believe in this hour for the man laying down his gun and lifting up his hands produces good works. Sir, the good works that are in store for you from God will demonstrate the love he has for you. In the twinkling of an eye, God can pour out new creativity in you to start a new life for you.

I believe for many men especially our young men the time is ticking on your decision on your hands. Your hands were given to you by God to do something with them positively that has never been done. When you believe in the guns down hands up mindset greatness is in your footsteps for glory. What I believe is you have just been discharged out of the devil's army into the army of God.

In the devil's army, I am watching young men marching in style to lockup serving a hard time. In the army of God with lifted hands, men can be marching in style to freedom. This freedom comes as a result of no longer allowing a gun to be the master of their future. As I watch the news and see the gun violence I literally see how the gun is the master of so many young lives.

When the guns are down and hands up in worship men can clearly see the master of our lives is Christ. What I discovered when my hands were up when clouds appeared, heaven dispatched the sun without notice. Sir, I believe without notice the moment you put the gun down and hands up a peek of the sun is near. Once you notice the **Sun** is near you will also notice God's **SON** is near to bring you hope. I want to let you know sir that the **Son Jesus** is near waiting on your hands to come up. Now here's what's important. You do not have to be afraid of what your friends are family might say. What I believe is about to happen for you is you are about to cause a change in others and you.

Yes, I believe your new life that is about to be changed by gun down hands up mindset will have a domino effect. The reason why I believe this is about to happen for many is many is ready to surrender. Again, I do not mean surrender in fear of giving up, I believe many are ready to surrender to Christ. In the prison what I have noticed about many of the men with gun violence some knew the bible well. What they didn't know well was the power that came with surrendering to God's will. I knew going into combat in Iraq I needed to surrender to God's will to receive success. In doing that I needed to not worry about my hands down on my gun but hands up in praise. Sir, I believe if you can put your trust in what you can receive with your hands up it could amaze you. What hands up also taught me in my trouble hour was wisdom invaded my insides.

I just began to see things in a much different light than I saw when my hands were down in any concern. God allowed wisdom to demonstrate to me that I truly can do all things through Christ which strengthen me.(Phill:4.13). I noticed that when I trusted God in all things he would do all the work when I used all my faith. I discovered also for the true man that lifted hands is also a call on Jesus name. The bible says "Thus will I bless thee while I live: I will lift up my hands in thy name.(Psalms 63.4). Yes, lifted hands by faith in Christ's name can get provisions that the world cannot deny. Men can become new with new results and new roads to become greater men for a greater world.

I spend a lot of time speaking to young men free and in lockup about making their world a greater world. What God desires in us as men is to change every dark corner in the world to become his light. What the devil has done consistently is forced the world's thinking on some of the greatest young men. What I believe is going to change that is moving men from guns down and hands up. Notice that the scripture above says "I will bless thee" which is honor and reverence also to God. Now, this takes on a new mindset that breaks the back of what the world expects. See, what the world expects from man is continued violence that is not of God or His ways.

The hands-up mindset brings men back to walking out why he is here the first place that he makes his mark. Now, the world wants the man to make his mark with gun marks that he makes a mark in lockup. I believe with lifted hands the man can make his mark that is God ordained. When the man's mark on the earth is God ordained everything in his path is heaven activated. What I mean here and have witnessed is heaven has already activated what has been spoken over us. This is what I experienced again in Iraq when I arrived that heaven had already settled my position as leader. I believe by faith that while I was in route to Iraq I had lifted my hands to Christ for wonders.

The reason why my hands were lifted is because I wanted light with me knowing that I would be facing darkness. Sir, don't allow again darkness to take away the light that God has ordained for you by faith. Your light that God has for you will pour out much more over you that you may have experienced. This is why you must understand the guns down hands up method that you can experience God. On March 24, 2018 we saw hundreds and thousands of students march in Washington D.C. protesting against guns. What I also saw in reality were these students saying guns down hands up. Now, what they were saying to me was Washington we need your hands up for all schools. It is my prayer that their plea to the leaders provide them the attention they deserve at their schools. For men as I am praying and my plea to you is to take a look at what a gun has done for education. I pray that you had one opportunity to look at all those students saying guns down. I can assure you that among all those students in the crowd one of them could model the heart of your own. What I am seeing in lockup daily are young men who lives are over from gun violence.

As all of these students are crying out for peace, and protection, and laws from Washington, let us all cry out. I pray that we all cry out that men would be saved with guns down and hands up that all may succeed.

Chapter 7

FISHERMAN OF MEN

Prior to coming to work at Kilby prison for men I was unemployed for three years spending much time with God. What I did hear clearly from God as He was working on me was that I would become a fisherman of men (Luke 5.10). After applying for many jobs the one that I would get would be a prison for men. What I began to see after working at the prison for a year was men are in real trouble. I say that because what the devil has done is opened a huge door for men to come to prison. In this amazingly huge door for men to find his way to lockup what I do see is there is hope. This is a hope that the enemy cannot identify with when this hope is the hope of almighty God.

In this journey and now this six year study while at the prison God has revealed to me some amazing insight. As a man of God, I must declare that all men can be free. What I also know is what God has deposited in me as His child is hope for men that change may come. In as much as I know that all must be punished for a crime committed my desire is to bring hope. I desire to bring this hope in the heart of men because with hope he can become like God. When I walk the halls of the prison daily I can see how the enemy has caused pain in the family. I believe the start to rebuilding families must start with the rebuilding of men.

The only way and I mean with true possibility of turnaround in men must come from the creator of men. What I believe God has perfected in me in all my pain is a word to perfect man from lockup. What I have discovered is most trouble that rises in young men comes from a different perspective. What I mean here is it is their perspective about them or their own situation that needs faith. I was speaking to a young man in lockup who is there because his best friends quit school. When this young man's friends quit, his perspectives about his chances were grim. What I was confirming in him was his purpose on earth is nobody's but his and not others.

I am on mission for God to tell all men that the world is hurting for the man who understands his reason for existing. Sir, you and I will never be too low in our problem or our situation that our purpose grows dim. The only way that this occurs is we have thrown in the towel on what God can do in us. I believe the moment the man can't see what God can do through him, the enemy takes command. When Simon said to Jesus "Master we have toiled all night and caught nothing"(Luke 5:5) his perspectives had to change about seeing nothing. I believe many young men are locked up because they have not seen nothing from their own efforts for years in their life.

I know what that feels like after working hard on my federal job for years and never seeing the promotion others received. When Simon acted on what Jesus asked him to do even though he had seen nothing results were different. Simon saw the blessing from God for acting on what never occurred for him. What I am speaking to all men is when you step out on blind faith you can see what you never have seen. I believe we are in a season where God wants to show who he is in real men. I believe there are many men across the country that is tired of natural results. My prayer is as a fisherman of men for God that he is about to lead me to open the eyes of men. My desire is to do that immediately because of the overflow of men that are in lockup through closed eyes.

Now, what I have found in these six years working in prison is men eyes are closed due to the wiles of the devil. (Epes: 6.11). What the devil has done in great men is caused him to grow weary over his failures. The way the devil has done this is to allow the man to see his dominion given by God fail. Remember the devil knows scripture and he knows God gave man dominion in the earth. (Gen:1.26). I believe the moment the man doesn't see his abilities given by God he can fall. I believe at this point his mind descends to a lower capacity and he began to function without a purpose. What those of us as men who believe can do is speak a word of hope and reel him. Now, when we reel him in through hope and by faith we can open his eyes to God's abundance.

This is what Simon received once he let down his net again he caught more fish that he called for his partners. (Luke 5.7). I have witnessed more than enough men in lockup that I must become a fisherman of men. As a fisherman of men I want to share with men that you no longer have to be a bait. When I say bait I mean you no longer have to be used by the devil to rob you of life. Sir, God has placed in you as a man hidden treasure that only needs to be launched out. Yes, it needs to be launched out into the deep where God can use you with what is in your hand. When I say that I mean whatever God has given you all you need is faith and hope working.

The only way that you as a man is giving in to the devil is you are staying in the shallow water of fear and deceit. Sir, you need to launch out into the deep with God on your side so that you may get a great catch. What I believe you will catch is a man who is desperate for a chance to discover a true God. The God who made you with gifts and talents that has been hidden behind the worlds view of a man. I believe what the true man in every man is saying right now is there is more for me than this. I am seeing daily in lockup how the enemy has trapped the best man into trouble when he is in fear. What I mean here is he is in fear of launching out for a catch not knowing what is at the end.

Sir, you need to no longer walk out of your life in that kind of fear because God sees more in you than you can see. When fear holds you to stay in the shallow water of the unknown trouble has your number. What the state is doing with those numbers is making a number on a prison identification card. Sir, your future is too big for a prison identification card that should read president of a bank card. I say this because I am speaking to young men in lockup with presidential destinies. What has tripped them up is the enemy has kept them in shallow water of no hope. I am here to tell every man that the hope in you alive is greater than the fear in you of the death of your dream. The enemy knows that the fear in you of death of a dream is literally a seed of fear in you to launch into the deep. Working at the prison has been a very clear revelation for me from God to be that fisherman of men.

I believe what the devil is doing in all of the violence among men is trying to spread a deep-rooted disease. What I want to do as a believer is to be God's messenger of deliverance for men that there is a cure. The common denominator I continue to see in the men at lockup (CPHD) is spreading. I have been delivered from this rooted disease I once had due to my environment and way of thinking. Now, with the power of God rooted in me I am fishing of men for God. What I know is I have been strengthened with God's deliverance therefore I want to strengthen others. The bible says " And the Lord said, Simon, Simon, behold Satan hath desired to sift you as wheat: But I have prayed for thee, that thy faith fail not: and when thou art converted, strengthen thy brethren. (Luke 22:31-32).

I believe most of the troubled young men that come to lockup daily just need to be strengthened. I say that because talking to them I am confident inside of them they have been weakened. The world around them in which they live unfortunately wiped away every positive vein they had. When this was done by the devil it took away their motivation to do good things to do bad things. I was talking to a young man in lockup that nearly brought me to tears the other day. What the young man said was if he knew that there was real hope his gift alone would have kept him. What the young man also said was he could be at home raising his boys if he knew of hope. Here's what I need to get to all men. Hope is a bridge between the worst in you and the best in you.

You and I once we connect with the hope in us given by God all of our days of being sifted by the devil are over. What I discovered is when we can get hope in our hearts trouble disappears in the grip of our dreams. Sir, you do not have to continue on that road of no hope which leads many to lockup. What I am trying to convince to you and hopefully your son or brother is that God is for us. Now, we must get a vision of hope that the darkness of no hope finds it's way out of our life. What I am seeing here in lockup among many great men is the world of no hope is getting them life. What I am saying here is life in prison without parole simply because hope had been lost.

I am on a journey for life as a fisherman of men to tell a story about faith and hope that they are not sifted as wheat. When men in this hour are sifted as wheat he becomes a suspect of losing his freedom. I say that because I have been in an environment where temptation tried me and failed. God desires you and I to be free that we do the impossible for him that his name gets the glory. Sir, this is what I want to say to you that may be going through a tough setback in your life. What I believe God desires from you right now is what I call a **cost of living increase** in your faith. The bible says " The just shall live by faith. (Gal.3.11). Sir, you can't live the life God has for you if the level of your faith is not able to move mountains in your life. I discovered when I deployed to Iraq I needed a **cost of living increase** in my faith to live. I knew I couldn't live in the battle around me in Iraq with the same level of faith at home.

My faith at home was in good condition but where I was going in battle it could not survive the enemy's attacks. I am on a mission as a fisherman of men to inspire men to get a cost of living increase in faith. I believe what the cost of living increase will do is equip the man in battle to win every battle. The reason I see so many young men coming to lockup is they are not winning the battles at hand. Many of the men across this country are losing on so many levels trying to win with no faith. I can easily tell when I talk to some men in lockup that they had no faith in what God could do. Jesus said how is it that you have no faith. (Mark 4.40). I want to say to all men your faith can take you far above what the enemy has showed you and told you what you can't have or become.

I want every man to know first that in your DNA lies in you creating something out of nothing for someone. Now, you might not see it or don't expect it but what I do need from you by faith is to believe it. Again, you and I were made from God and we are not supposed to allow the world to control us. God created this world from nothing when nothing was around to become something. What the enemy is constantly doing is causing men to become nothing that he may land a spot in lockup. The way the enemy is causing some men to become nothing is by pushing them to become trouble. Sir, you no longer have to fall for that from the devil if you understand my message to you.

When you get a cost of living increase in your faith you will see that you are the wrong man for the devil. The reason that you will become that man is you know you are much needed in society. Now, what is important for every man is how I get a cost of living increase in my faith. The way that I received my cost of living increase for Iraq and came home greater than I went was by prayer. I went to God in a way that I never have come to God but this time I released all concerns. When I released all my concerns including death a new spirit came over me of change. This new spirit for new change brought me much closer to God and my faith was increased to purpose.

This cost of living increase in my faith now is authorized daily to say things only that I expect to come to pass. Sir, this new direction now for your life can change the course of the routine that you may live. By faith, you can commit to God and watch how God brings you promotion from a place you never knew. I am a fisherman of men that is encouraging men to take a step that they may have never taken. The reason why I desire to do this in men is that many are taking steps that lead to lockup. Now, some of the steps that they are taking are covered well in the pathway to lockup. I have spoken to more than enough men here that is locked up that never saw it coming. Sir, I am here to tell you that if you are uncertain right now that you are a winner for God there is a problem. What the problem could be is that the devil could be showing you a life of losing. You and I as a man do not take losing very well because we were made by God to win. The devil knows this therefore when any area of our life appears to be defeated anger can invade us.

What I have seen in the past six years working at the prison is how anger sat in and caused a negative reaction. What I have discovered in men is it doesn't matter what the challenge is the negative reaction is winning. When this type of reaction occurred violence or some form of illegal transmission takes place. Now, the judge is not hearing it, all he wants to hear from you is how do you plea. The judge of the universe who is our God(Psalms 75.7) wants to know do you know him. I am on a mission for the rest of my life to be a fisherman of men that they get to know God. I have gone through many tough roads in my life and knowing who God is has made the difference. You and I as a man is designed to make a difference. I shall be this fisherman of men that the world might see a difference in those that I shall find.

God's Make A Difference Man

I am a believer that every man who truly knows God and knows who he is in God is a make a difference man. The reason why I believe this is because I don't think that we were placed on the earth to just exist. We as men were put here to bring the love of God, His presence, and His power. The way that we are able to do this is to know that he lives in us and we believe that he is for us. What the devil works hard daily in men is to close his eyes to his image of God and open his eyes to the world. The moment this is set in stone in his heart trouble is at his footsteps. When the devil plants this seed of closed eyes to the image of God in him he can be a whisper from lockup.

I discovered that God thought a lot of me to put His son Jesus through what He would eventually endure. Now, what I know without a shadow of a doubt is I didn't deserve what He did for me. What made a difference in me not dying due to my sinful state was Christ took my punishment so that I could be free. What I desire to do with all that is in me is make a difference in a life where they may be free. Sir, I have witnessed a lot of young men that are bound in lockup that missed an opportunity. Now, what they missed was an opportunity to allow the freedom they once had been accounted for. Yes, God desires every man created to make his life on this earth worth living.

The bible says "I come that they might have life and that they may have it more abundantly. (John 10.10). For me, part of abundant life is for me to make a difference in the earth that I affect life. Sir, what you need to know is when you have been given a new day the atmosphere is set for change. You as a man can't look back on yesterday or tomorrow but right now for that right now miracle. When I began to know that I did not have to sink into my world of not enough my world changed. I begin to see that I had been misled long enough by my world that I was not capable. One day I had an encounter with God that changed my thinking that I didn't belong to the world. Once I picked my head up from where it was I was able to see the life that was given me by blood.

It is by the blood of Christ sir that you and I as men can look toward heaven for strength and strengthen our world. What I see in our world as well as at the prison where I work is many men need an encounter. The men in our world need an encounter with God that they may be loosed from trouble. Sir, I am here to say to you that an encounter with God can shake any trouble the devil brings. Now, you do not have to keep thinking that your life is all about trouble and misfortune. What I have discovered is that the enemy is working hard to prevent you from the encounter you need. The reason why he is doing that is he knows once you have this encounter with God you are free.

Yes, you shall be free and loosed from the devil that you are on your way to making a difference and telling your story. Now, what I believe is that man that can embrace this revelation shall be set free. Yes, I believe this with every ounce of resurrection power in me (Ephes:1.19-20) that you are next. See, here's what the enemy is doing he is celebrating while our young men are shooting each other. Now, the devil knows that is not of God but of the devil and desires more new recruits. What I am saying to every man is that God has a greater plan for your life that is worth celebrating. The devil has a plan for your life in lockup that is not a celebration but major frustration.

I believe God has a makeover for the man who trusts Him that will place Him ahead of the devils tricks and schemes. During this makeover in your life there shall be more than enough coming to you. God will do it for you because of your obedience to submit to him and you willingness to make a difference. I believe sir you will be one of God's greatest men after the makeover because of your new heart. When I saw what God was doing with me I felt as though I had a spiritual heart transplant. In the development of the new heart that I received from God I received a new determination. With this new determination I saw God make all of my crooked places straight. (Isaiah 45.2).

When God makes the man crooked places straight by faith he can walk straight into his destiny designed for success. Now, what the enemy is doing in the life of men of no hope is keeping them in crooked places. The crooked places that are of the devil are those places that are filled with lockup potential. Sir, you are walking in crooked places when violence is at the forefront of your mind. The good thing is that you were never made to keep walking in those crooked places. The only way you are still walking that way is you think that you are far gone from a turnaround. Sir, the God I serve is willing to make your crooked places straight to see you make a difference.

The moment God picked me up from the crooked places I was walking I found my place by faith in God's army. When I looked around after being put in that straight place all of my problems were being straightened out. Now, not saying everything became perfect for me, but I began walking straight toward God's promises. The devil no longer had a hold of my future that could freeze my moment. God gave me a new mind that I am a man to make a difference wherever I plant my feet. Sir, this is for you as well because you don't have to stay in that crooked place of doom and gloom. God wants you to come from where you are now to where he sees you forever in the kingdom.

You and I were born to be kingdom men for our families as well as for our communities that other men be free. What we must know is whether we are winning or losing in life somebody wants to be like us. I discovered as a young man living in the projects that others were watching every move I made. I know this because twenty years after I left the projects I would run into neighbors that remembered me. Now, what they remembered were the highlights of my life that were worth remembering. Sir, I promise you that those that really know you will have visuals of you and your legacy. What God wants to do in you will shatter every rough place in your life you ever experienced. I believe as a man with new determination making a difference in your world shall be imminent. The trouble that ever thought about sending you to lockup will be that place that gets you a move up. What I believe as a new man with hope God is about to take you higher than before. Now, sir I need you to believe because the enemy needs you to believe as well that your past is better.

I am here to tell you that your past is not better because your past is history while your tomorrow is future. God is looking for world changers and you and I are the right **makeup** for the **shakeup.** The way that men of this season shake off those lockup potentials is to put on this new man potential. (Coloss:3.10). The way that you put on new man potentials is to put off those old man habits of bad environments. God desires you to be among movers and shakers that are ready to do those great works. Now, what trouble has done for many great men is caused them to underestimate their own potential. I have talked to many young men here in lockup that never saw greatness in them.

What caused this misconception were environments that were prone to trouble due to time spent on site. When you spend much time on **site** in bad environments **your** mind takes a **bite** that destroys futures. I watched this as I grew up in the projects and even in my adult life how the mind worked with this. This will always have an effect on the man when he is on the edge of uncertainty. Now is the time for every young man to discover who he is as a man or the mind will take a hit. I say that because the goal of the devil is to work your mind on a quick fix for life's journey. Sir, let me tell you that there is no quick fix and the only place success comes before work is in the dictionary.

Now is the time for you as a man to turn away from trying to get it the wrong way and seek after God. When you seek after knowing God you will see all alone that God was with you all the time. Now, God will not be a part of disobedience, but he will be a part of changing you for doing right. The bible says "Seek ye first the kingdom of God and his righteousness and all these things shall be added to you. (Matt:6.33). Sir, the moment you began to seek God you will discover great things will be added to you. What every man must do in this season is seek God with great intensity. Sir, all this requires is you find the time with God that you don't find yourself doing time.

I discover daily that great men are **doing time** mainly because they did not **find time** with God first. I had a man sitting on the bench at the prison the other day stop me and said sir I can tell you are a Christian. I said to him thank you sir and I began to witness to him that God is with him even in lockup. One thing that I caught in our conversation was he said had he found Christ first he could have changed his world. Now, I told him to keep seeking Christ and he can do great things now in him. Sir, what I am saying is what the enemy would love for you to do is to find out you are great after lock up. What I am saying to you now is you are great now and can make a difference now. What is important for you as a man now is to know lockup for you will lockdown others. I say that because I believe what God has in store for you is much bigger than for you only. I truly believe that what has been growing in you even in your struggle is a **territorial exchange.** This is an experience where I believe one man's encounter with God affects and influence lives over a huge area.

The difference in this man's life causes an exchange of bad living for the devil to great living for God. This is the power of God given in the life of a man to reach lives across boundaries to make a difference. Sir, I believe this can be you if you believe and know that life is not over for you and your family. God is ready to do those mighty things for you so that your life is not a reflection of defeat. I believe if you would increase your moments with God in the study and in prayer increase shall come. There shall be increase in opportunity for you to be the man most men dream of. I truly believe that you are possibly that man that is one praise away from seeing God close up.

What I have discovered about a lot of great men that I have counseled were so close to a breakthrough. What I mean here is if they would have held on a little while longer the miracle was there. Brethren, what the enemy desires for you is to be overtaken by the pressures of this world. What I am saying to you is God has already provided the blessings for you if you believe. The moment you commit this much needed time with God a make a difference moment is for you. I believe God desires for you to have a **close up** with God while the devil desires you to have a **lock up** with the devil. The reason man needs a close up with God is to see his image.

What made a difference with me as a believer was when I had a close up with God everything changed. Again, the bible says God gave me his image (Gen.1.26) but I needed to see for myself that it is so. When I began to study the word of God and to obey his teaching his power began to overtake me. See, what made the difference for me with this is when I understood that Jesus became flesh. The bible says " And being found in fashion as a man, he humbled himself, and became obedient unto death, even the death at the cross. (Phillip:2.9). Sir, I believe Jesus became that man that you and I could endure our cross in the world and still win. I hurt all over when I see young men give in to their cross.

Many are giving in to their cross with violence that is destroying their lives due to a lack of ability to endure. I discovered when I could endure my pain that I may suffer in the world payback is coming. With the payback that is coming I can make a difference in the world and in the life of another. Sir, God wants you to endure your suffering and believe him for a breakthrough moment for you. The way that you make this happen for you is to desire to make a difference. I believe when you come to yourself with the mind of Christ working in you it shall be done. You as a man no longer have to live a life of a troubled man with lockup within your reach. You can turn your life around and be a make a difference man in your community right now. All you have to do is say to yourself that I am from this point forward the man God called me to be. When you say that you need to say it in faith and believe God that he has already made a way. Sir, let me say to you that it is never too late for you to make a difference in this world.

Regardless to what you have done in the past you can repent to God and look for the future he has for you. Many young men are showing up daily in our prison not knowing that God had a bright future for them. What presented a cloud over their future were their current circumstances of doom. Sir, don't be blinded if your current circumstances look doom and no way out. God has a plan for you that is about turning your doom circumstances into a life worth living for. What God desires for you is to bring you out of doom and putting you ahead of the class. I believe if you would just trust in the God who can deliver you there will be a great celebration. In your celebration you shall become a difference maker in your world that no one ever knew.

The Restored Man

One thing that I believe for certain is that if men would be restored from their trouble world they can be free. What I see walking the halls over our prison daily are men that are still bound by their natural state of mind. As I watch this daily to me it is a metaphor of how most men are walking out their life. What I am convinced is that if we as the church don't reach this man to change him lockup awaits him. The bible says "Brethren, if a man be overtaken in a fault, ye which are spiritual, restore such a one in the spirit of meekness; considering thyself, lest thou also be tempted. (Gal:6.1). In lockup all of these men has been overtaken in a fault and convicted for their fault.

I believe there are many men in the free world that have been overtaken in a fault by the devil. Some of these faults I believe come in the form of their way of thinking that they are a nobody. When this occurs in the mind of a man I believe he is out of control in his way of functioning in the earth. Now, this man is suspect for any abnormal way of life for survival and is suspect for lockup. This is what I have discovered in my six year study while working in the prison among men. I am totally convinced of this discovery as I have talked to many of these men from all walks of life. When the man is out of control his natural man accepts what appears to be easy to survive.

This is a trick of the devil because we know that everything that appears to be easy to survive is not legal. Now, let's remember the god of this world (the devil) blinded their minds (2corr:4.4) that they stay bound. This is where we as believers come in with our faith and restore this man that he can be free. What I am always blown away with is the fact that God has put restoration power in us who believe. This is why when I talk to young men today and they appear lost I am on the job to restore him. This is what the bible says. As I see the men at work in the prison I can only think of the many that may yet come in. I believe to restore the man shall take away the devil's ability to rule and control a man.

Restoration causes the man to get back up from his fall and his fault to the place where God can work in him. I believe restoration is what caused me to come back from a way of thinking as the world had labeled me. Growing up in the projects the world had labeled me as **below the bar** and less likely to succeed. When this is settled in the mind of a young man growing in this environment it could spell trouble. That is exactly what has happened to many young men as prison overcrowding is out of control. I believe until men can be restored to the point that they can win overcrowding will continue. Sir, it doesn't matter what the situation looks like you can be restored for greatness.

God desires you as a man to walk upright that you represent him on the earth without staying in trouble. There are too many young men I am watching daily coming to lockup due to the wrong way of thinking. The restored man I believe is a man that has been renewed by the works of God for his glory. In this restored man is a man with a new walk with an identity that is shaped for greatness. I believe the devil works hard on the old man that restoration never is established in a man. The reason for this is the devil wants the man destroyed that all he is involved with is trouble. When I look at the makeup of a man daily on what I see in lockup is trouble. Now, I know this is not what man was made for but this is the product of a troubled man.

All you and I ever see mostly on the news about the average man is a troubled man doomed by his trouble. I am convinced in these last six years working in the prison that the enemy really has mastered a plan. What I see is the enemy has mastered a plan that the man stays troubled without change. What the devil also knows is if he allows one man to slip into the restored mode hope is back. Sir, I knew that I needed restoration coming from my background filled with worldly defeat. All my defeat was in my mind because most of what was in my eyesight was being a success. What I mean here is success as a child for a man came only for athletes or a movie star.

As I began to grow in God and understand his word I then began to understand that the devil was a lie. I began to see in this knowledge of God why so many men were living in defeat. When I was restored by God and his word I began to see that I can only rise to higher heights through him. Sir, it is not about where you come from or how much money you have on you. What determines who you are and where you are going is all in your thinking and in your mind. A restored man now by faith has the mind of Christ and can become all that he can dream to become. Now, you as a man have the ability to dream as restoration takes place in you now.

In my restored mind, God began to allow me to dream dreams that my natural mind would have thought impossible. The reason why this thought would always surface was the world blinded me from greatness. This is what the world is doing to most of the young men coming to lockup right now. Since the man's dreams are shadowed by his environment his thinking is aligned with troubling thoughts. When I look at the gun violence and all the school shootings this is evidence of the man's thoughts. Now, I believe even the world does not want your mind restored but relevant. What I mean here is the world wants the man's thoughts relevant to the posture of it's design.

God desires you as a man to be not relevant only to the world but for His work that you are the best in the world. Yes sir, you were made by God to be the best at what you do for Him that He gets the glory. When the man gets this restored mind he now comes under God's plan for His purpose. I know that it has been a restored mind in me that caused me to rise above every failure. The only way that I was able to endure even in combat in Iraq was my restored mind would not worry. The restored mind only relies on God to shield him and protect him in the worst situation. I believe this was for me because in the battles for me in my life the hills were too high to climb. My natural mind was in no way able to handle what the pressures of this world could lead a man. What I see daily in the troubles of man is the pressures of him trying to please the natural mind. Sir, as a man you can be restored but you must believe restoration is possible. I believe there are even many men in the church right now who never even consider being restored.

This is why I believe many in the body of Christ are still bound because they never even think or talk about restoration. The bible says " But this is a people robbed and spoiled; they are all of them snared in holes, and they are hid in prison houses: they are for a prey, and none delivereth ; for a spoil, and none say **Restore**.

(Isaiah:42.22). Men, it is now time for us to say **Restore** that we may do God's will. I truly believe that God has blessed me in such a way that by faith I shall witness great men restored. My job is to get men to believe they can be restored and to say the word **Restore.** I truly thank God for what he has done in my life since being restored and I must help another.

I know without a doubt that God sent me to a men's prison to help bring restoration to those that are lost. I also believe God also desires me to bring restoration to men that are free in the world but lost in knowing God. Saints, I am fully persuaded that God has put restoration in my hands by faith to expect results. The results that I expect through restoration have been already paid for and released. What I am on a mission for in this hour is to get men to see the impossible coming their way. I believe God is looking all over the earth for that man who has embraced restoration in his heart. I was truly blessed while working at the prison to meet great men who believed in restoration.

One of these men that I was blessed to spend time with was a man that I know God sent me there to restore. Now, let's remember this is what the bible says for the spiritual to do (Gal:6.1) and we can. While working at the prison I get to see so many men locked up and some just have a Godly appearance. Now, when I say this I mean the man of God just has a uniqueness upon him that is noticeable. This is the light that shines upon him that even dressed in the prison whites it can be seen. My first conversation with this gentleman after I saw him was a confirmation right away. I say that because I saw military discipline and he confirmed it and we were both graduates of the same academy.

Yes, this man was a graduate of the Warrant Officer Academy and had fallen into a fault and my job was to restore him. After speaking with him about his fault and he repented I began to speak restoration over him. As believers and as the spiritual God wants us to speak restoration over his people. When we speak restoration over those that are bound God can set them free that they walk upright. Now, I am not saying that those that are bound for crime do not do the time. We know if convicted they must do their time while God do great work in them. Now, this gentleman that I am speaking of that was a graduate of the academy he completed his sentence. The job that God has given me again is to reach men and set them free from lockup by being restored. My point here is God can do a mighty work in the man and for the man when he says **Restore.** When this restored man was released from prison I prayed a prayer of restoration over him. Now, what I want to say is this man was a pilot for the military as a warrant officer. His goal was to get back into flying upon being released from prison but many said it would be impossible.

I had even the Christians that worked with me said yes he is a wonderful man but he will not fly again. Well again, remember the bible says none says Restore and this is because none believe in being restored. Well, I believe and so did this man and I said to him Mr. Jay you and I must believe when we pray. Once this gentleman arrived home and applied for the job as a pilot we prayed a powerful prayer over the phone. The job didn't come right away therefore he worked other small jobs. One day I received a text from him and he said Jeff, I am landing from my last flight of the day. Sir, I do not care what your issue is in your life let me declare restoration over you.

Restoration can take you away from the troubles of this world that are causing lockup in the lives of many. You no longer have to live a troubled life now that you know restoration is available and is real. My new friend Mr. Jay is flying all over the east coast and is living a restored life from God. Praise The Lord!! I believe what God is doing in Mr. Jay's life is through restoration flying high above the enemy's attempt on his future. Sir, I don't know what has grounded you and is keeping you from soaring. God has a plan for your life through restoration that you may fly high above the enemy of lockup. The restored man has the ability to get back all that the enemy has stolen.

What the restored man receives that the devil hates is his identity which puts him back in on the path to success. Now, this man can get back to what God created him to do and do it with expectations. What the enemy knows that he has done when the man is troubled is robbed him of his identity. When the man's identity is robbed then can succumb to robbery to fulfill his manhood. The problem with this is he is out of sync with reality and finds himself in lockup upon convicted. The enemy is doing this in men in various ways as long as he strips him from true identity. The devil cares less whether he does it through sex crimes, drug crimes, etc.. as long as identity is affected.

Sir, the restored man is a powerful man and you can make a difference in your world when restoration is upon you. This comes by faith after receiving Christ as Lord and allowing restoration to overtake you. Restoration by faith gives this man a new life that brings upon a new walk of life. My goal in life is to speak and declare restoration over every troubled man that he overtakes his opposition. Yes, as a man we are able to overtake our opposition because we have the power of God in us. Sir, it does not matter what has happened in the past you have an opportunity. What I mean here is you have an opportunity to turn away from a troubled world to a new world. I witness men coming to lockup daily from a troubled world that watches them escape restoration. God is a good God and he desires to do well in you that you might do very well on the earth. The trouble lies deep in the earth and is on the path of taking great men down really quick. As I watch this on the airways via television I also am watching it daily while working in the prison. Sir, I pray Restoration over you that your future keeps you flying high above your failures.

The Wise Man

I believe in the season that we are in right now it is imperative that all men learn the significance of wisdom. When the man walks in the wisdom of God he is able to endure the devil's tricks. I am confident that if I did not learn to embrace the wisdom of God my future would be dim. I believe if most men that are locked up would have known of God's wisdom their outcome would be different. The reason why I believe every man's outcome will be different it was for me. When I received the wisdom of God happiness came over me with power. The bible says " Happy is the man that find wisdom, and the man that gets understanding. (Prov:3.13).

I received this happiness that came from God and I saw myself differently with the gifts God gave me. Now, I didn't try to compare my gifts with anyone but received understanding on using what God gave me. Sir, I believe if you get to know God and pray for this wisdom your gifts will come forth. When your gifts and talents come forth trouble will no longer grip your way of thinking. Many men are being locked up daily because wisdom from God has never consumed their life. What I discovered was with the wisdom of God I could rearrange the devil's intent on my life. I can do this because now I have a different perspective when it comes to applying God's truth.

Applying the wisdom of God I discovered that I can get a greater understanding of why I am here on the earth. When trouble attempts to take me away from my purpose understanding resets my image. When I was unemployed for three years under much pressure wisdom grounded me in hope. I began to understand that God made promises to me and I must wait for the promise. Now, what this began to do was to reset my image and my future that God is not going back on his word. My job was to stay strong in my understanding and don't give in to my flesh and thoughts. What I witness daily is how men are not applying wisdom under the pressure of the world.

A wise man that gets this understanding from God can walk out God's promises and defeat the devil's attack. What this requires is a man who is constantly seeking a greater understanding of himself and of God. What I am seeing daily in many men that come to lockup is they really have little knowledge of themselves. I am convinced that a man who has little knowledge of himself has no knowledge of God. What the devil is doing daily is keeping a blindfold over the man that wisdom and knowledge escape him. Sir, I am here to tell you that as wisdom and knowledge escape you law and order embrace you. The world and its temptation is much too strong for average knowledge.

I see great young men with average knowledge but that knowledge was not strong enough for the pressure. One of the strongest temptations I see taking great men with average knowledge is sex abuse. Some of the greatest men ever known in their craft are going down not embracing the wisdom of God. What I am confident about a man of wisdom is he will always make the best choice. I say that because wisdom takes the man out of his natural way of thinking into the wise council. God is calling men to seek his counsel so that we all can make the best choices in life that can keep us free. The bad choices that are being made daily by men are spreading into the family structure. When the man decides that he is the head and not the tail wisdom can be a platform of hope.

What I discovered was as a wise man with wisdom from God can change the course of difficult situations. Situations can change I believe because the wise man's words carry elements of change for the good. Sir, when you walk upright with the love of God you have the opportunity to help others greatly. One day at the prison I saw a young man who I had been encouraging handcuffed sitting. This young man was sitting with his hands behind his back on his way to be put in a single cell. I later found out that he had been in a fight with another dorm mate which is a violation. When I spoke to him and gave him wisdom from God that touched his situation change took place.

I saw this young man ten minutes later he was a different person without handcuffs and was cleared from punishment. What I shared with him while he was handcuffed was wisdom from God of contentment. What I am trying to convey to young men today is the importance of wisdom in life. A wise man has a way of receiving heaven's council that stirs him from trouble to triumph. God desires every man to turn away from wickedness to righteousness so that he may be free. I have witnessed on a daily basis how the lack of wisdom can rob a future and cut short many dreams. The wise man is granted access to a path that is full of life that he can reach every goal and vision.

The man who has no wisdom and leaves himself to his own understanding has a clear pathway to lockup. I see too many great men that were in great spotlight but that light was a doorway for bad choices if allowed. Education is not an anchor for sound wisdom because many smart men are losing the battle. Wisdom comes from God to a man that he can function with grace in all areas. The bible says "O Lord, how manifold are thy works! in wisdom hast thou made them all: the earth is full of thy riches. (Psalm 104.24). When the man can receive the wisdom of God a mighty path is discovered. While the man walks on this new path he has the key to victory and freedom.

What the devil does continually is darkening the man way of thinking from wisdom and leads him astray. The man without this wisdom finds trouble and strays away in deception that breeds lockup every time. Sir, God has much work for you that can be accomplished that truly is filled with his wisdom. You no longer have to allow the devil to feed your thinking with bad choices of the devil. With the wisdom of God operating in your life, you can stand with confidence in your future in the earth. I am confident that God can take you far above your own thinking with his wisdom as a guide. Now, you may have a background that is similar to mine in that I came from the projects. I began to walk in the knowledge of God and discovered that his wisdom can rearrange my direction. The moment God's knowledge comes and overtakes man's ways new doors open. After joining the military and following God's direction he showed me sights I have never seen before. Sir, what God desires to do with his wisdom is show you sights that you have never seen or experienced. Many young men are never witnessing these new sights because trouble has blackened their view.

When trouble clouds the view of man he now wallows in the low perception of the natural man's thoughts. I am here to tell you that the natural man's thoughts alone have many great men in lockup. God desires the man to be totally dependent on the wisdom of God which reveals success. The bible says "Give instruction to a wise man, and he will be yet wiser: teach a just man, and he will increase in learning. (Prov:9.9). I believe with the wisdom of God man can grow exceedingly toward greatness. This shall come as a result of the counsel of God that keeps him soaring above his abilities. Sir, God can bring you the wisdom that you need that could lead you out of trouble.

The wisdom of God that comes with studying his word can increase your learning that can get you that job you desire. What the enemy is doing to young men now is decreasing their learning to quit school. I consistently see the devil's pattern with this as I watch school dropouts flooding our prisons. Sir, when you get to know God his wisdom can reset the margins of your mind. You get to see the real you operating under the power of a mighty God who gives you strength. When we as men seek the wisdom of God we are seeking our purpose for being on the earth. Many men that find themselves overtaken by trouble are really overtaken by no identity.

Sir, you have not come even close to where God desires you to be until you get to know the power of God. Now, I must say that I was blown away with where God wanted to take me as I learned of him. When I began to know God personally I no longer wanted to keep up the pace I started with. I say this because my environment kept me thinking at the pace of what I saw with little wisdom. God entered in the equation of my thinking and launched me to learning for greater accomplishments. This is why I knew that when I entered the Warrant Officer Academy I was under new learning. The learning I grew up with taught me that my past would keep me from such a blessing. Sir, now is the time for you to walk away from your past of trouble to your future of success through wisdom. The men that I see in lockup daily I believe were a breath away from the wisdom that leads to success. When I see the trouble that overtakes the best of men I witness men that are broken. These men are broken and are in need of restoration that can turn their entire life around.

The wise man takes on a life that will not be sidetracked by the troubles that can lead him to trouble. I believe I am speaking even now to a man that realizes he has been sidetracked by the devil. Yes, the devil will sidetrack you with domestic violence, drugs, robbery, or anything knowing that is not you. The reason the devil will do this is he knows in trouble or tests the man's wisdom will be in a battle. God will never give up on the man when he is totally committed to serving him. I discovered when my heart and mind are in tune with the spirit I can receive all God has for me. Now, sir, you are too great of a man to be a candidate for lockup.

I believe the devil hopes that you fail to become wise as God desires you to be so that you can recover what's lost. Let's begin today by telling the devil that he is a liar and that he is too late. The devil is too late because you and I have had a spiritual connection as a man to man about your future. The wisdom of God by faith is upon you now that shall grant you much hope and blessings. This is a call once again for the man who has been fed up with average and just enough. The devil can no longer bring you this plate of food seasoned with failure that shall grant you lockup. Many men in lockup right now have eaten from this table and wish they knew of the wisdom of God.

Knowing God shall give you the confidence to avoid the trouble that you can become the wise man he desires. I believe as you begin to study the word God shall reveal to the man in you the blessings for you.

Chapter 8

FAITH OVER LOCKUP

I truly believe that God has given every man the faith he needs to keep him free from lockup. What every man has to know is in order to access the faith he needs a connection with the giver of faith. The bible says "God has dealt to every man a measure of faith. (Romans 12.3). Now, since every man has been given an amount of faith his faith must be lived out in every area of life. When the man understands that he has the image of God when faith is activated circumstances can change. What the devil can do when the man has no faith is he can flash negatives images of defeat. When this is done in the man all hope is gone and it appears he is without.

When we can learn as men to operate in the God kind of faith we can cause trouble to bow down at our faith. The way we cause this trouble to bow down at our faith is we know God will provide. The devil knows that when it appears that all hope is gone to sustain us the natural mind takes over. The natural mind is unaware of an all powerful God who can do the impossible. Now, the man with this mind of no faith is overtaken by his flesh and he acts upon natural reasoning. I am here to tell every man that natural reasoning for man's desires are leading many to lockup. All of this is a part of the common denominator in trouble men Poison Hope Dysfunction. I believe faith is so powerful when the man applies it that it can drive his need directly to God.

The three years of unemployment was really devastating as a man desiring to support his family. The devil really was trying to work on my mind and my image that you are less than a man being without. Now, these are the words that the devil tosses at the man to force him to do the wrong thing. Faith in God opens the ears of the man who believes that he can hear the spirit saying wait. What kept my ears open to the spirit was reading the word daily that I can see myself coming out. Sir, now is the time for you to walk in faith in order that you can overcome every temptation. Once the man is overcome by the temptation of the flesh he is led to a dark path. Too many of our young men on a daily basis are led to this dark path and are being locked up.

When I walk down the hallway in the prison every morning I am seeing a world of men from 18 to 80 of little faith. The issue is that it didn't matter what the trouble was his faith could have kept him in control. I believe if it was robbery because of little faith he thought if he didn't take it he would never have. I also believe if it was taking another life this man lack of faith robbed him of what God said. The bible says love your enemies (Matt5.44) and I believe when we do this he will protect you. What it takes to walk in this is strong faith in a strong and all mighty God who is able. I had to walk this out daily while in Iraq because I knew Iraqis were working with us but shooting at us. I begin to speak to God and said to him Lord I will trust you by faith to sustain me. When men can trust in God to sustain him God can provide for him that he know God cares. Sir, I am here to tell you that God cares for you and he has a way out for you if you will only trust him. Now, the important thing for you as a man to get developed in you is faith over lockup. When you develop some **faith over lockup** you are now in a **setup** that God can **pick you up**. Yes, what God can do for you and I through faith is pull us up from the snares of the devil that troubles us.

What the devil's goal to do is to keep men troubled bound that he may never discover his full potential. Faith can move not only mountains but if necessary it can move time that God's man needs are met. One thing was certain, I was unemployed in 2009-20012 during some tough financial times in America. I knew there were some huge mountains of financial storms that could bury me. When I began to pray a prayer of faith I began to feel and experience some shifting of time. It appeared that I was about to really lose everything but through the blood of Christ I didn't lose faith. When I began to pray in faith time was pulled back and I was employed and nothing was lost.

Sir, I can understand if things are really tough for you but I am here to tell you your faith can be tougher than your problem. The enemy will try to push the wrong button on your anger and frustration that yields lockup. Your faith is not far from your frustration because the both require a decision. I decided when frustration was at my entry door while unemployed to choose faith in God. Faith overwhelmed the frustration that was prompted and provision came knocking. Sir, I would rather for provisions to come knocking than the police to come knocking at your door. Many men are going down at an alarming rate at the prison due to the wrong knock at the door.

Faith over lockup has a power pull on your decisions that give you hope in making great choices in life. This is because faith over lockup can breathe hope in the man that he is much bigger than what it looks like. What this faith will do is give you spiritual insight on the blessing that God has ordained for you. Now, in order to grasp this you will have to learn to live and believe you already have the blessing. This is what separates the true man of faith that can overcome a horrible setback. This man has the spirit of God working in him that is invisible but is very much present. God continually speaks to this man and he hears his voice by faith that he will not be defeated.

What I have learned about the men in lockup is the devil put a blanket over them mentally that defeat is not an option. Sir, as a man who has been given a measure of faith you do not have to settle for that lie. By faith you have everything in you especially breath and faith that can bring you peace. This is the peace that you need in the storm that lights the fire in your faith to get up and move. This is what I had to do in Baghdad Iraq because the pressure was on me to be in fear of dying. What kept me strong in the battle was I have a strong relationship with God for every battle. I believe in the hour that we are in as men we must be strong in faith as we give glory to God. The bible says " He (Abraham) staggered not at the promise of God through unbelief ; but was strong in faith, giving glory to God. (Romans 4.20). I am confident that in war I could not stagger at the promise that God would keep me. Faith in God can keep a man out of **lockup** when he **lookup.** As the bombings were coming after me daily in Iraq I was not giving in and be bound.

Sir, there may be bombings of much trouble coming after your future but faith over lockup is in you. The reason why I believe it is in you is because I believe the best of you have not been tampered with yet. I say that because you have not seen possibly the goodness of God living inside of you. God has a master plan for you that you and your name become a household name in your community. Sir, do not be moved by what you have done including the trouble you may have experienced. God is looking at you by faith through his blood. When I walk through all those men at the prison daily I see someone else. What I mean here is I do not see them for what they **have done.** I see these men as who they **can become.**

I believe by faith that this is how God sees all of us who trust and have faith in him that we make a difference. Faith over lockup among men today I am confident can fix the overcrowding problems. This is the God kind of faith that can tear down walls of tradition and boundaries that holds us hostage. When men can walk in faith to the mighty promises of God there will be no lack of joy. When joy is present and faith is on the breastplate of his heart God can do some SUDDENLY BLESSINGS (ACTS 2.2). I believe once men are saved they can suddenly change from a burglar to a businessman. **I believe as men get to know Jesus they can suddenly change from stealing cars to part owners of dealerships.**

How this will take place is a new mind to believe they can go **higher** as men when we look to a **higher** power. Again men will have to be strong in faith giving glory to God for what he is well able to do. What I will always remember after my six year study at the prison is the abilities most men have in lockup. What I always noticed was these men just needed to activate their faith over lockup. I spoke with a young man sitting on the bench the other day before leaving to go home. I asked him what is it that he will be doing to keep him from coming back to prison once he is at home. This young man said I have a clothing company that I sell for ladies and I have customers across the state.

I said to this young man that I don't know why you are here and I am not interested and it is not my business. What I did share with him was that it is important for him to learn and know the power of God. I also said to him that God is a faith God and if he get to know him he can take his business to higher heights. What I wanted him to know is the devil desires for him to take his eyes off his business. I said to him the devil wants to keep your eyes on him because he is intimidated by his possibilities. Here's what the devil knows about this young man. I told this young man that if you walk by faith and trust in God he can pour his miracles on his business and bless him. The devil is intimidated by every man that has the abilities to think outside of the box of a job. I said to this young man that I believe you have a gift to do what you do but the enemy is mad. Now, I said also to him that he cannot look back at his past but his future with faith over lockup. Sir, the devil is mad at you and all men when we desire to do something big and impossible.

I told this young man that I believe if he go home and pray and have faith in God his business can flourish. I told him that this is the year of 2018 and 8 is the number for new beginnings for those who believe. This young man is getting out of prison with an opportunity for new beginnings in his life. I also told him that his faith in almighty God has the potential to be number one in the state. I want men like this young man to know that this is the year that God shall exceed expectations. I saw in the eyes of this young man saying give me more. What he said to me was I really needed that and thank you so much. I believe faith over lockup planted a seed in his heart.

Now, what I am praying and believing is for God to do a work first in his heart then a work in his business. When I left this young man I said to him remember it is not about what you've done but what you can become. I told him that I believe he can become something wonderful for God and his family. This is all I believe need to be spoken over the life of troubled men that they can overcome. What will be needed in their lives as men is a powerful walk of faith that they can be all they can be. What the system has done and is doing is allowing men to destroy themselves with no faith. The devil knows again that men with this measure and faith knows not to give no thought to lockup.

I believe God is searching the house of hope for men to learn to live by this kind of faith and he can be free. I found a way to defeat the devil in my life when I learned to walk in this faith and have dominion. Men can have dominion over the devil when faith has connected to his heart and his walk. When faith has invaded the heart of a man who believes he no longer looks at the mountain. A faithful man who knows of the faithful God looks at the one who moves the mountain. Sir, this is a word for you and your moment that it is faith that you need to rule and reign. God is standing by waiting on you to call on his name and walk in faith that the walls are coming down.

You can have this faith over lockup and turn your entire world around and see how marvelous your God is. This is what I discovered about God when I decided to believe what God said about me. Jesus said that I am the light of this world (Matt:14) and by faith my light is not to be hid under pressure. My faith in God with my light of hope in me as a man can reverse every curse the devil had on me. This is what took place as I walked the stage as Chief Warrant Officer and broke the curse. My battle that I was going through with three failures at the academy appeared as a curse. God turned the curse into a blessing as I was able to do mighty things for God as a warrant officer. Sir, it may appear that your troubles may appear as a curse upon you as well. I believe with the faith the size of a mustard seed (Matt:17.20) a man can develop faith over lockup. By faith this release open doors for the man as his life takes a massive turn for the good of God's glory. Now, this same man can began to see himself as God sees him and do great things for society.

The Law Of Faith And Law Of The Land

I believe when a man learns to walk by faith and not by sight the land can have no hold on his future. Remember, the bible says this man was given dominion (Gen1.26) over the earth by faith and land is on the earth. Now, this does not mean that the man can disobey the law of the land because he must obey. Yes, if you violate the law you can come to lockup. What is important is if the man connects with God through faith he can become a great man in the land. I discovered that my faith when active can cause many obstacles to obey the law of faith upon the land. The bible says "Where is boasting then? It is excluded. By what law?. of works? No, but by the law of faith. (Romans 3.27).

The law of faith can work for a believer when they understand the power of faith wherever they plant their feet. Sir, regardless of where you live you do not have to break a law of the land and face lockup. You are much greater than what the trouble around you in the land is trying to bring your way. Wherever you live in the earth by faith the power of God can give you a strong advantage if you believe. When I planted my feet in Iraq where there was much trouble the law of faith was working in me. Yes, even at war there were some laws that we had to abide by or we could face lockup. The law of faith which was working in me was working in my behalf over the law of the land.

The way this was working for me was my faith that God shall supply all of my needs (Phill:4.19) and the land must obey. Sir, you do not have to break any laws of the land that send you to lockup. When you know your God and how big he is your land where you live must give in to the law. What I mean here is the law of the land must give in to the law of faith which is of a faithful God. This is the faithful God that created the land and has given the earth and the land to children of men.(Psalm 115:16) Sir, you are a child of a man, and that by faith puts you in the right place. Now, what you need to do is to get your thinking and your faith in the right place.

In the bible there was a woman from the land of Canaan who daughter needed healing from being demon-possessed. (Matt:15.21-28). The real issue here was she was from a different land and not welcomed. This woman kept pressing in to Jesus with her faith that the law of faith won over law of the land. Now, this was not her land and it was not her time yet to see the power of God. Sir, the law of faith can change time restrictions and land restrictions when you have the God kind of faith. What we see here in this story is how your faith when it is bold steps into a new time zone. Jesus says to this woman "O woman, great is thy faith: be it unto thee even as thou wilt". The woman daughter was healed as the law of faith was over the law of that land. Sir, you are not waiting on God, God is waiting on you and your faith.

What I am witnessing daily are many men coming to the wrong place (lockup) not knowing the law of faith. Iraq in all of its troubles bowed to the law of faith that was in me even though I was on their land. I had the opportunity to watch God show himself strong by the law of faith over the law of the land. I was not about to let the law of the land in Iraq dictate my purpose in the earth as a man. As men with purpose we can still achieve great things even when we appear to be at a disadvantage. When the law of faith is at full throttle we are never at a place without provisions. God will provide for you sir if you would just trust him for every need and you shall be free.

The devil's goal is to get you as a man to be just like him by causing you to kill, still, and destroy (Matt:10.10). Now, again we know that the devil knows the word and he knows that God wants you to be like him. What the devil has done is switched the script on men who has lost their identity in trouble. God through his word has provided a way of escape by his law. The bible says "Open thou mine eyes, that I may behold wondrous things out of thy law. (Psalm 119.18). I believe what God desires are for all men to see and operate out of his law and win. When we believe and walk in faith our eyes can be opened to miracles and wonderful things from God. This is what God has allowed me to see with my eyes even when bombs in Iraq were coming. By faith I could still see God doing wondrous things as long as I trusted and obeyed his laws.

When you as a man can learn to know God and obey his laws I believe you can easily respect the law of the land. This is because there is something on the inside of you like God that demand obedience. Now, I say easily but I this does not mean temptation will not be knocking at your door. Growing up in the projects and around temptation to do wrong came plentiful on a daily basis. What I believed kept me on the right path was my father's laws and the laws of God that he taught. When the opportunity came to steal from the store as it did I began to think about my father and lockup. One gave me much fear (my father) the other gave me much concern.

My concern was I didn't like the thought of being locked up because I just believed that I could rise above my surroundings. I believe sir that you can arise above your surroundings understanding the law of faith. The law of faith I believe can send you miles high above your every pitfall. You can choose by faith that you will obey God and his laws and discover your purpose. Coming out of high school with average grades I knew that the world had labeled me average. When I joined the Army and began to obey God and follow him faith began to open my eyes to hope. I believe what trouble does when much of it is committed is closes the eyes of faith and hope.

I believe this is why the devil desires men to continue in trouble as he closes in on him rather than God. I talk to many men of all ages that return to prison as repeat offenders and ask them what is the problem. I discovered that when most of them were trying to do right wrong gave a greater presentation. The devil does this to men especially when they are vulnerable. What do I mean here, remember when Satan tempted Jesus after he had been in the wilderness for forty days and he was hungry. (Matt:4.2) Now, we have to always remember as men the devil is coming very strong at the point of our weakness. The enemy does this just to get the man in a place where he can be bound.

The bible says " Again, the devil took him up on the an exceedingly high mountain, and showed him all the kingdoms of the world and their glory. And he said to him (Jesus) All these things I will give you if you fall down and worship me. (Matt:4.8). What I see here is the devil is showing Jesus a greater presentation based upon him doing right. This is what the enemy is doing on a daily basis to men of no faith. I believe these greater presentations are coming through , sex crimes, drugs, robbery, etc.. that leads to lockup. When I look at all the great men who have fallen in sexual harassment I see a problem in their law of faith and the law of the land. What I see is how the enemy has blinded their minds to faith and opened their eyes to deception. The enemy does not want men to walk in faith but only rely on his own strength. When man is confident that he has to rely on his own strength his heart bleeds deception and confusion. Now, the devil can present and easy way out on the surface but is loaded with deception and lockup.

What God desires in the man is to obey his law that the law of faith enters your heart and mind that you trust him. I believe when this occurs in the heart of man he no longer have to be tricked by deception. The world is good at this upon men to present financial gains covered with schemes. When we are in faith through the law of faith we can know that God is our refuge and hope. The bible says "The law of your mouth is better to me than thousands of coins of gold and silver.(Psalm 119:72). When we as men believe the law of faith God's word is much greater than a profit. The word of God has the power in it alone to cause us to soar above the world's deception.

I believe we are living in a time right now where men who know the law of faith shall see the miracles of God. The reason these miracles and blessing will appear is because their oppressors will bow to the law. The only way that the devil is winning over the man now is he is unaware of God's law. I believe when the man began to study about God and know who he is the law will overtake him. I watched the law of faith bring me new ideas and discoveries the moment I learned of the law. Now, with the law of faith working in my heart and in my life I can walk with God and him with me. When men began to activate their faith in God even in their troubles they can endure the law of the land.

We were made by God as men to dominate our world but only when we abide by the laws of God. I knew without God there was no way my family and I could survive during my three years of unemployment. My faith I knew needed to be in place where I could see through the hurdles of the law of the land. The law of the land said to me in writing that in six weeks your house will foreclose. The law of faith said to me if you if you believe God he will show you how his law is greater. In less than six weeks the law of faith yielded me a new job and a new contract on my home. Child of God, your faith in God can have the enemy at awe of what God can do.

What God desires is for his people to get to know him in order that he can establish his laws in your heart. I believe if men began to make the decision right now to know God faith will lead them home. What my prayer is right now is for every man to cry out to God that his heart embraces God's law. The law of faith can turn the man from his trouble world that he can obey the law of the land. I believe the enemy is setting new traps daily that the man fall in the pit of lawbreaking. The problem with this is the enemy knows exactly what season to **stir up** that **lead up** to **lockup.** When the sexual harassment charges were stirred up the devil knew the season was just right.

This is because the devil knows exactly the right timing and right source to bring men to disobedience. I believe with disobedience and no relationship with God in men is a trap for failure. Now, the devil knows this therefore he will always feed the man's sexual desire who is blinded. What is even more fatal to the man is the blindness has no symptoms upon his natural eyes. This is why even the millionaires have fallen with the sexual crimes because they didn't see it coming.

Sir, you will not see it coming either with your natural eyes until the law of faith is working in your life. The law of the land is very serious in this matter (sex crimes) and God desires us to be men of discipline. Now, is the time for men to be upon their best behavior while the devil is as that roaring lion. (1Peter 5.8). This roaring lion is seeking I believe every man who is unsure of himself and God. The law of faith is so powerful that it can bring you in remembrance of who you once were. By faith you and I as a man once had the same image God has (Gen.1.26) and lost it in sin. What the devil has done very well is kept men walking as though there is no God in heaven.

When we walk by faith and not by sight we can walk in the knowledge of God and regain our rightful place. Our rightful place as men in the earth is to live by faith and discover our purpose that gives God glory. The devil desires men to continue to live in the natural world as he live a life of hopelessness. Often as I walk the halls in the prison I easily see and hear men speaking with no hope. What I do as often as I can is to give them a word of hope to turn around their thinking. I said to a young man today that God is not mad at you but what he desires is for you to be changed. The law of faith I believe is also filled with restoration that the man can live in the law of the land.

The law of faith when it is embraced can stand us up with confidence that our destiny can come alive in the land. When we live by these laws we can be obedient and our ways filled with hope can keep us free. The enemy will not stop his attempts on the life of the man especially when he is walking upright. Sir, you need to know that you serve a faithful God and you do not have to seek trouble. When you seek the ways of the devil the roads in the end can lead you to lockup. As a man created by God the man has the potential to make history in his world when he knows the law. The law of faith is what makes the difference in man's entire world that he can win in the law of the land.

The devil is able to close the door of hope when trouble comes to bring the man to lockup. By faith, God can open the door. When we get to know God and walk in faith the law of faith reminds us of what God has said. The bible says " I know thy works: behold , I have set before thee an open door, and no man can shut it: for thou hast kept my word, and has not denied my name.(Rev:3.8) Sir, I believe if you get to know God and keep his word you can keep lockup under your feet and succeed. God has a plan for your life that is greater than handcuffs and shackles on your feet. The devil is a liar and he wants you to always think that you are a loser and can never achieve your dreams.

God desires you and I as men to walk in faith and to trust him to do exactly what he said he would do. Now is the time to learn the importance of the law of faith and how much power is in this law with God. Sir, let me encourage you to walk away from that trouble that is trying to hinder you. All the enemy desires for you is to bind you and your dreams that lockup keeps you shut out. What the devil is doing in the minds of the greatest men is pushing them to the edge of failure. The law of faith wherever land you resides can put you above the trouble that your life receives double. Yes, God can give you double for your trouble if you trust him and allow him to be Lord. (Isaiah 61.7).

Faith And Yes I Can

I truly believe the moment the man gets the yes I can in him he can turn around his troubles in record time. What this requires is the man understanding that faith is much more powerful than his thinking. I say this because in his natural mind there are many things he believes is impossible. Jesus said to a man name Peter to walk on water which appeared to be impossible for him. The bible says "And when Peter had come down out of the boat, **he walked on the water** to go to Jesus. (Matt:14.19). What I saw in this is this man did something impossible as he was coming to Jesus. Here's the key, sir, it doesn't matter what you are facing when you look to Jesus I say yes you can.

What I have witnessed in my six year assignment working at the prison are young men with the I can't mindset. What really concerns me is how many of them have said I can't in the classroom and quit school. Sir, this is a setup by the devil that if man can say I can't in school he says I can't in life. Now, what I see every day in lockup is the I can't spirit is dominating the minds of our young men. What we all are witnessing on the news is how even great men say I can't control my sexual desires. What this has led to is a great number of men fall to sexual harassment. Sir, you were created by God who is a faith God and yes you can take authority over your sexual desires.

What the devil has a habit of doing is coming after the man where he knows he can **lose sight by sight.** What I mean here is the man can **lose sight** of his identity by having his **eyesight** on the wrong thing. This is what I see happened when David saw a woman from a roof bathing and beautiful. (2Sam:11.2-14)**.** David began to lose sight of identity by having his eyesight on the wrong thing. The only way that the man can keep sight of who he is and destiny is when faith is activated. The bible says "The just shall live by faith (Gal:3.11). When we live by faith we can come out of the natural process of living. We can become agents of change that the world knows that we are of God. What the man has to do in this hour is to know the importance of faith and yes I can. I believe when the man has faith with yes I can he becomes a force for the devil.

The reason this can happen is when we come into faith we get heaven on our side and an amazing force. Now, what I discovered is while this is working in our lives we can't be moved by the pressure. Sir, you do not have to be moved by your setback that it forces you to commit to trouble. You serve a more powerful God than that who desires you to be in faith and say yes I can rise. You can rise above robbery, drugs, shootings, etc. only when faith has erased your past for the future. Now, faith is powerful enough to do that but only when you are in agreement. What you must be bold enough to do is to say Yes I can in faith and trust God for what he has said.

I love sharing with the men in lockup as I did today while many of them were sitting on the bench in processing. What I was sharing with them was their faith will have a huge role in their outcome while in lockup. This was an amazing moment that God allowed without interruptions of a lockdown. Sir, what the enemy is doing with power right now is coming after the man who has no faith. Now, since the enemy knows this man has no faith he knows this man is full of words like I can't. As long as this man is saying I can't the enemy knows all his hidden abilities takes a big hit. The man's abilities take a big hit and the greatest hit is his faith and his hope while he perishes in trouble.

I am witnessing on a daily basis in lockup a large number of men who faith and hope died while on trial. Yes, their faith and hope died on trial while they were going through the test of look like it's over. Sir, I have a question for you? Are you going through something in your life and it looks like it's over?. Let me submit to you that by faith 99% of that is to get you to throw in the towel and give up. I believe right now if you come into faith and say yes I can you will see the hand of God. Sir, I'm here to tell you that it is nothing but a test that takes faith to pass with words like yes I can. I believe when the man can say yes I can and the test has said no you can't a miracle can take place.

I believe God desires me to say yes I can in faith knowing that God has the ability to do anything he desires. What I must do as a man is to let the devil and my situation know that I am of God and I can. I truly believe most test, trials, and setbacks that send the man to lockup needed a word of faith. The word of faith easily could have been if I wait on God I can be the best man for the wait. Sir, if you wait on God with faith and yes I can what you are trying to obtain you will see was yours anyway. All you have to do as a man is say yes I can long enough and soon your wait is over. Now, it may appear that it is taking a long time for you but God is not going against what his word says.

The bible says I can do all things through Christ which strengthens me.(Phill:4.13). The issue is for the man to know this that he can be free and many free from lockup. I have talked to many men in lockup that are here because they relied on their thoughts. Sir, your thoughts is no match for the devil when he is the author of confusion. What the devil is doing is confusing the man who has little knowledge of God and no education. I see this again among our young men who are coming to prison at an all-time high that can't even read. Young man, I'm here to tell you if you can't read get back in school. It doesn't matter what the situation was when you quit there are many opportunities to finish.

Trust me when I say after my six-year study in the prison that the devil has a confirmed reservation for dropouts. These reservations are being made every day by the devil as we take them in. Sir, it is time for you as a man to get some faith and yes I can about your life. I know that you can win if you just believe you can and stop the devil from saying you can't. When God made man he equipped him to win every battle that comes his way. I believe this is because the man has God's image inside of him but requires faith and confidence. I knew the moment that I said I can't become a Warrant officer because it's too hard the devil would celebrate. The reason that the devil would celebrate is now I can't becomes my way of life.

Sir, what you must know as a man is whatever you say out of your mouth it is so. The bible says "Death and life is in the power of the tongue. (Prov:18.21). I believe when man says I can't he speaks death to his dreams and destiny. The roads of life begin to get dark and lockup begins to get clear.

Faith and the yes I can mindset can bring hope back to his memory that he was created to overcome. We can overcome what the world brings our way but we can never do it thinking we are defeated. Every act that is against us in the flesh is against what we were made to be in the spirit. Now, it is time for every man to realize that your flesh is always going in the direction of this world. This is why I am seeing so many young men coming to prison for the same thing because flesh is at work. I truly believe one of the most devastating things with this we are seeing again is with school shootings. These are young men with flesh at work, hope is lost and I can't is alive.

Sir, your spirit operates in faith and saying yes I can and you can see miracles come your way and bless you. I know that tough times appear to run you down in the worst moment to ruin your entire day. God is keeping a watch over your life and desires you to become the greatest comeback report. I can only imagine how hard things may have been if it seems as though you can't see your way. Trust me when I say now is the time for you and that time is right now when you only believe. I believe if you begin this day saying yes I can even if it hurts in a moment there will be joy. Yes, I was hurting when I was unemployed and bills were due and I had no money.

I kept looking up to heaven with tears in my eyes and faith in my heart saying yes I can make it and God showed up. I am here to tell every man that you were born to be a yes I can man for your family. What I have witnessed at the prison is a generation of men of I can't do it. The issue is yes they can't do it on their own because it takes their faith and their yes in God. I am on a mission to get in the minds of men with a passion to get in the faith and in the game. I say this because far too many of our young men are on the sidelines of I can't and make the roster of lockup. I look at the roster in lockup on a daily basis and I am amazed by the offenses I can't brings.

I am pleading to every parent to be the best in your effort to tell your young man that yes he can. I say that because once he gets here to lockup he is in unfortunately more I can't than he will be in yes I can. Now, I do have some of the greatest young men here who are yes I can men that just made mistakes. My goal is to have as many young men this year to know and believe that they are yes I can men. When you walk in faith and become a yes I can man you can change the course of life. The reason why this can happen is you now have the confidence to defy natural laws. What I mean here is those natural laws that say you are a failure because of where you come from.

Faith and the yes I can attitude can bring heavens blessings that the world can't stop. Sir, all you need to do is decide right now that you are in no way going to end up in lockup. When you make this decision you are paving the way for God to do something amazing in you. What happens to most men that have experienced failure for so long is failure adopts their past. When failure adopts their past it puts a blanket of no hope on their future and settles in their mind.

Now, this young man has no visibility of a future because failure has given him a new name that brings him comfort. Faith becomes an essential tool attached with yes I can to dismantle the stronghold. Many of our young men do not know of this tactic that the enemy is using to target the best of boys. This tactic the devil is using is nothing new because the enemy tried it on me as a young teenager. What the devil has done over the years is camouflaged his identity behind quick money schemes. Now, the devil is allowing it through schemes that are quick and rapid arrests. Young man, you can't outsmart the system forever and soon you will be caught unless you change now.

Faith and yes I can takes on a new dimension that destroys the devils plans due to God's intervention. Yes, God intervenes the minute you believe that he is able to do it for you and for his glory. Sir, this is your hour to get your best game face on to where you desire to go in the earth. When you desire to go as high as God desires you to go there will be no turning back to your past. I believe this will be because you will not believe where faith can take a man who has been defeated. This is where my faith took me when I began to trust God and walk in faith and say yes to God. I know when I came into the faith I felt heaven all around me saying I am backing you always.

Sir, this is what God wants to do for you when you have faith and release out of your mouth yes I can. I said this while the enemy was shooting at the helicopter I was on in Baghdad but heaven surrounded me. When the man cry out to God in faith for what he is believing for the enemy can't contain him. Young man you can cry out to God about your situation in faith and something must change. What I can assure you will change by faith is the way it was before you called on him. I am here to tell you that when I called on God in faith and believed my situation changed in a mighty way. It may not have changed the way I wanted it but it changed for my good and my purpose.

Faith and the yes I can man in this hour will notify his purpose that a shakeup is stirring up his identity. This is the man that God has been looking for to say yes Lord in all of his work that God can reveal purpose. Sir, now is the time for you to call on God now that trouble take a back seat to your future. Let me say that if it will not glorify God with what you are doing STOP NOW. Let God start

Jeffery Mathews

something new in you with a made-up mind with purpose and faith with a yes I can spirit. I believe you are on your way with the new beginning that has been waiting for your decision to change. Now that by faith change is upon you chains are coming off you of lack and not enough. The devil thought that he had you in a place that your trouble will last you all the way to lockup. Not so, I believe and declare that you are spiritually pregnant with twins called faith and yes Lord. Upon this new birth in you there shall be celebrations for new heights, new visions, and much new life.

Chapter 9

SATAN'S DEMASKING OF THE MAN

When I look at the crisis that the enemy is bringing in the lives of even great men I am seeing a demasking taking place. The way that the enemy is doing this is by literally removing the image off the man given by God. Now, he is doing this by causing the man in any way he can to violate principles he knows is not of God. The moment the man violates the principles and laws of God Satan moves in. The first thing Satan wants to remove quickly as possible is any appearance of righteous living. When the man demonstrates the likeness of God in his walk, talk, and actions, he is a threat to the devil. Now, it is time for the devil to cause this man to violate God's ways by an act of violence.

In the devil's eyes when he can cause this man to bow down with any act he has just removed or demasked this man. When I sat down and spoke to many of the men in lockup a lot of them said I don't believe I did that. Now, many of these men were great educators, lawyers, doctors, and yes preachers. Here's the key, the devil doesn't care about who you are in the world as long as he can take off your mask. Remember, the devil knows scriptures and he was one of God's angels and lost his identity. What I keep trying to bring to men is Satan is mad about that and is after every man's identity. The devil cares less about the fact that I preach the gospel or teach at the university.

Since the devil lost his identity he is working overtime to get every man demasked that he could lose his identity as well. First, the devil is after those men who walk humbly before God but is on the fence with relationship. Secondly, he is after those who have yet committed to Christ that they never know Him. Now, yes the devil is after all of us but some of us have made up our minds that we are serving Christ only. With this made up mind to Him only does not mean that we have arrived. What it does mean is that every day we keep our eyes in His word and meditate day and night while we worship. What I discovered in doing this I am not giving the enemy any downtime with Christ.

See, what I have discovered is the moment I get idle this is the time I open up for Satan to go to work on me. Young man I am here to tell you as a believer in Christ you can get the power that is unmovable. When you get to know God and walk in faith and trust him he will meet all your needs and cover you. What I discovered is when I develop a relationship with him the devil must come through God. Many great men are in lockup because their ability to not be demasked was stolen. The way it was stolen was they were uncertain about themselves when they had a choice to make. I am a witness that when you commit to God and walk out his promises your mask is unmovable.

The reason that the enemy could not remove the image or demask me was I had taken away my own thoughts. Sometimes we as men have a tendency to trust our own thoughts to be a product of perfection. This can raise our level of confidence in ourselves from how the world around us perceives us. When I received Christ in my life my thoughts no longer had rule over me or my future. Sir, when you come into a new life with Christ you have a new identity that Satan is after. Now, when you are functioning on the earth on your own you have no worry about being demasked. Satan is allowing you to have your way because he knows you are a blink from trouble.

The bible says "because as he is so are we in this world (1 John4.17) and the devil know this is crucial in the earth. Yes, the devil knows that this man who walks by faith in this verse has much power in the earth. This is a man with a relationship with God with an identity that the devil desires to demasked. This is a man also that has totally committed to God's promises and all of his provisions. This is where God desires every man of faith to walk in and live by and the devil can only threaten. Now, what the devil has done in the lives of many men of no faith is threatened them and stripped them. When this took place men didn't even know who they were and fail the test.

Sir, when you and I know that as he is (Jesus) so are we this strips the devil of his rights in our life. The only way that we do not have authority over our situations is the devil has demasked us from purpose. Young man, you do not have to continue to think that you can't be all that you can be right now. When you walk in faith and call on God you can reclaim destiny and get back into the game of life. Now, the devil desires you to get in trouble that you get life from the judge at the court. You as a man do not have to settle for that any longer if you can embrace your true destiny. By faith you can recover right now with this verse alone in faith and watch life become new.

I have witnessed enough men from many territories come to lockup with their true destiny demasked by their trouble. Now, their trouble was an act of the devil because they were not the original author of their demise. I say that because as a man they came from God originally but were demasked under pressure. The pressure of this world has demasked so many men that the prisons are overcrowded. I say they are overcrowded due to the pressure brought by the devil to remove their identity. This removal of identity has led great men to robbery, murder, and many we see now to sexual harassment. Now come on man, we know this is not normal for so many men to go down at once.

I am here to tell you after these six years working in the prison I have seen the face of men that is different than on their I.D. card. Now, I am not seeing this in the natural but I am seeing this in the spirit. Here's the key, yes this is the same man but the difference is his identity is demasked and replaced by a number. Sir, here's what I am saying, the devil is now in the business of demasking identities with numbers. Now, what the devil is doing with this is putting the true man with the number of troubled men. I am here to tell you there are a huge number of troubled men. What the devil also knows is the best place to get this done is in lockup. Yes sir, the devil wants to strip every man of his true identity to lockup that he loses sight of destiny. The devil is into details and he is also into numbers as I saw them while working at the prison. Now, not every man loses sight of destiny in prison but many have and many will because they lose hope. I am here to expose the devil to men of destiny and who desires to be all he can be for the glory of God.

I received revealed knowledge from God while working at the men's prison that is vital to the whole man. By faith I received it based on hearing from God with a deep relationship I have with him **personally.** I will say it like this, my mother name was **Mary** (like Jesus) my father name was **Joe or Joseph** (like Jesus) and I rose on the **3rd day** of June from my mother's womb like Jesus rose on the 3rd day from the grave. Now, I can go on and on like my last name is Mathews symbolic of the first book of the New Testament. I said all that to say this, once again the bible says "as he is so are we in this world. I take this personally and believe this by faith and use it on the devil that I belong to God. All this I received by revelation knowledge from God for the earth. (Ephes: 1.17).

Now, by faith, all of us belong to God who believes in him and has made him Lord of our life. The call on my life as a fisherman of men is to empower all men that we are the image of God and he loves us. In doing that I must walk in the power of God that is in me and receive from heaven spiritual insight. I have been doing this study for six years in men and everything is crystal clear. I am on a spiritual journey for God to bring men into the knowledge of God that they may be free. As I do this I am careful that I do not get too deep that I might sound too far out for the natural mind. Sir, all I am saying again is the devil is after everything that is like God in the man.

What one of his main goals is to get us comfortable with the unstable and compromising world as men. Yes, he is trying daily of getting us to look like the average man who has no real knowledge of God. What I have also discovered in lockup is how the devil has a snapshot of nearly every man. Remember, we take in an average of 40 new men a day in prison without fail. Now, think about that, this is a lot of images or snapshots on a yearly basis that comes to prison. Here's what I am saying, there is somebody that has come through our prison that looks like you and me. One day the intake nurse came to my supply room and said she needed a knee brace for an inmate.

Now, she asked me did I have a certain size and she would send the inmate to me to pick it up with an order slip from her. As the nurse walked out my door she said the inmate that needs it looks just like you. I said to her YEAH RIGHT!. When the inmate came to my office with the order I looked at him and nearly passed out. The reason why I nearly passed out was that it was like I saw my twin. Yes, this guy looked just like me and I thought the intake nurse was joking. What am I saying, the devil is not playing with his tactics of demasking the man. Sir, this is just one intake prison in Alabama where overcrowding is at an all-time high and running over. My encouragement to every man that desires to be great for

God is to stay with God. The man that desires to be on his own I am here to tell you that the devil has our images on lockdown. All he knows that he needs to do is to push your button of pressure and emotion and you are in lockup. Guys, this is all the devil has done to get all of these big-name personalities into sex crimes. Sir, you know you are going to jail if found guilty in this.

Let me give you another real example of this like image. There was one gentleman also at the prison I will just call him Mr. B. that really blew my mind. I say this because the first time I saw him I ran to get a co-worker of mine Mr. Swinney. I ran to get Mr. Swinney because I wanted to show him the man who was the exact image of my father. Mr. father and mother went to be with the Lord. Now, this was so clear to me that it was scary. This gentleman has my father's exact facial features, exact short stature of 5'6, exact demeanor, exact salt and pepper hair color, etc. God did not reveal to me at that time what he has reveal to me now regarding what Satan has done with images of man. Here is what's so real about this. I have worked at this prison for six years and this person has been there my entire time.

What is unusual about this was it is not often at this facility that many inmates stay here that long of a period. They usually get transferred to other facilities. God is amazing at his work. Now, this guy is a wonderful gentleman and I told him how much he reminds me of my father. When he would come down daily to get his medicine he would make sure he stops by my office to say hello. I loved talking to this gentleman because it was almost as I was talking to my father again. Here's what I do know about all this, God reveals in the spirit the deep things of God. (1Corr:2.10). Sir, you may not get all this but I believe God. What I desire to do is to get the man to know that now is the time to walk with God and pray.

I want to speak with the power and authority in me to the man that is on the edge to submit to God now. You and I know that you are too close to making a big mistake that can cause you to lose it all. Now sir, listen to me for a second, I can hear what the spirit is saying to us and the church real clear. The bible says "He who has an ear, let him hear what the spirit says to the churches. (Rev:3.6) Sir, by faith we are the church and God desires us to take heed of what he is saying to every man. Now is the time for you to get closer to God and walk with him that your identity remains in him. The enemy is more powerful than what we think and can cover more territory than you and I.

One thing is for certain, God can cover you and I and the whole universe and put the devil where he belongs. I believe that we are living in a time where the man that desires true destiny and true life needs God. The devil is after I believe every man that he freezes him in his tracks of purpose and dismantle him. What he wants to dismantle is our identity and get us demasked from who God called us. The only way to stay with your identity is to stay with God as he leads you. Now, unfortunately the devil is doing a decent job on having men with him that leads them to lockup. Sir, you can still realize your dream regardless of what it looks like, but it does matter where you are looking. If you are looking to the world or the devil to meet your needs it could lead to great disappointment. The bible says "Looking unto Jesus, the author and finisher of our faith (Hebrews 12.2). I am confident that if all men would look to Jesus they can accomplish their dream against the odds.

I want to say to all men this is not the time to walk in uncertainty because this says to the devil here I am. Sir, you need to walk in confidence and in faith that the devil is not demasking you of your gift. When the devil strips you of your identity he can strip you of your future and this has spelled trouble for men. Sir, I believe today you are on your way to that place that you were born to be. That place is at the top of your mountain that was designed for nobody but you with only your image.

Who Are You To You

I discovered in talking to many men in lockup that it is important to know who you are to you in the earth. I say that because many of them came to prison with no clue of a positive image of themselves. Most of the young men only knew of themselves from the damage done by their troubled world. I am here to encourage men that you were not born to be judged by the makeup of your circumstances. What purpose requires is establishing the reason of your birth and the power within it. What I knew was critical as I was going through my pain was who am I to myself in the pain. I began to think about the fact that I am not going through alone therefore I am still somebody.

Sir, I know the mountain could be hard to climb all alone but you are not all alone when you are in faith. The trouble that may be tempting you to lockup has an underline factor of you knowing who you are. What you need to know is that you are more than a conquer in Christ Jesus and you are not alone. There is hidden talent all in you that is covered by the perception you have about yourself. Here's the question, who are you to you not when things are good but when things are a mess? What most of the men that are here in lockup were locked up when things were a mess somewhere. The problem will always arise with your freedom when the pressure point is on your natural man. Now, it will not come against your spirit man or the real you because there you know who you are.

When I was just hanging around the crowd of religious folks who just went to church I accepted what they accepted. What I am saying is listening to their stories if they accepted average so did I. When trials came at the people I was around they would say things like It Is What It Is and they accepted it. Well, the problem with that is that would go against God's word and they saw themselves as average. Once again the bible says we are more than conquerors

(Rom:8.37) and I must see myself that way. I no longer as a man and a believer have to cave into the slave mentality from Egypt. Sir, you were made by God to have your identity paved on the breastplate of your heart.

The devil will keep sending a great number of men to lockup until they know who they are to themselves. Now, the importance is there must be a method in the mind of the man to reprogram his thinking. I have watched so many young men come to prison held hostage before they arrived. Most of these men were held hostage by their world which never allowed them a chance to meet themselves. I saw this coming from the projects because it is hard to identity greatness from a **poverty platform.** The only way that this can be done is if there is a dream inside of you that overrides your natural platform. Not many young men get this opportunity unless he is some outstanding athlete.

God is calling men from the highway of conviction that you are much bigger than the world you came from. Now is the time for every man to take a good look at not just who he is but from whom he came from. I am here to tell every man that you are the greatest when you say you are with your mouth. The key is this, the moment you call yourself a winner a winner's identity began to take shape. This changed everything for me knowing that most of my life appeared to belong to the what's left generation. When this takes root in a man he can began to back away from who he is. Now, the world can begin to present a world of **Come and Get It** and when he does he gets it and gets locked up.

Let me encourage you sir to daily step into that mirror with faith and declare that I am a new man today. Declare that you are a new man with a new vision that will allow you to break out of your zone. What the world may have done to you is what it did to me while I was in my zone of not enough. One day I heard the voice of God saying when are you going to say about you what

I say about you. I said "O MY GOD" Lord forgive me for my lack of knowledge about who I am in you. What happened next? I rededicated my life to Christ and I came into a new beginning with God and me.

I was reaffirmed by God that I was the salt of the earth (Matt: 5.13) and was making no attempt to make a difference. The problem was I was not salt of the earth to me because of how I saw myself. Now, I see myself by faith because of who I am in Christ with a new determination as a difference maker. NEWS FLASH!! Sir, you owe it to yourself to think about yourself as God thinks of you. Now, once again you can't focus on what's before you but who is for you that you make a difference. I am confident that many men lose their freedom and come to lockup because of this very thing. In the world that we live in today men that are not sure of themselves are found in lockup.

I believe sir when you come into faith you can come into discovering who you are to you right now. I am confident that knowing who you are to you now can redirect your past and define your future. I saw this work for me quickly once I came in agreement with God that I was not just here. What causes so many of these young men to come to lockup is they just think they are here to breath. No sir, as men we are here to start new worlds of families with our wives at our side. In doing this we must come to know our selves and see ourselves just as God sees us in him.

I am on a mission to get men to study the word of God that they may know who they are to themselves. This was critical for me going into combat because I could only rely on God and how I saw myself. This is symbolic of the worst battle in your life that will have an outcome of who you were in the battle. Now, I am here to tell you that I knew who I was to God first before I knew who I was in this battle. I believe every man can cause the devil to tremble when we discover who we are in God. When we do this I believe we have the devil on the run trying to find us. The reason why the devil can't find us is we have found ourselves in Christ and in new identity. The issue is God is waiting for us as men to know how they are to themselves that he can use us. Now, remember the devil wants to use men especially young men in the way they are seen now. When the devil use young men he is using them to commit crimes that lead to lockup. This is why I was very consistent on speaking a word of hope especially to the man who was being released. What I wanted to make sure was that I reminded him that he is somebody that God can use. I especially wanted to spend some time with him to find out who he was to himself.

God is calling us as men to know him deeply that we can walk and talk with him that we learn of ourselves. The more that I began to know of God I began to grow out of systems that were not for my good. This also included relationships that were hindering me from discovering all I am to God. Sir, it just might be time for you to look to new and greater influences that may be holding you hostage. What is so dangerous right now among men is they can hold themselves hostage unknowingly. What the devil can do is make you so comfortable in your state of mind that it feels right. The problem with that is just because it feels right does not make it right for your future.

What is right for your future is for you and I as men to know who we are in the battle and the battle can be won. It doesn't matter if your battle is a job problem, marriage problem, addiction problem, God is able. You have the potential right now by faith to change the direction of your storm with words. Your words as a man who is confident of himself can touch the airways of heaven and get results. When I was living in the projects I said I was going in the Army to make a difference as I am. Now, I said that shortly after I didn't make the cut on my high school basketball team. I said that with confidence because I was disappointed and I knew that disappointment could ruin my identity.

I knew that I had the gift and talent to make the team but not necessarily the size to compete with the rest. What I decided to do was to use my God-given gifts and talents that I always live by faith. When a man lives by this kind of faith he can stand against the odds if he only knows who he is. Knowing who I was to God and myself allowed me to break a color barrier as a Chief Warrant officer in Alabama. Sir, you can break barriers in your world when you know who are you to you. Now, like I was you may not be much to the people around you but I am here to tell you that does not matter. What God wants to know from you and me is whatever you desire do you believe he is able. (Matt:9.28).

Sir, let me encourage you to spend this entire day saying to yourself with confidence I am the man God's been looking for. What you are doing is building up what is already in you to knock down walls. Some of the best young men that have come to this prison I believe were three words from never coming to prison. Today I believe those three words are I Am Somebody. I say that because I believe when a man say I am **somebody** you notify the devil in hell that I am not just **anybody**. Sir, I believe you cause hell to tremble when you declare that you are somebody in the sight of God. Now, you must stay in this mindset for the rest of your life because there is more for you. What the devil will try to do is rob you because you don't see it yet. You and I must be men of patience that we allow God to be God in us at his appointed time. What I am here to tell you is that yes, there is an appointed time for you and I to reign on the earth. What I also believe is that time is at the end of our faith in knowing who we are to ourselves.

I knew once again what the system thought of me that I worked with for twenty years and that was incompetent. Now, I looked up the definition of incompetent and it says not fit or capable. That didn't make me feel good about how the system thought about me but it was up to me to fix that. I begin to think about where God had brought me from coming from the projects and enduring in combat. I refused to be defined by the systems identity of me and began to know what I thought about me. I began to think I am strong in God and I have strong faith. I began to remember that the angel of the Lord appeared to Gideon and said The Lord is with you, you mighty man of valor. (Judges 6:12). I believe by faith that God sees you and me sir as a man of valor.

What must be done now with confidence is for us to see ourselves strong in determination and character. A man of valor is a man of strength who can overcome the pressure from any outside force. I believe the first step in turning your life around as a man is having a strong mind and strong faith. One of the things that I discovered takes great men down to lockup is a deceived mind of character. This mind can lead the man to act on any form of crime because a deceived mind is blind to obedience. Hence, this is a mind that will not conform to laws but act of impulse. Sir, when you know who you are to you now you can take authority over the impulse as well as the act.

I am watching crimes committed daily on the news and can see through the man that this is his condition. These acts are no different than the large number of inmates that I speak with on a daily basis. As I study most of their cases in the spirit under the anointing God reveals to me the underline issue. What I do know is this, that man that is lost in who he is to himself is in real trouble. The reason why he is lost in himself is because he is lost in God but with God he can be found. The devil is opening up many cans of opportunity for the man to go down right before our eyes. It appears sometimes that even some churches are missing the importance of their people knowing who they are.

I am a firm believer that there is no way that I can know all about myself until I know God personally and intimately. I am so grateful that the first of our growth track in our church is to know God. Knowing God I believe clears the airways that the word of God can do the impossible now. Sir, the impossible can be done in your life if you can keep hope alive in you for greatness. I am here to tell you that you are not average even though your circumstances may say differently. If you can say I am somebody with deep conviction trouble will no longer enter your mind. What will enter into your mind is I am a man who now knows that there is hope for me. God wants you to know him personally that a new light comes upon you. Some of these crimes in men that are coming through this prison came through a doubled-minded man. (James 1:8) This was a man that meant well one moment then in a flash meant for bad.

One of the ways the enemy is using this in men today is with his ways that lead to sexual harassment. Sir, now is the time to think yourself into that man in control of who he is and not out of control. Lockup is full of men who allowed a confused identity to cause them to make the wrong decision. The way that you and I prevent that in this season to is to be confident of who we are and who we are called by God.

The Man And The Masterpiece

The bible says " we are God's masterpiece created in Christ Jesus for good works(Ephes:2.10 NLT) and I believe if a man can embrace this he can overcome. What most of us is accustomed to is accepting what the world has presented before us. What I am encouraging men is there is something about us that God decided to make us great. Now, what our world around us is continuing to do is to push us over the river of not good enough. When this takes place all the energy I have to accomplish a dream could wither in the sea of doubt. What I have to believe as a man and God's masterpiece is I can go back to school in faith. When I go back to school in faith all of the dreams I lost in doubt are restored back to my view.

When I can believe that I am God's masterpiece I believe I am fitted to be the best at what I commit to do. It doesn't matter that the world say I am incompetent God has a master plan for my life. Now, I did not get the promotion in the system I worked for twenty years but God promoted me in his kingdom. God later showed me in the spirit that his master plan for me was much greater than that system. I discovered that God desires all men to walk in faith that his master plan is alive. When God's master plan is acknowledged in the life of the man, God's masterpiece is active in the earth. Sir, you and I must get to the point that we recognize that God has favored us.

When God placed his favor upon us we were able to do the most amazing things in the earth with confidence. What the devil has done is created a mixture of barriers to keep men from walking out his masterpiece. These barriers come in various forms that the man steps his feet in a trap. Once the man is trapped he wonders in the darkness of pity and shame and Satan stills God's plan. Sir, you may be wondering in pity and shame of the setback but I am here to tell you it's not over. When we were made as a man and God's masterpiece an ingredient of comeback is in you. This is what makes us strong and able to turn it around if we never give in and quit.

I truly believe that if the man can embrace his identity as God's masterpiece he can be revived and restored. When I walk in the prison daily and past all these men I often say if they only knew and believed. Now is the time sir for you to know that you are God's masterpiece created for good work. Now, the work that is in you is only waiting for you to believe that it only needs activating. I believe when the man activates the masterpiece in him we can fix the overcrowding in prison as well. I say that because when we realize we are God's masterpiece we truly have much work. What is so amazing about knowing you are his masterpiece is all the tools you need to succeed are available.

God will pour out favor over the life of the man that his honor shows up as we reach other men with honor. I believe the work that God has for us when we know what we have can turn young men around. What young men are looking for is someone who they can admire and imitate that is worthy. My heart would hurt as I talked with these men in lockup as to what really troubled them. What I am fully committed to in this hour is pouring out my heart upon men with compassion. What I know about the young men in lockup was some never had a father to mentor hope. Our society of young men is being trampled with false persuasion that is robbing them one by one. I want to speak to every young man that has never witnessed that man in your home. There is an image in you given by God for you to be the best man as well as the best father in your community.

The image that is in you is the image of a masterpiece that you can imitate that can bring you hope. I know that things might have been very blurry but there is light at the end of the tunnel for you. You are filled with an image of **hope** that the devil would like to fill with **dope** and cause you to **mope**. Now, what I have witnessed in lockup is when this took place trouble was at their fingertips. The reason why trouble was there is that the enemy knows the next step from mopping. The pathway for the man becomes a cloud for poor decisions and a footstool for deception. In a twinkling of an eye you can be rescued with a decision of I am God's masterpiece.

When I made the mistakes that I made coming out of the projects what kept me was I knew God wasn't mad. I begin to feel like I still had a chance to recover from the inside that my outside wasn't hindered. Sir, let me encourage you that God is not mad at you because of what you may have done. If you can think and know that repentance is available from the inside, your outside can be changed. I am daily troubled by the men that I see in lockup whose outside has been hindered. Lockup hinders your outside that you are not able to take your dreams to the people outside. When you began to know that by faith you can be God's masterpiece on display you get a new mind.

When I walked away from the old mind that I once had I developed a new mind that I might be a witness. When the new man grows and matures in the new mind hope began to reveal new insight. I began to see some things that I never saw that the world kept from me again that dashed hope. Yes, there is a lot of hope dashing going on in the world and the devil is the master artist. When I see all the robbery and murders going on from the news I say to myself I know what that is. What I discovered talking with all these guys who have done those very acts it is amazing. What I found out is a man with little or no hope in his heart to win is very strong in his head for failure.

What I also discovered is this failure in his head has overtaken his ability to **refocus, recover** and **reload.** You see, when you and I as a man hit **bottom** by faith we have what it takes to **refocus** to the **top**. We can do this as a man because we have been given by God as his masterpiece power to **recover**. Now, when we fall we do not stay down because we have God's image and we **reload**. This is what Joseph did when he hit the bottom of the pit when thrown in by his brothers.(Gen:37.24). I am confident that when you know that you are God's masterpiece there's hope. With this kind of hope, you will see that there is still much room for you and your dream. The world's system may appear to you that there is no room but this requires great faith. This is where you can refocus and see yourself through a new set of lenses you never discovered. When I was turned around for my third failure at the academy I went back with new eyesight. I knew that I must refocus in order to graduate that I no longer will be laughed at.

The moment I refocused and went to the academy as God's masterpiece I began to see myself in recovery. I began to recover after I graduated and the first thing God showed me was I could be used by him. God allowed me to be in a leadership position that the people had never seen by my race. I began to feel the glory of the Lord allowing me to recover all that I had lost in all my failures. Sir, now is the time to not look at your failures and disappointments but how God can allow you to recover. When God allow you to recover he will bring you the blessings you though you have lost. God's man as his masterpiece can be recovered with grace that the world will never know.

I believe we are in a time right now when man began to pray to God for forgiveness he can recover much. As I stay in contact with some of the men that were in lockup I see how God is so amazing. When man can come to know God and ask for forgiveness God can wipe his slate clean and use him. I shout for joy in the lives of these men when I see them recover what was lost in time. Sir, what I want you to know is you have the opportunity to see God's amazing hand now. I desire for you to stay free by staying connected to God and watch him work out your troubles. You do not have to think that because you may not be rich that your troubles are everlasting.

You may feel that you are poor and live in the projects like I did and God doesn't hear you. The bible says "This poor man cried out, and the Lord heard him, and saved him out of all his troubles. (Psalm 34:6). Listen to me sir, God loves you and still care for you so much that he see you as his masterpiece. The only way that you don't recover from where you may be is you lost hope, God have not lost you. I believe there is much ahead for you in your future when you decide to do the right thing. What I discovered with some of these men in lockup was doing the right thing was doing anything. The problem with that is when you just do anything you must face consequences.

What I want you to know sir is you were not born to just do anything; you were born to do mighty things. These mighty things are things that can be a blessing to others as you bless God in the process. Now, I know that may sound churchy but I want to speak to your **real man** with **real words**. When I say your real man I mean your inward man that was made to respond to the things that are spiritual. I am so tired of seeing great men go to lockup because of responding to natural things. Listen to me guys, robbery, murder, rape, domestic violence etc.. these are all natural things. What is happening daily as I watch the news men are responding to natural things that are not you. Yes, when these are carried out or committed by the man he must face the charges. What I am saying is this is not what the man was made for and the devil knows it so he speaks. When the devil speaks and says "punch that woman" that came from a natural perspective for natural consequences. The natural consequences are after the punch comes rough results and possibly lockup.

One of our top city officials were arrested the other day for punching his girlfriend in the face with his fist. This is a man who is well respected. He later resigned. Now, this could have come from a natural perspective that yielded natural consequences. Sir, again what the enemy wants from the man is a quick response to natural things. Now, your spirit man would walk away from the things not of the spirit. I truly am praying that men learn how to identify the things that are of the spirit. Remember, Jesus said the words that I speak they are spirit and they are life (John 6:63). I know that Jesus is not going to speak and tell me to punch a woman or rape her therefore it is the devil.

In order for the man to position himself to identify these is always having a desire to do the right thing. I love thinking that I am God's masterpiece because it keeps me having that desire to bring change. My desire was to bring change to the thinking of men in lockup when I uttered one word. You see, when men think long enough on who God called him to be the likeness of God by faith shows up. My prayer to God now is for him to allow my words I speak to men touch their hearts. What I mean is I truly want their hearts to burn with conviction from the word of God. The bible says "And they said one to another, did not our hearts burn within us while he talked with us on the road, and while he opened the scriptures to us. (Luke 24:32).

I believe in this hour God is looking for men that can pour out his love and care upon one another as hearts burn. I loved to do this at the prison because many times I would see tears of joy in men. I would see this often in them especially when I would pour into their hearts God's love. Like Jesus, this would happen as I talked with them. I believe as I pour out the love of God in men that they are God's masterpiece change will come. I am confident that the numbers are dwindling daily of men of standards. What I am saying here is we need more men with the masterpiece spirit. I believe God is searching the entire earth for that man who is willing to be different for his kingdom.

What this man is going to require is kingdom minded footsteps that are willing to take fiery darts. These will be darts that may even be fired from your own people who are mad that you are not like them. I have decided that I am going to be that man to tell another man like you that you are amazing. I mean that you are so amazing to God that he has stacks of blessings for you regardless of what you've done. What I want to speak to the man today is hope can cut you a new set of orders. I know that it may have been a little dismal for you in the past, but again a new set of orders are cut. In these orders God is calling you a new man now and the benefit package is great. You are called by faith God's masterpiece with all rights and privileges granted that you lack nothing. Don't think about your past now, because your past is under the blood and to never return. What this is for you is that day that you have been hoping for and the day that you can only dream of. Now sir, I am speaking words that are straight from heaven straight to your doorsteps.

These are words by faith of cleanup that are designed to clean any man's heart up as his life gets cleaned up. I can feel the spirit of the Lord in my fingertips as I am writing this just for your good. I am confident as the man writing this book that I am God's chosen vessel to make men hearts burn for him. Remember, Jesus said he that believe on me, the works that I do shall he do also, and greater works than these shall he do. (John14:12). My goal in the earth with this assignment is to reach men and perfect them in his word from lockup.

Chapter 10

MAN UP OR LOCKUP

I am confident after this six year study on the job at lockup that man must either man up or face lockup. I say this because at the pace the devil is on in the lives of men there are not many choices for men. What it really has come to is either we man up to be all God called us to be or trouble is near. Remember, the bible says "Man who is born of woman is of few days full of trouble. (Job:14.1). Guys, from what I have seen in my six-year journey working at the prison trouble has our number. Now, when I say that I mean we are walking in a world full of trouble that has power to lead many to trouble.

Now, you and I may not be personally affected with trouble, but I can assure you as a man trouble will try us. Trouble especially will attempt to try those of us who tries to fully obey God and laws. What I have discovered in lockup is this thing called trouble has a hidden agenda that flares in a second. What I am saying here is one minute the man was free and in seconds he is in handcuffs. Sir, all I am saying is this is the time for you and I to make up our mind as to who are we going to serve. Here's why I say that. I have seen some of the greatest men of influence come to jail. Now, some of them were not for long but the fact of the matter they came and established a record.

You and I as a man was never created by God to establish records in that manner, but establish a legacy for his name. The reason I believe I am seeing so many great men going down is they are under some delusion. When I say that I mean they believe either their title, name, money, etc..they are untouchable. Sir, **EXCUSE ME, NEWS FLASH**, in lockup I have issued shoes and eyeglasses to all these guys. Yes sir, and guess what they had all the above but they realize now they did have much. Most of them I talked with personally told me that they did not have connection with God. What they were all living by was their own identity and status and bowed down to the devil.

Now is the time for man to man up and understand that his abilities alone are not enough to out-think the devil. Here's what's key, all your money, fame, status is far beneath the devil when he wants you. Let me say right up front here that the reason he wants you is he sees your worldly honor. Now, let me say here nothing is wrong with having success because we are children of God. Success belongs to us. What the devil wants to see is we are all about the world that he can redirect out thinking. When the devil redirects our thinking it is never the direction that is pleasing for God or mankind. I am confident that as men we must open up the eyes that really matter.

The eyes that I am speaking of are our spiritual eyes that we can see the man that God desires us to be. Guys, I am here to tell you that your natural eyes only care about the natural world's perception. The problem is when the natural results shows up from natural trouble perception is absent at the courthouse. When this occurs in most cases the man is lead out in chains on his way to lockup. When I think about all those names of athletes, news anchors, actors that fell it must open our eyes. Now, I am on a mission for God like never before to open the spiritual eyes of men that they see. The bible says "To open their eyes, and to turn them from darkness to light, and from the power of Satan unto God, that they may receive forgiveness of sins, and inheritance among them which are sanctified by faith that is in me. (Acts 26:18).

What I am confident about with this is that the enemy has kept men eyes closed intentionally that he falls. Right now what we are seeing is how devastating the fall has become among men in America. What I have witnessed in the last six years working at the prison is what this scripture above is saying. When man is in darkness he is of the power of Satan and believers can turn him to God. Sir, I don't know where is your faith but what I do know is without some faith its only a matter of time. What I am saying here is a test will show up that will ask you who is your God. Now, it will not be said that clear but when you clear the smoke that is what is being asked.

What I am also seeing very clearly in these last days is the effect of the common denominator among troubled men. I am witnessing Poison Hope Disorder rule in the lives of men that is leading to lockup. Again, some with this disorder that I discovered is taking away lives due to hope is gone. One day in a small city in a small city outside Montgomery we witnessed a terrible trauma among one man. For me this was a clear case of Poison Hope Disorder among a man with no hope. In this case a man killed his wife and two of his children, and two of his children he also shot. The two children shot are in serious condition and the man also set the house on fire with the children inside. Now, after he finished his shootings of his family and burned the house he killed himself. All this happened after the wife filed for divorce a week earlier.

Here's what I am saying guys, many men are troubled and we are facing some really difficult days ahead. With all that said, there is much hope within our reach that requires men reaching for the right source. Our source is our God who is more than able to sustain us when it appears hope is gone. What I am pleading to all men now is the importance of getting our eyes focused in the right direction. Again, what I am saying to the man is you do not have to throw in the towel on a bad day. All we have to do as men is to **Man up** that we can **Stand Up** and say I Am **looking up**. When we say in faith that I am looking up you can walk away and trust God that he has it.

You see, what we are doing as men is destroying seeds that we may have planted but are dying because of no water. My walk with God as a man of hope and faith can be the water of hope for a seed that I pass. As we all know young boys today have few men role models that are within their reach. Now, what I mean is there are not many that they can call and say I need you now and I will be waiting. We know it will be unlikely for his professional athlete to show up on his behalf. My desire is to be a brighter light daily in my every walk because I am not sure who is watching. My prayer is for the young men that I can encourage they feel my spirit of compassion for their future.

I truly believe that it is of great importance that as a man call for me he knows that I will be there. I believe that if the man that killed himself and his children knew one man of integrity, we may not have his story. This is why I cry out to God saying Lord teach me daily how to be that upright man. You see, if I can be that upright man I can help that other man that he can man up under fire. We are living in a time now where we must as men know how to Man up when the heat is on. Now, it doesn't matter whether our heat is in our home, our job, our finances, we must live. Yes, I say we must live and not die under pressure because legacy is at state.

God is calling for us to institute our legacy right in the midst of a bad moment that we can stand strong. Sir, I'm telling you now that you were not born to create an atmosphere of shame but an atmosphere of dignity. The way that this happens for you and I is we stand firm right in the midst of the pain. Now, what this is going to take is some boldness on our behalf as men. Yes sir, you and I know what it is to be bold when we have been convicted on a matter we believe. This is not the boldness as the natural man but the boldness of a righteous man. The bible says " The righteous is as bold as a lion. (Proverbs 28.1). When we as men get right with God things change for us.

My job as a believer and a man of God was to be bold in Iraq right in the midst of attacks coming nightly. Now, that was tough, but I had young men in my section that needed to see righteousness at work. Sometimes God put us as men in the worst conditions to see what will come out of us. What I am seeing that is coming to lockup is not of a good report neither of a good effort. What I have seen that is coming out of men is no faith, no hope, and no patience to endure. All of this that I see in some of these men are the things that get them locked up under pressure. In Iraq I knew it would take some boldness in my walk and my faith that could change the course of my direction.

Again I wanted the young men to see someone who trusted and had an interest in their inward man as a man. When others see us do something out of the ordinary I believe it sparks a light of hope for their future. Trust me when I say a lot of our young men need that light right now more than ever. God is calling men from every corner of the universe and you especially to let's man up for the journey. This will be a journey that will be worth taking that will change lives forever. One of the ways that we can be that light is to be bold enough to be a greater man today than yesterday. I mean now, I get up every day saying God desire a greater determination today to serve. Now, I am going to start at home because I believe God want me to grow daily as a husband. When I grow daily as a husband I hold a higher standard than I did yesterday towards my wife. What I discovered here is I just might be causing my neighbor to Man Up as a husband and love his wife. After nearly 40 years of a great marriage I still believe there is a place in me to Man up.

I believe when I Man up by faith I come up to a greater level with God where I am worthy to be imitated. This is because when I Man up I have invited the fullness of God to be displayed before my very eyes. Now, as I am displayed before my eyes I am also displayed before the eyes of men. I believe as all men call upon God to Man Up before him we only desire the things that glorify him. I am on an all-out bliss to get men to see the fullness of God that they spend time with him and not in lockup. You see, after spending time with these men in lockup for six years I saw something. What I saw was whatever man can see in its fullness is where he is willing to sacrifice everything.

I talked with some of the inmates that stated they saw clearly or the fullness in a robbery and was willing for lockup. The reason they was willing was because they had never seen fullness at that level. The bible says "And of his fullness we have all received grace for grace. (John 1.16). I believed as I planted my feet in Baghdad Iraq I saw the fullness of God that I never saw at that level. Now, I was willing to sacrifice it all not only for my country but for what I believed in from the fullness. At this point now as a man I am willing to Man Up to a place that a new work can be done in me. Sir, if you want to see this new work done in you I say Man up that you are far from lockup.

What the enemy is doing now is trying to constrain the ears of men that they don't get this kind of word. You now have an edge on many that have yet to get this revelation that I am bringing from heaven. Sir, it is in the name of Jesus that I am bringing this as a gift from God which is me by faith. You have yet to experience the hand of God as a man until you can Man up and embrace his name. What your situation or circumstances maybe have not seen you in the fullness of God. I had to understand that when I was tearing about my situation when I was out of work. Then I had to take a step back to what I had witnessed that my situation had overwhelmed me with.

Then in a twinkling of an eye the word of God came over me to Man up and look up for all your help. I began to think of all that God had done for me when I was at the worst place that I have been. You see, also what happens when you man up you free up blessing God has for you that has been blocked. Now, what the enemy does is block them out by bringing clouds of disappointments. These disappointments the enemy brings are blockers from the neck up hoping the man doesn't man up. What I am saying is they are all in the mind until the man resets himself. When I reset myself back to the place I knew God from I began to see hope through the clouds.

What I am seeing in many young men is when these clouds show up trouble is attached in the clouds. When the man never resets himself to his place in God trouble overtakes him and lockup is imminent. This is when a rage is stirred up in some of our men and they get violent and out of control. What the enemy does in this case is feed into what I call his disposition of thoughts. Now, the enemy knows at this point his disposition is not in favor of doing something good but bad. Sir, stop letting the devil do this to us because we are much greater than what the trouble has brought. God is calling you to come to him with the best Man in you that you get the best in him.

This is what I witnessed when I gave God the best of me in all of my sorrows and pain that I can get his best. Now, I am on a mission impossible to bring hope to men that they might give God their best despite failure. I believe in every man there is a man in you crying out that you Man him Up before God. I have seen enough of great men coming to lockup with the best of him never got a chance. The reason why the best of him never received that chance was because the best of him was never asked for. God is standing by waiting for you and I to ask that we might receive all he has. Child of God, it is time for the real man to Man up because if we look around we can see where man is headed.

The enemy is leading the man to his worst nightmare one sexual harassment, domestic violence, murder etc. at a time. What the spirit of the Lord revealed to me to tell all men is this. The devil hopes that you think that you are excluded from the manhunt that he is on in this world. Yes sir, he hopes that you think that you have it all together while he comes to still all you have. This is why I keep my eyes on Christ and his word by faith is my shield. Brethren, let us Man up as men that we turn the hearts of young men as they see us make a difference.

The Call On The Man

When I look at the world today I am confident that there is a call on the man that requires the total man. I say total man because this requires every part of him that was given to him from his creation. When man was created by God every part of God was given to man to construct his likeness.(Gen.1.26). When we as men were created by God we were made to hear from God and heed to his call. Now, regardless to what our circumstances are the man is made to make a difference as he is. The reason that I can make a difference is when I know that I am called of Jesus Christ. The bible says "By whom we have received grace and apostleship, for obedience to the faith among all nations, for his name: Among whom are ye also the **called** of Jesus Christ. (Romans 1.5-6).

Sir, as a man in this hour it is not the time to be on the sidelines to represent who God called us to be. I know without a shadow of a doubt from what I witnessed in lockup that only the strong men will survive. When I say strong I mean men that have decided to be strong in faith and strong in endurance. Now, I must say even those men until they understand and know their calling they are at risk. What God revealed to me in the spirit is there is a call on the man from God to thrust him into spiritual dominance. That is, he is about to be placed far above his natural strength and abilities. What this dominance shall be about is his calling and who it is who is doing the call.

I believe when that man hears his call and come forth I believe that we will see change in troubled men. I believe we will see change in troubled fathers, sons, brothers, even preachers which are locked up. Now, the preachers in lockup, that's a book in the future so stay tuned and stay with God. Guys, I am here to tell you that the enemy cares less about who you say you are until he knows who you are. We are called by our creator as men to walk with a lifestyle that is worth living. What we are seeing day after day on the news are men that have lost their direction through darkness. Now, what we have to know as righteous men is that the enemy is after our light forever.

What this must do for us is to keep us so focused on the call from God that we never have to fight the battle. With the dominance the call will do in the life of the man who obeys is cover him and shield him. Let me say this, the call that comes from God has a covering over you to do God's perfect will. Now, I believe God's will is for you and I to demonstrate on this earth that in him all things are possible. I truly believe that it is possible for a man to be restored from his dark world to light. I also believe that the troubled man can come to be a righteous man if he sees enough right men. God is placing a call on men by faith to answer his call that we can be a tower of hope

Sir, it has nothing to do with where you were **raised up** or where you were **torn down** God is calling you up. Yes, he is calling you up from doing things that you know is not right that is destroying you and others. I remember seeing nearly an entire neighborhood of men come to lockup for the same problem. Now, why is that, because sometimes doing the wrong thing has a face of a copycat spirit. Sir, if your son see you slapping your wife very often his spirit is consuming that as the right thing. What your son will eventually become is a son slapping his wife and gets locked up like you can. Trust me when I say in six years working at the prison I saw this in abundance of father and son like spirit.

The call on the man from God is to be set apart from darkness of violence to the light of love, joy, peace. Domestic violence cares less about who decides to copy his spirit as long as they become cellmates. I believe the call upon man now is to be that man who is willing to have a heart for God. When we have a heart for God we can be humble and compassionate enough to help all in need. Sir, there are many young men in need of a helping hand on how to be a man of honor. What I discovered from many young men in lockup is everyone one else is not real so why should they be. Many have said they have even given up on the church because of being looked down upon.

The call upon man is to never look down upon a man for the exception of looking down upon him to lift him up. I believe as a believer I carry something and someone in me that display a spirit of compassion. By faith I believe I carry the power of restoration and that someone is the Holy Spirit himself. When we as men can be confident of this I believe we can reach one young man consistently daily. What my prayer was daily at the prison was Lord, let me reach one man today of change. Now, even when I am in the grocery store I say Lord let my light affect a young man greatly. I pray that the call on my life is so strong that it changes a man's mind from stealing at that store.

Sir, the call on our life can be that strong if we ask God for that kind of life that can be yours for the asking. You as a man who believes can have this and get this if you are willing to be that example. I truly believe that the call is on right now to the men that are ready to live right before man and God. Now is the time sir. I am telling you now that I am tired of seeing men go down due to unrighteousness. We must understand that God is a just God and he can release his judgment. God is a forgiving God. This is why I am on such a journey to get men to receive the call of righteousness and be blessed.

The bible says "For God's [holy] wrath and indignation are revealed from heaven against all ungodliness and unrighteous men, who in their wickedness repress and hinder the truth and make it inoperative. (Romans 1.18amp). When I look at all the sex crimes among famous men it concerns me. Yes, I am also concern of all the other wickedness that men are doing to bring them to lockup. Sir, as men we do not want the wrath of God we want the power of God to make a difference. What I believe is the call of man in this hour is to get right or get ready for what is to come. I believe that there are men out there that are ready to repent that he may be restored by God. I must say when I was restored by God there was no looking back but looking forward. When I began to look forward I no longer had guilt in me for what I had done in the past neither did God. Sir, when you answer the call of God on men today your future will trample your past greatly. I began to see myself as someone that God could use even though my peers could not.

I am grateful to God this day that he saw me fit to go into another nation as Iraq proclaiming to men that God is. Now, I must say I had to say this to men and women that they could receive it for their right now moment. God would give me a word to preach to them that heaven knew they needed for safety. I believe God has given me a word for men that heaven know they need for their safety and their freedom. My prayer is that men would hear from God as he is calling all men to lend him their ears. When I watch the news I know men right now are not listening to what God is saying. Sir, let me say this to you, I would blot out those things that are not worth hearing for your future.

God is calling you to turn your ear to him that he may speak your entire future and purpose to you now. When you do this in faith God is going to reveal to you that he has you in the palm of his hands. Now, this is going to take obedience and commitment to see your entire life getting a spiritual makeover. Here's what I do know, God did it for me and by that I know who I am and know my future and purpose. What is so amazing about this is God daily reveals to me that I am on track with his plan. The way that God does this in me is as I read his word daily he unfolds my daily duty. This really is effective for me because when the natural appears to **hold** my future, God **molds** my future.

What I mean here is when the enemy brings chaos of any sort God use that to strengthen me and open my eyes. God opens my eyes through the test and in the end pour out his wonders in my favor. Now, what the enemy tries to do is crucify my dream and my future by bringing failure or pain. What the devil don't know is by faith everything in me including my future is in Christ. Knowing this I can keep moving with God. The bible says "I have been crucified with Christ, it is no longer I who live, but Christ lives in me: and the life which I live now in the flesh I live by faith in the Son of God who love me and gave himself for me. (Gal:2.20). Let me say to all men that it is your flesh that is troubling.

God has a plan for you that you need to hear but your flesh can cause trouble to keep you from hearing God. What I have witnessed in lockup is how men are in church but the word was on deaf ears. We as men must crucify our flesh that the word of God falls fresh on us that we are free. You see, the old man in me I no longer know because that man was crucified by faith. I now live in Christ that I can change the entire atmosphere of the things in my life. This is where God wants you as a man that you can gain access to the keys to the kingdom. The call of man in this hour is to change the atmosphere that displays darkness. We have that power when we can hear from God and follow his command. What I desire is to see men follow God's command for their life and each one can change one. What I am saying here is each man can change the atmosphere of his world where trouble lies. I am confident on what I witnessed in lockup that trouble will bow to change.

I discovered that trouble bows to a change in heart from God that heard the voice of God saying sin no more. I watched this happen in the life of men that came to prison and received Christ while in lockup. After being released from prison and I keep in touch with their progress it was amazing and clear. Now, I do not hear from all but the ones I do their lives changed and they are making a difference. What I do know and they often share is hearing the voice of God calling for change. I believe now is the time more than ever for men to get their breakthrough from a troubled world. The prisons for men in our state are increasing in enrollment while college enrollment for men is decreasing.

What I do know for a fact is the university where I am on the ministry team men's enrollment is not what it once was. The enemy knows exactly what he is doing and now is the time for men to know what to do. This is the problem that I see in the prison, men just didn't know what to do upon decision time. You see, what the enemy is doing as I have said is keeping the man unlearned with no abilities. The enemy's main focus is to distract abilities that man never understands the importance of higher learning. As the enemy keeps the man unlearned he rambles and rage under pressure. Upon the man's last stance in the flesh, he strikes with a vengeance that leads to lockup.

Sir, it is time for us as men to discover now that there must be an alternative to the fall we are undergoing. What I mean here is nearly every high place the man can hold has been bitten by the bug of disgrace. God is calling for the man to see how his voice can move us from the thorns of disgrace to grace. I know the devil desired me to go down in the pits of disgrace by listening to wrong voices. What the enemy tried to do with me was workplace deception that is robbing millions across the country. Once again, that is a book from me in the future after 40 years in the workplace. What God is calling men to know is it is him alone that bares all of our burdens that we may live.

The world has done us a true disservice as men by allowing us to walk in disgrace due to positions. Once again, as many men have come fallen down in disgrace in sexual crimes we must refocus. Where I discovered the greatest start in this process was hearing the call from God on next steps. What I begin to recognize was there were some exchanges taking place in me upon saying yes to God. All of a sudden what the world thought about my destiny had no impact on my future. I just focused on how God saw me vertical rather than how the world saw me horizontal. Yes, the world saw me as I was knocked down by their words and perception of me then. God saw me when I stood up from being knocked down and declared that I am a child of God with favor. I rose from being knocked down by hearing God calling my name saying arise for thy light is come.(Isaiah 60.1). Brethren, I truly believe God is calling the man to arise from where you may have fallen. There is a place for every man who is ready to be that man that the world is hurting for. I believe sir, your name is at the **top** to bring you from where you are to place you on the **top**.

New Man New Life

I believe right now with the trouble of the world today there is a need for the new man that he receives new life. I believe in order to get that new life the man must know that change is very significant. What the enemy is doing to that young man in his troubled state is to keep him from changing. This is what the enemy desire in all of us that we live in that world that keeps us bound and defeated. When I would see a man coming back to prison again it was evident that change demands attention. Sir, if you know that your life is not where you desire it to be your attention is consumed by your present state. In order for you to see the new man come forward, change is required and new life unfolds.

I knew growing up in an average environment filled with tough times something in me must take a new route. I say that because

I knew if I stayed the same, my mind would perceive that as life. Yes, that is life but not the life that I believe I was created for by God to make a difference. What my goal was coming out of the projects was to make my father proud of his son's decisions. When I joined the military my goal was to embrace a new life so that I can become a new man. What I didn't like was what I had seen in my rearview which was the trouble on the hearts of men. I witnessed enough trouble that spoke volumes that by faith a new man can bring new life.

I believe as men working together with faith and hope we can change the life of other young men one at a time. I believe when we do this in faith we can create an atmosphere for new men new life. On July 15 2018 I watched on the news where a car fell from a ramp in New Orleans and landed down below on its back. A New Orleans saints football player with 10 others flipped the car over to save a man. What an amazing rescue to save a life. The spirit of the Lord revealed something to me in the rescue. Notice that 10 men came and rescued one life that he might live and have life abundantly. What I saw was God showing us that it may require several men to reach one man that he have life.

The bible says "What man of you having an hundred sheep, if he lose one of them, does not leave the ninety and nine in the wilderness, and go after that which was lost, until he find it. And when he hath found it, he layeth it on his shoulders rejoicing. (Luke 15:4-5). I say unto you, that likewise joy shall be in heaven over one sinner that repenteth, more than over ninety and nine just persons which need no repentance. (Luke:15.7). Sir, can you see the importance of reaching one. I believe like those ten men help saved that one man from the falling car, we must act as well. I believe heaven rejoices as well when we can save one man from a life of destruction. Destruction will soon lead to lockup.

When I pour all that is in me to bring a man from darkness into light by faith I am working toward a new life. Sir, this is why you need to know that you can't give up on your son even if he has been disobedient. God is calling all of us as men to go after that one and trust him that he can receive new life. What our own effort will do is make us tired of trying to turn our own around. What God wants us to do as men is to not rely on our own strength but to produce this new man and new life. I am here to tell you that God knows about a new man from the beginning of time. What we need as men is a willing heart to encourage others that trouble will not overtake them. It appears as we watch the news that trouble has overtaken men at an alarming rate. I believe this is because some men think that a new man in them is highly unlikely.

What I believe is much of their life they have only been in a desperate survival mode. This can be the thought when you grew up in the projects and this environment was a way of life. The inward man in me began to speak in a way that my heart can beat in rhythm to what is said. My inward man which is my spirit man began to open up new ideas that I could relate too. Sir, there is a greater in you that can thrust you to higher heights that you can be a door of hope. God can bring favor your way in an instant if you believe as you can become a new man with new life. God has been mighty good to me and I am on an intense journey to pick a man up.

I desire to pick the man up that he acknowledges to God that he is in need of him as new life comes his way. The reason why new life is needed for the man now is his old man has tarnished his image. When the old man is tarnished by darkness his footsteps is in line with trouble and lockup is imminent. I believe there are many men that desire to do right but in their eyes right is not possible. The enemy has tarnished right living in the eyes of the natural man as a square or a sign of weakness. What this is doing for the natural man is keeping him in the old man(Colos:3.9) that he never becomes new. God has established blessings for the new man that he overcomes failure. Sir, this is a new man that you need to meet in you that can change your world.

I believe what this is going to take is the man desiring to put his past in his rear view that newness come alive. I am confident that newness will not come alive if old things are still alive in the man. Nearly every man that I have witnessed return to lockup in less than a year was overcome by the old man. Sir, there is more of you that is hidden within the new man that is crying to come out. Here's what I do know, when I became a new man, new life unfolded gifts in me unheard of. If someone would have told me years ago that I would write a book I would have said No Way. Now, I would have said that out of the old man view that has no vision for the new man.

The reason why I believe so many men are troubled is they are troubled by what the old man is doing in them. When I talk to some of these guys in lockup that have families and are great I discover they are being hindered. Yes, the devil has hindered them from crossing over to the new man for the new life. The devil does not mind you being a great man as long as you stay in the old mind. The reason the devil don't mind this is because he know in the old man you only get old things. When you come to know God in the new man, you have new things coming including a new mind. I truly believe dreams begin to take shape in the man the moment newness takes over. This is what took me to newer heights and the devil was mad that I didn't desire the old things. What is taking place as the man is challenged with life struggles is frustration breeds trouble. What brings this frustration is while the struggle is going on in his flesh, his spirit is about newness.

When the flesh is continuing in the old man his flesh responds with negative responses to robbery, murder etc.. Remember, the bible says For the flesh lusts against the spirit, and the spirit against the flesh: and these are contrary to one another, so that you do not do the things that you wish. (Gal:5.17). Sir, the enemy do not want you with the great things that awaits you in newness. What you will have to do now is get your hope and your faith working at its full capacity. I promise you when I got my faith activated with where I believed I was going my past died suddenly. My past died because my future was now alive and the new man began to walk a new life.

As I watch some of these young men daily walking in chains in lockup I think of how blessed I am by God. I say that because I think of again the temptation that tried to strip me of the new man I desired. Yes sir, I desired the new man even in the projects when the old man was pulling on me hard. What is happening every day is the old man is pulling on great men daily and taking him down. Yes sir, he is taking the man down and unfortunately he is taking him downtown and to lockup. What I am trying to convey to the man is you must come to yourself that the old man is not you. God has a much brighter future for you that the old man in you in no way can comprehend.

Today is the day to decide that you and I have no place in the world as the old man who brings trouble in us. We are to get to know the new man that we can become the best of the best among our neighbors. When we do this we can please God and shame the devil as God gets the glory for his work. Yes, there will be a new work in us that will bring this new man and new life for new things. I really believe the world has not yet seen or experienced the WOW factor in this man from God. What the spirit has revealed to me that in the years to come greater inventions are on the way. These great inventions and new technology will be coming from new men with new life.

Sir, if you would take heed of this word from God I believe you are one of his chosen men to do the work. Yes sir, I know that you may have come close to giving up but you have just been promoted by God. Now, walk in faith that this is for you and know that promotions come from God.(Psalm 75.7). I am here to tell you as a man that you have been living in the old man long enough missing your blessing. God has a blessing so big for the new man that his old troubles will never be remembered. I see men walking in their old defeated nature at the prison that haunts their future. What I would do as a believer even when I saw that was lift him up that all things are possible. I was after his new man that I believed was deep down in him looking for a way of escape.

I believe there are men haunted with bad choices that the old man approved without consent from the new man. I say that because the devil is not considering my new man and not waiting on my decision. Sir, as a man there is a way of escape from the troubles that are robbing many young men today. I have seen over and over daily here in lockup men that are not aware that they can escape trouble. One of the ways of escaping trouble is not giving breath to the thoughts of commitment. You see, when trouble comes to the man it comes uncommitted needing life to it. When the man breathes in to the trouble he buys in to the thought and before he knows it it's done.

I received this from several inmates that never could see themselves committing such horrible crimes. The easiest way also for the man is to again walk away from that old man as you walk away from the environment. We are in a season for men where they are committing some of the unimaginable crimes. Sir, what I am certain about right now about man it is critical for us to guard our new man. What I mean here is again the devil is after us because he knows we are after the new man. Yes, I am after reaching and perfecting the man from lockup because we are needed in our world. I truly mean we are needed and we are needed in the new man because the old man is present.

What my calling is as a man of God with this amazing exciting assignment is to **Perfect The Man from Lockup.** I am again certain about this calling on my life that it is significant of why I was born and yet live. God sent me to Kilby Prison for men as an employee with purpose to bring deliverance to men. I am confident that even getting pounded nightly by bombs in Iraq couldn't stop this purpose. I am on a mission impossible for God to see men free by way of trusting in God that they may have life. In the life that man has on the earth I am confident that his life is to glorify God at his best. Well, in my years with boots on ground at the prison I am confident the man is not at his best.

Yes, there is a great ministry at the prison as I witnessed and was deeply blessed as I saw purpose come alive. What I believe is God desires us to take the good news to the highways and compel.(Luke 14.23). When we are a new man with new life there is strength and power for doing the right thing. I am sure that there are men that are hungry for breaking free from the bondage of lack. Lack is a hidden seed that can bring violence to the natural man who footprints are of old. This is what I see when I see the violence that men are carrying out in his violent state. What I believe as I watch all the violent act of men on the news are footprints that are poisoned. Yes, these are footprints that are poisoned with Poison Hope Dysfunction that I discovered. With these footprints and the old man he is destined to step in the line of fire with trouble to lockup. When this man comes into the knowledge of God his footsteps shall become new like him. As we walk in the newness of God as men something extraordinary takes place on the inside. What that something is as I discovered in my life is again that old man died that I became something new. The bible say "Therefore we are buried with him by baptism into death: that like as Christ was raised up from the dead by the glory of the Father, even so we also should walk in newness of life. (Romans 6:4).

Sir, as you walk out and think about what I have shared with you I am celebrating with you on the new life ahead. Now, what the enemy desires is for you to stay right where you are but we have news for him. You are not looking back but looking far ahead for what is about to come your way in newness. I believe God has set aside this special moment for you and him as you draw closer to him. What the enemy is subject to do is turn up the heat to trouble you that lockup is for you. I believe that you are one of God's chosen that he is perfecting that blessings overtake you now and forever more. God Bless!!